MESSENGERS
OF DAY

BOOKS BY
ANTHONY POWELL

NOVELS
Afternoon Men
Venusberg
From a View to a Death
Agents and Patients
What's Become of Waring

A DANCE TO THE MUSIC OF TIME
A Question of Upbringing
A Buyer's Market
The Acceptance World
At Lady Molly's
Casanova's Chinese Restaurant
The Kindly Ones
The Valley of Bones
The Soldier's Art
The Military Philosophers
Books Do Furnish a Room
Temporary Kings
Hearing Secret Harmonies

BIOGRAPHIES
John Aubrey and his Friends

PLAYS
The Garden God and *The Rest I'll Whistle*

MEMOIRS:
To Keep the Ball Rolling
Vol. I. Infants of the Spring
Vol. II. Messengers of Day

The Memoirs of
Anthony Powell

Volume II

MESSENGERS
OF DAY

HOLT, RINEHART AND WINSTON
New York

Library of Congress Cataloging in Publication Data
Powell, Anthony, 1905–
Messengers of day.
(His To keep the ball rolling; 2)
Includes index.
1. Powell, Anthony, 1950–   —Biography—London
life. 2. Novelists, English—20th century—Biography.
3. London—Intellectual life. I. Title. II. Series.
PR6031.074Z52   823'.9'12 [B]   78-4703
ISBN 0-03-020996-X

Messengers of Day is the second volume of an autobiographical
series by Anthony Powell entitled To Keep the Ball Rolling.

First published in the United States in 1978.

Printed in the United States of America.

10 9 8 7 6 5 4 3 2 1

Decius	Here lies the east: doth not the day break here?
Casca	No.
Cinna	O, pardon, sir, it doth; and yon grey lines
	That fret the clouds are messengers of day.

Julius Caesar II i

CONTENTS

Illustrations follow page 118

MESSENGERS
OF DAY

I

Dawn in Henrietta Street

In the autumn of 1926 I came to work in London. I should be twenty-one in December. Clichés, says Jarry, are the armature of the absolute, and no figure is more tritely familiar, at the same time more truly archetypal, than the young man setting out on a metropolitan career. Balzac and Stendhal especially love his situation. I had read no Stendhal then, only dipped into Balzac's *La Fille aux Yeux d'Or* (Dowson's translation, acquired by my father for the Conder illustrations), where the hero is a fully fledged man-about-town; the lesbian and transvestite scenes largely lost on me at the age of sixteen. Accordingly, I was not inspired to identify with Rastignac or Rubempré, and their high standards of ambition. The best I could do in the way of Balzacian (or Stendhalian) ambition was that of every reasonably literate young man of the period; vague intention to write a novel myself one of these days.

The first thing to do was to find somewhere to live. No Oxford friend seemed to be in the same position at just that moment, some already installed for a year or more in London flats, others lodging with parents or not yet down from the University. During the final year at Oxford I had to some extent lost touch with a lot of people known there earlier. That was partly due to the relatively withdrawn undergraduate life Henry Yorke and I had lived out of college in adjacent sets of rooms; partly because contemporaries were beginning to branch off along paths for various reasons—social, economic, sexual, intellectual—not my own. Yorke's first novel (*Blindness*, by Henry Green) was to appear the following spring. He had not yet gone to work in his family's Birmingham factory.

I possessed no household goods, so something furnished was required. Several possibilities presented themselves. A cluster of Oxford acquaintances, several belonging to what might be called the middle era of the Hypocrites Club, was settled in Bloomsbury (mainly the Queen Square/Great Ormond Street area, little way from Bloomsbury brahmin territory), where they had reconstructed a somewhat Oxfordish mode of life. In principle I was reacting against Oxford and Oxford ways; that part of London in any case comparatively unexplored terrain. There were adherents to Ebury Street, Chelsea, Campden Hill, regions further afield. As to *quartier* I had my own ideas, though I might not have admitted to everyone that the Shepherd's Market seduction scene which opens Michael Arlen's novel, *The Green Hat* (1924), chiefly caused me to set my sights on that small village enclave (also described in Disraeli's *Tancred*), so unexpectedly concealed among the then grand residences of Mayfair.

(By an odd chance I found myself giving luncheon to Arlen tête-à-tête thirty years later, and was able to reveal what had prompted my first London *garçonnière*. Small, slight, neat, infinitely sure of himself, yet somehow set apart from other people, he twice repeated at the table a personal definition: 'I, Dikran Kouyoumdjian, an Armenian'. Dikran is the equivalent of Tigranes, the name of several kings of Armenia in classical times. Arlen talked entertainingly of books and sexual relationships, saying among other things that, unlike most men he knew, he did not believe in sleeping with friends' wives.)

Even today (1978), in face of ruthless knockings down, scarcely less ruthless smartenings up, Shepherd Market—more frequently called Shepherd's Market by those who lived there—has kept vestiges of an old stylishness. At that period all the traders were 'little shops'; the pubs, down-to-earth pubs; the prostitutes, as such, differentiated from the merely raffish by segregation in one large forbidding block of flats. Even a few years later—soon after the initial demolitions—this primitive innocence had begun to dwindle, but, when I arrived with the object of trying to find somewhere to live, the Market's air of seedy chic perfectly suited my own post-Oxonian mood. Chiefly on grounds of price I had not much hope of achieving this aim. On the contrary, the first door bell rung supplied an answer.

Shepherd Street crosses the lower levels of the Market east and west, from which, at right angles, the short cul-de-sac of Carrington Street runs south, terminating even at that date in a busy all-night garage. A pub, The Old Chesterfield Arms, still remains on the north-east corner of Carrington Street; on the opposite corner then stood Carrington House, a building going back at least to the 17th century, perhaps appreciably earlier. Reputed former town mansion of the Earls of Sefton, Carrington House could never have been of inordinate size. The courtesan Kitty Fisher (painted by Reynolds) is said to have lived there ('Lucy Lockit lost her pocket/Kitty Fisher found it'); later, Lord Nelson. At some time not at all recent the structure had been divided into two houses. These traditions, true or untrue, were all unknown to me, when I rang the bell of Carrington House's easterly wing, by then simply 9 Shepherd Street.

The door was opened by a lady, handsome, full of attack, who wore a rather dashing hat. She turned out to be the wife of the owner, Commander Williamson, an ex-naval officer employed at the Air Ministry. Mrs Williamson (I suppose in her forties, though she looked younger), undeterred by a dilapidated exterior, had made that half of Carrington House their London home, letting off a couple of rooms on the ground-floor, one above. The former were vacant; with breakfast, someone to make the bed, two pounds a week. In a matter of minutes they were engaged.

It should be emphasized at once that my suite was neither large nor luxurious. In fact, as an airing-cupboard divided into two compartments, the extent would not have been thought excessive, even in a moderately sized house. Nearly half the tiny sitting room was taken up by a vast glass-fronted bookcase reaching almost to the ceiling. A miniature sofa set against this elephantine piece of furniture allowed just space for a chair and folding table, the table kept in a corner when not in use. An outdated set of the *Encyclopaedia Britannica* took up most of the bookcase, the upper shelves of which were stocked with technical manuals of inconceivable dryness. The bedroom, even smaller than the sitting room, was an irregular pentagon (otherwise unmagical in character), three of its walls on the street. In one of these outside walls a nailed-up door, perhaps former tradesmen's entrance, had been made partially draught-proof, though retaining within and without the appearance of offering additional ingress to the house.

2

It had been arranged through my father's friend, Thomas Balston, that I should learn the business of publishing—a mystery to be attained within the span of three years—at the firm of Gerald Duckworth & Co. Ltd, of which Balston was now a director. I was perfectly amenable to becoming a publisher; indeed could conjure up no more plausible means of attempting to earn a living. During the years of apprenticeship I was to receive a certain allowance from my father, a certain salary from Duckworth's. I do not remember the precise proportion each party was to pay, but, as year succeeded to year, my father contributed less, the firm more; the amount I received, three hundred pounds annually, remaining a constant. Finally, I think, my father was paying half that sum, which he continued to do later as an allowance.

Duckworth's, one of the smaller London publishing houses, had been founded in 1898 by Gerald Duckworth himself, a man at this time in his middle fifties. The firm's offices were at 3 Henrietta Street, the Covent Garden end of what still remains a publishers' alley. Hogarth's allegory, *Morning* (a chill winter scene in about 1736), shows part of the heavy Inigo Jones portico of St Paul's Church, Covent Garden, on the right; on the left of the picture, Duckworth's premises seem to be just beyond the (since disappeared) building with pillars; though Hogarth either took liberties in representing four windows in a row, or these were reduced to three in the course of much architectural maltreatment of the street's 17th century symmetry. Dingy without, only a few finely ornate door-fittings recalled better days within.

The three directors of the firm were Gerald Duckworth, George Milsted, Thomas Balston. Gerald Duckworth, himself not specially rich, came from a decidedly well-to-do family. His widowed mother had married a widower, Sir Leslie Stephen (founder of the *Dictionary of National Biography*), producing further children, who included Vanessa Bell and Virginia Woolf. This last circumstance has caused chroniclers of 'Bloomsbury' to focus attention on the two Duckworths, Gerald and his elder brother, George (knighted civil servant of the official art world), both of whom being accused by their half-sister of indulging in unbecoming fumblings with her as a little girl.

4

Such imputations on the part of a person of Virginia Woolf's mental condition are to be accepted with a certain degree of caution, but there can be no doubt that her relationship with the Duckworth brothers was a complex one, arousing all her own ambivalent feelings about sex, money, and the social life to which, when old enough, her more affluent half-brothers introduced her. She always stigmatized them as 'clubmen', but, notwithstanding forebodings on that score, submitted a first novel, *The Voyage Out*, to Gerald Duckworth, who published it in 1915; her second, *Night and Day*, four years later. These two books (straightforward in style, arguably her best) were ceded to The Hogarth Press when set up by Leonard and Virginia Woolf; a sense of relief probably felt on both sides at this rearrangement.

The Virginia Woolf/Gerald Duckworth connexion has bearing on my own circumstances only as illustration of the manner in which Duckworth's, in spite of this blood link with all that was most modish in literary fashions of the Twenties, was by now entirely out of touch with anything of that sort. There was no contact between the two firms, and it could have been a year or more before I even heard of the Virginia Woolf relationship. Gerald Duckworth had some reputation as a rackety Edwardian bachelor, and the varied sexual promiscuities of Bloomsbury were generally known. Nevertheless, the notion (true or untrue) that either of the Duckworth brothers had indulged in erotic scufflings with Virginia Woolf—at any age—would in those days have seemed grotesque beyond words; my own generation regarding Bloomsbury as no less elderly, stuffy, anxious to put the stopper on rising talent, than the staunchly anti-avant-garde Duckworths.

Gerald Duckworth (who remained childless) had married and settled down only a year or two before I came into the firm. I do not remember a first presentation to him. I dined at his house in De Vere Gardens, Kensington, only once, I think, when, without any strong sense of conviviality, a memorable amount was drunk. He was a big burly man, slight grey moustache, small rather baleful eyes behind steel spectacles, a vaguely dissatisfied air. Some suggestion of a love affair gone wrong was hinted (which late marriage might endorse), but I never heard any details of his personal past. Like Marley's ghost in more gastronomic guise he moved gloomily through the office, a haze of port fumes and stale cigar smoke in his wake; probably showing greater amiability among cronies at

5

The Garrick, where—reputed on a good day to dispatch a bottle of claret at luncheon—he undoubtedly earned his half-sister's label as clubman.

Though I have heard a literary agent describe him as devious in negotiation, the truly extraordinary thing about Gerald Duckworth was that he had chosen to become a publisher at all; much less founded a firm for that purpose. His interest in books, anyway as a medium for reading, was as slender as that of any man I have ever encountered, though he had some liking for the Theatre, a milieu where the legendary love affair was by tradition placed. If the virus of bibliophobia is dormant in the blood there is nothing like a publisher's life for aggravating the condition.

Nevertheless, the firm's earlier lists contained conspicuous names: Henry James; August Strindberg; John Galsworthy (as John Sinjohn); Hilaire Belloc; Edward Thomas; Ford Madox Ford; D. H. Lawrence; a lot more too. This vigour on the editorial side had been almost entirely due to employing Edward Garnett as Duckworth's reader between 1901 and 1920. Why a talent scout of such ability was ever lost I do not know. Perhaps twenty years of brilliant recommendation became at last altogether unendurable.

I never met Garnett, but by an odd chance was familiar with his name before joining the firm. When we were both still undergraduates I had suggested to Yorke that he might show the manuscript of the novel he was writing to Balston. Balston, not greatly impressed, turned it down. Somehow it reached Garnett, then working for another publisher. *Blindness* was not issued by Garnett's then firm, but, liking the book, he carefully went through the manuscript with Yorke, who would often talk of 'old Garnett's' attractive character, odd mannerisms, invaluable hints about novel-writing.

Among other authors of the Edwardian period whose books had been polished up by Garnett was Galsworthy, though friendship barely survived Garnett's parallel use of the term 'clubman' in connexion with Galsworthy. Notwithstanding Galsworthy's protests that he had never made a friend in a club (certainly his own writings about clubs display strange ideas of how he supposed they are run), he got on well with Gerald Duckworth, whose family was by no means without Forsytean overtones. It is unjust to say (as has been stated) that Duckworth's let go *The Forsyte Saga*. In fact, after two unsuccessful John Sinjohn books, Galsworthy (under his own name this time) published with another firm two more unsuccessful novels; even after those books, signs of his becoming a bestseller stemming less from *A Man of Property* (1906), than *The Country House* (1907), not a Forsyte novel at all. Duckworth's continued to publish Galsworthy's plays, quite a valuable item, and he was one of the few authors with whom Gerald Duckworth dealt personally.

Others of that elect were Elinor Glyn, Belloc, Ford Madox Ford, all of whom could claim a recognizable social life apart from their writing. Elinor Glyn's *The Visits of Elizabeth* (1900) remains funny to this day, recalling the wit and manner of Nancy Mitford; the scenes from French aristocratic life (known from the author's French cousins) perhaps more convincing than parallel Mitfordian ones. These early Glyn novels, brought out before large sales in the US turned her almost into an American writer, are said to have been issued without written contract.

By the time I arrived Belloc's work, except for the comic verse (illustrated by Basil Blackwood and Nicolas Bentley), had mostly passed from the hands of Duckworth's. Ford Madox Ford's leaning towards modern forms might have been thought to militate against him with Gerald Duckworth, but Ford's own determined clubman pretensions, even if a trifle precarious when closely examined, were held to excuse a too insistent modernism.

3

George Milsted, second on the mast-head of directors, had been with the firm since its early stages of inception; though away in the army during the first war, while Gerald Duckworth kept things going on his own. Small, thickset, white-moustached, Milsted's turn-out was always intensely sporting. Together with a brown bowler, he wore, all the year round, tweeds of the loudest check, most uncompromisingly horsey cut; in winter, as for hacking, a short fawn covert coat.

I could not imagine who this figure from the race-course might be, when I first caught sight of Milsted pottering about the room in which I worked. He was examining the file copies with apparent surprise, as if never seen before, and he were browsing round a secondhand bookshop. The ensemble, suggesting a prosperous bookie on the way to Newmarket (his air perhaps too grave for a bookmaker's), was not unlike one of Evelyn Waugh's favourite outfits in latter days; though Waugh's bowler was grey, his tweeds apt to be spongebag, or that Household Troops pattern, intended by the designer in the first instance for tweed caps, rather than complete suits. In Milsted (contrasted with Waugh) these outwardly aggressive garments did not in the least denote a rebarbative nature. On the contrary, Milsted's demeanour was always quiet and cordial.

In legend, Milsted is said occasionally to have arrived at the office driving a phaeton—no easy undertaking among the also horse-drawn fruit wagons of Covent Garden—but I never witnessed the ribands in his hands. He and his wife lived modestly in a house they had built for themselves somewhere south of London, only a jump or more ahead of the suburbs. They too were childless. Milsted would sometimes remark: 'As long as a man owns a horse, and a gun, and a dog, he has no cause to complain of his lot in this world.' Appropriate clothes undoubtedly played an important part in this philosophy of life, and he once confided to me that (as a Gunner officer of fairly mature age) he had preferred to sport a khaki stock, rather than the more militarily conventional knotted tie.

Unless devoting himself to some such demanding labours as proof-reading *The Collected Works of Ronald Firbank*, Milsted did not very often show up at Henrietta Street; indeed scarcely averaging once a week. He was a zealous proof-reader, taking pains to check points like Firbank's sometimes hazardous Latin; for example, in the administration of Last Rites to the Archduchess in *The Flower Beneath the Foot*, or when Latin snatches (apparently also liturgical in echo) are used in an exchange between the footmen in *Valmouth*. The latter passage proved beyond all Milsted's industry to amend with certitude. His general knowledge was considerable. So much so, that—like Brougham and the Law—he might have been said to know a little about everything except the business side of publishing.

4

When, a few years before my own appearance there, Thomas Balston became the junior director of Duckworth's, that (so he told me) had been on the strict understanding that Milsted would be dead in six months. What (or who) was to finish Milsted off, I do not know, nor how he so unexpectedly escaped imminent mortality. Milsted's later career has no particular relevance here (he lived, in fact, well into his eighties, seeing the firm through another war, showing interest in its doings within measurable distance of his own end), the point being merely that, when Balston took on this directorship, he supposed the business was his for the asking: Gerald Duckworth, if allowed to hobnob with the two or three authors he found possible to tolerate, would show little or no interest in what names were added to the firm's list; Milsted, if not soon dead, would at worst live on as a moribund colleague, seen at the office with increasing rarity. After a few years of the hard work Balston was only too anxious to bestow, Duckworth's could reasonably be envisaged as an over-ripe fruit about to drop into his lap.

If Gerald Duckworth came close to detesting books with all his heart, Milsted to regarding them as no more than a pleasantly civilized adjunct to stables, kennels, gun-room, Balston felt a passionate dedication to the publishing trade and its manifold obligations. He had always wanted to be a publisher, and at last some fortunate circumstance—possibly demise of a brother—had put him in the way of sufficient capital to invest in the Duckworth partnership. He was unmarried—his sexual proclivities always remained enigmatic, apparently non-existent in physical form, though he was capable of being stirred by emotional attachments of a sentimental sort towards both sexes—so that all his energies could be freely devoted to building up what was undeniably a thoroughly tumbledown concern.

Tall, thin, black–moustached, jet black hair standing up on end, Balston, who was in his middle forties, gave expression to a mass of nervous tensions. He moved with jerky precipitancy, never closing a door without slamming it. Something of a classical scholar in his youth, other literary tastes were less easy to define. A delight in argument and contradiction required such preferences to be varied from one hour to the next; sometimes total reversal of his normal point of view on any given subject. On the one hand, he favoured modernism, being attracted by any chance of shocking the old-fashioned or straitlaced with perverse philosophic, political, above all anti-religious views; on the other hand, too much sexual frankness could provoke in him embarrassed giggles.

In the latter mood he would show strongly traditional, even prim, frames of mind. Among writers of a then new sort neither Proust nor Joyce appealed to him, while at the same time he wanted the firm to

9

engage in the latest thing, and by implication one of my jobs was to bring in the bright young men among my own contemporaries.

In the former mood, when in the same month (January, 1928) Hardy and Haig both died, Balston liked to tease literary people by saying that unquestionably the soldier would be remembered by history as a greater man than the writer. He was, indeed, an admirer of the Field-Marshal, whose words he had found on some occasion during the war deeply moving. In this same connexion, Balston approved my own proposal that— to avoid recurrent controversy as to whether or not such-and-such a poet or novelist should be buried in Westminster Abbey—an Unknown Author might be interred there once and for all.

5

To get some practical experience of publishing himself Balston had worked for a time in the office of T. Fisher Unwin; a firm with the distinction of commissioning a poster by Beardsley in the Nineties, and (again at Edward Garnett's instigation) of having published the early works of Joseph Conrad. Fisher Unwin graduates often cropped up in the publishing world, the acceptance of trainees probably a recognized policy.

Whatever the mutual arrangement, in Balston's case that had not been a success; terminating in a letter from him to The Fishy Onion—as he always designated his former boss, giving at the same time an imitation of Unwin pulling at his goatee beard, while considering some monetary saving—a communication of his own departure, which included the phrase 'reducing your staff to the duties and emoluments of the office boy.'

Nevertheless it was at Fisher Unwin's that Balston came across, on the managerial side there, a future henchman, who was to mean a great deal to him, also to Duckworth's. This was A. G. Lewis—I believe his christian name was Abbot, but to have called him that would have been unthinkable, or indeed anything but 'Mr Lewis'—whom, when in a position to do so, Balston installed as Duckworth's manager. Balston possessed for Lewis a kind of hero-worship that (in business terms) approached passion, causing Lewis to become a preponderant figure in the office, especially my own corner of it, as we shared a room.

I am not, unlike many people I know, a great fan of *The Diary of a*

Nobody (1892), but I recognize the Grossmiths' book uniquely pinpoints a certain level of life in its day. Lewis himself was not in the least like Pooter, but Pooter's background was entirely Lewis's, making him prototype of a race all but departed even at that date, anyway in so unmodified a form; the old-fashioned middle-class, when the term really had some meaning. There was no one of Lewis's many cronies on the non-editorial side of publishing less prepared than he to move with the times, become assimilated with a contemporary scene in which social differences had begun to become blurred. Lewis would have none of that. He allowed absolutely no adjustment in relations with those he considered above or below him. He knew precisely where he stood himself, desired nothing else, and neither by demeanour nor dress would alter his own stance in the smallest degree.

Slight in build, skeletally thin, with a small toothbrush moustache, Lewis always wore a black coat and striped trousers, the jacket fastened in the Victorian manner by only its high top button. A deep reddish complexion in all weathers made him seem either flushed by drink, ominously dehydrated, or just come into a warm blaze from an outside climate below freezing. In point of fact no one could have been more moderate in eating and drinking. Lewis liked an occasional glass of wine, but told me that he could never eat game when served at trade banquets.

At times rendered irritable by the vexations of publishing life, particularly exacerbating on the production side—suffering too from digestive troubles, probably why game was to be avoided—Lewis was a very nice man, straightforward, kindhearted, absolutely reliable, who knew his job exceedingly well within certain terms of reference. At the same time he had his limitations. Where the editorial side was concerned, the most unassuming of managers—in the sense that he would stick word for word to Balston's, or my own, description of a given book, when dealing with, say, an American publisher—Lewis would also, if to some extent waggishly, always bemoan anything taken on that had the air of being highbrow, or required presentation in what he regarded as a highbrow manner.

This was a standpoint that caused a kind of chronic attrition. Naturally Lewis was Balston's subordinate, but Balston, if not exactly afraid of Lewis, never liked to cross him too far. Accordingly, compromises were made that might at times have been better unmade. That was especially true in the way Duckworth books were produced. Lewis, quite rightly, was always keen on economy in printing and binding; occasionally a trifle parsimonious about the number of review copies sent out. Such things are all very well in principle; moments come when exceptions must be allowed. Some highbrow books, especially when well produced, turn out to sell very well.

Authors go to a small publisher to get individual attention. Sooner or later they are likely to be bribed away by advances larger than a small publisher can afford to pay, or by the prospect of a more extensive sales organization. Economies may be necessary; they must be made with understanding. In those days—before wartime austerities resigned everyone to novels that look like school textbooks—writers thought more than they do now about their work appearing in elegant form. In such matters young and farouche authors could find Lewis, who was painfully shy, difficult to deal with. This might hasten departure to another firm.

6

That the picture in my mind of Lewis—particularly as belonging to a species all but extinct even in the Twenties—was not an exaggeratedly subjective one was confirmed forty years later.

Towards the end of the 1960s, in an old established bookshop off Piccadilly, I came across first editions of two early novels of mine. A gratifying price was being asked. Both were inscribed to Lewis. I enquired if anything was known of their provenance. It turned out that the bookseller to whom I spoke had himself negotiated their purchase. He was eager to tell the story. He seemed scarcely to take in that I had once known Lewis well.

Although a middle-aged man himself, the bookseller had been astounded by the antique air of this veteran, from whom he had apparently bought several 'collectors' items' in the past. For some minutes he spoke animatedly about the house (in Streatham, I think), its lace curtains, old-fashioned atmosphere, above all the clothes of its owner, recalling an antediluvian epoch. Lewis must then have been in his late eighties. These two books, the bookseller said, had long been refused. He added that times were hard for those on fixed pensions, so that in the end he had persuaded the obstinate old fellow to part with them. I felt very touched.

7

The premises at 3 Henrietta Street to which young writers were to be lured were not outwardly inviting. The front door, kept open during the day, gave on to a shabby uncarpeted passage with a staircase at the end. On the left was another door inscribed with the name of the firm; possibly followed by the word ENQUIRIES, though I am not sure about that. If so, the hope was not one to build on. Within stood simply the trade counter (where booksellers' representatives collected copies from publishers' stock), no focus beyond that barrier existing to which an enquiry might specifically be directed; nor, for that matter, was any one individual responsible for answering the telephone.

Three or four breezy young men, invoice clerks, would be engaged in caustic conversation among themselves at their long high desk on the far side of the room, and their attention had to be caught. That was not always easy. Out of sight to the right lay the (one man) packing department, from which a Dickensian ancient kept up a fusillade of cockney banter with the invoice clerks, with whom he was perpetually at war.

In theory all arrivals at Duckworth's came to this bar of judgment: authors; visiting American publishers; literary agents; book-jacket designers; travellers in printing, binding, papermaking; sellers of advertising space; not least, the steady flow of the mentally deranged, whose routine was—no doubt still is—to call regularly on publishers. If clients had to wait, there was nowhere for them to sit. Later a kind of hutch was constructed between counter, wall, and window, furnished with a couple of hard chairs. Writers familiar with the severities of ground-floor conditions would not bother to be announced on the house-telephone (a concession to modernity), but come straight up to the room of whomever they wanted to see.

On the first floor, a small room at the top of the stairs was occupied by Balston. Cramped, austere, there was just room for two visitors. Balston's room overlooked Henrietta Street, where it approached the south-west corner of Covent Garden. The considerably larger room next door, with a small view of the market, was shared by Gerald Duckworth, and, when on duty, Milsted. Their roll-top desks were set back to back, so that each had a window from which to watch what was happening outside, but they were hidden from each other by a towering wall of dust-covered books, accumulated on the space between since the foundation of the firm. More books and manuscripts, usually a newspaper or two, littered the floor round Gerald Duckworth's seat, beside which, for the use of a potential caller, stood an armchair in the last stages of decomposition. Dust was everywhere, disorder infinite.

Order was only a little more apparent in the room behind this one (its outlook on to the backs of houses), occupied by Lewis and myself. Lewis's roll-top desk faced the door, but he could not see who entered without craning round a stack similar to that set between the two partners; in this case, recently published books, proofs of books, 'dummies' of books, estimates, invoices, letters currently to be considered; everything else that could find no other place to rest than the top of the desk.

Further into the room stood my own smaller (non-roll-top) desk, beside it another crumbling armchair, unearthed from some cubby-hole, after energetic efforts on my part, and installed—not without all opposition—for visitors. Formerly authors had been required to stand in the presence of their publisher's staff.

This room was lined from floor to ceiling with the dust-wrapped file-copies of the firm's output since the beginning; a record not too scrupulously kept over the years. Beyond the office in which Lewis and I sat was a tiny closet, where a succession of secretary-typists lived out their usually disgruntled being.

Some aspirants to the publishing profession are, at the opening of their career, charged to enact a season in the packing department. I have always regretted no such obligation was imposed on me, since everyone whose life is concerned with books is likely to spend a good deal of time tying up parcels of them, an art I have never properly mastered. Professional instruction would have been invaluable.

As it was I began my novitiate writing invoices (for which I showed little talent), sitting on one of those high office stools that must have been in the mind of William Johnson Cory, when, in the *Eton Boating Song*, he wrote of weather that tempted their abandonment. I would indite invoices in the morning; in the afternoon ascend to the first floor, there to learn about seeing books through the press; composing ads; reading manuscripts; dealing with authors and agents; all the things that make up a publisher's day.

At Carrington House, when I returned there, Mrs Williamson was the quintessence of goodwill; sending down a cup of tea and slice of cake 'last thing', which I had to countermand, because—so it seemed—strong tea kept me awake. Tea and cake probably had nothing to do with insomnia, because I continued to sleep badly for years, and have never achieved anything like an Abou Ben Adhem standard of deep dreams of peace.

Nor could I eat the hearty breakfasts Mrs Williamson provided. I had not learnt then to ask for one piece of toast in the Continental manner, even in those days perfectly normal behaviour, though perhaps less common than nowadays. These things disturbed Mrs Williamson. I, on my side, felt embarrassed by her extrovert kindnesses. I was going through a period of ineptitude at dealing with people. She must have thought me a very odd young man.

An excellent pub dinner was to be had at The New Chesterfield Arms, opposite Carrington House to the north; three courses for half-a-crown, where a dozen or more persons sat round a large table on the first floor. The doings of the clientèle (mostly Shepherd Market residents) were unguessable. Some looked as if they might have a story to tell. The tone of this communal table was formal. I never made any acquaintances there, though I would sometimes come across other young men who occasionally made use of the place. The room above mine at the Williamsons' (single but larger than my two) was inhabited by an Etonian about four years senior to me; known by sight on account of some eminence as an oarsman. Relations as neighbours were never carried further than saying good-evening or goodnight on the rare occasions when we met on the doorstep. I have no idea how he occupied himself.

I would sometimes try to settle down to a book after dinner, but my sitting room was not a place to encourage reading; still less writing. The contents of the giant bookcase offered small appeal even for so compulsive a book-examiner as myself. When, after the best part of a year, I took down one of the faded Encyclopaedias, a crumpled French pornographic paperback, concealed and forgotten by some former tenant, lurked behind them. It was a work of no great merit even in its own genre. In order not to seem its furtive owner (if someone looked up an article in the Britannica when I was out, or after I had moved to other accommodation), I passed the volume on to some friend.

Said to be haunted, Carrington House certainly projected that heavy overcrowded atmosphere common to most very old inhabited dwellings. Nothing spectral ever came my way, though in the night bemused drunks, or tarts hoping to make contact, would knock on the illusory door of the bedroom that gave on to the street.

The local tarts were themselves inclined to drink a good deal. It was not unknown to find one of them, surrounded by sympathetic colleagues, totally passed out on the pavement in Brick Street, the narrow alley flanked by huge buildings, which linked the Market with the tarts' nightly beat on Piccadilly. After midnight, two small male prostitutes would sometimes linger, humming gently to themselves, at Brick Street's Piccadilly end.

The mansion-block on the opposite side of Carrington Street was a kind of tarts' barracks. It contained at that period only one male inhabitant, but that a distinguished figure, Sir Ronald Waterhouse, the Prime Minister's Principal Private Secretary. Possibly he was moving house in the neighbourhood, and required temporary accommodation not too far away. Whatever the reason, this eminent public servant (who in similar capacity had worked under several other administrations) must have required all his official *sang froid* to cope with the neighbours, in general not at all well-behaved.

One night, a rumpus in progress at the flats, the landlord or manager, who, perhaps wisely, lived not on the premises but round the corner, came to see what was amiss. One of his tenants, looking down like Jezebel from her window, exclaimed: 'Why, there's that little bugger so-and-so! He's had every woman in the block, including myself.'

II

Sea Air

'This sea air makes one very hungry', remarked a Central European professor, taking tea with me in London some years ago. Without going so far as to regard London as a *plage*, I feel well there as a rule. The place suits me. None the less in those early months, the weather foul, I seemed out of sorts. I look back on the period without nostalgia. Perhaps embarkation on life in the Balzacian manner is a kind of shock to the system, which different individuals sustain in different ways. I had wanted to come down from Oxford, begin the great experiment. Now things appeared difficult to organize. At the University, whether you liked them or not, people were just round the corner. In London, special arrangements had to be made to see the most casual acquaintance.

When I came out of the office I was often at a loose end, unable to decide what on earth to do with myself. Balston, a very hospitable man, would quite often issue invitations to dine at his flat; occasions likely to have a business basis. Decorated with Staffordshire figures (on which he wrote the first major book), pictures by Mark Gertler and Ethelbert White, Balston's service-flat in Artillery Mansions, Victoria Street (close to the scene of my birth), was more than a trifle claustrophobic.

Recurrent guests were G. S. Street, the (in effect) censor of plays; Rose Macaulay, a writer not published by Duckworth's; Charles Ginner, Camden Town Group painter; G. U. Ellis, who worked in Lloyd's bank, in his spare time writing novels for Duckworth's.

George Street (another bachelor inhabitant of Artillery Mansions) was in his sixties, deaf and grumpy. His name was associated with the Nineties, but—as one of W. E. Henley's circle—in an anti-aesthete capacity. Among Street's various books, *The Autobiography of a Boy* (1894) had some success in its day; a satire on Wilde and his friends, which I have never read. I see now that, tackled in the right manner, Street could have produced interesting information about the past. At the time I did not have the good sense to grasp that. I remember inadvertently shocking him by saying 'about half the people one knows are homosexual'.

Ginner, middle-aged, worthy, inarticulate to a degree, painted the sort of pictures I now recognize as capable work; then judged not very exciting. I don't think Ginner would ever have risen to anecdotes.

G. U. Ellis, Balston's discovery as an author, was always hoping to make enough by writing to enable him to leave the bank, work he disliked. He hovered on the brink of producing a popular novel, in what was even then a somewhat old-fashioned genre, but never brought off that ambition. Ellis's critical tastes were more go-ahead than his own novels. After he left Duckworth's (in circumstances he was to feel rather bitter about) he wrote *Twilight on Parnassus: a Survey of Post-War Fiction and Pre-War Criticism* (1939), the first study of that sort to devote an appreciable amount of space to my own early novels; something for which I have always felt grateful.

By the time Rose Macaulay used to visit us at Chester Gate, Regent's Park, in the late 1940s (chaining her bicycle to the area railings) I greatly liked her. In those early days at Balston's dinner parties she seemed prim, chilly, forbidding, the embodiment of academic spinsterhood. Such a judgment was inept, though true that she enjoyed emitting an impression of Cambridge severity.

In fact, prepared to consider all human behaviour in the coolest most objective manner, Rose Macaulay was unusually flexible in revising her own statements. Referring to some recently published novel—possibly Waugh's *A Handful of Dust* (1934)—she said to me: 'I have not read it yet. Not a very interesting subject—adultery in Mayfair.'

'Why should you think that an uninteresting subject?'

'You are quite right,' she said. 'It was a silly thing to say. Subjects are entirely a matter of how they are treated by the writer.'

2

It was Evelyn Waugh, in about March of the New Year (1927), who cheered up what remains in my mind as a rather dreary introduction to London life. We had not seen each other since his sporadic visits to Oxford eight or nine months before; quite a long gap in acquaintance when you are that age. I can't remember whether we ran across each other by chance, or if I wrote to him with the deliberate object of trying to arrange a meeting that might result in a book for Duckworth's.

In principle still earning a living by working as a schoolmaster—which he had been doing on and off by then for two or three years—Waugh had just been sacked out of hand from whatever was the school of the moment. Finding himself in the lowest of water financially did not in the least impair his spirits outwardly, though no doubt there were gloomy moments when alone. He took the line that he was an adventurer, prepared to do anything; and that sooner or later the right opportunity would turn up.

Waugh possessed one substantial advantage. Although he might speak condescendingly about the world of his novelist elder brother, that world was always open to him. Alec Waugh's affiliations—roughly speaking, competent middlebrow professional writers, and the less stage-bound end of the Theatre—were quite lively ones. Nevertheless, even if freely available, like everywhere else they demanded a certain amount of money for overheads.

This was the period when I knew and liked Waugh best. We must have met at times elsewhere, but I chiefly remember invitations to cold supper on Sunday nights at his parents' house in North End Road; even then still a comparatively unbuilt up locality, linking Hampstead with Golders Green.

I can think of no other notable writer of Waugh's generation who came from so unequivocally 'literary' a background; books—their writing, editing, printing, advertising, marketing—the normal way of life. His father, Arthur Waugh (always called Chapman & Hall, from his chairmanship of that publishing company), is naturalistically outlined in *A Little Learning*; more fantastically projected in several of his younger son's novels.

Waugh *père* was not only a 'man of letters' of somewhat old-fashioned sort, as described in these projections, but, having a taste for self-dramatization, played that rôle with considerable verve. Although he kept his firm quite successfully afloat almost singlehanded, and must have possessed a vast literary acquaintance dating back to the Nineties, he, the whole Waugh household, gave an agreeable sense of remoteness from modern life. Arthur Waugh, as a publisher, made Gerald Duckworth seem more than ever clubmanlike; Balston, a thrusting youngster of alarmingly modernistic tendency. This Pickwickian *persona*, assumed with such determination, was at once irritating to his younger son, yet also in a manner sympathetic to the side in love with Victorianism.

If Waugh—as he himself records—was sometimes on bad terms with his father, no sign of any such awkward relationship ever appeared during North End Road visits. On the contrary, the two of them seemed to agree uncommonly well. Arthur Waugh's air of mildness was perhaps a little too good to be true, and he was apt to begin sentences with the jocose opening: 'Speaking as a member of the lower-middle classes . . .', but, if a fancy for exaggerated humility sometimes grated on his younger son's nerves, that was more for its implied lack of adventurousness, than on account of any explicit social ambition at that date.

Where smart life was concerned, Waugh himself would speak with a love/hate not unlike Thackeray's; a state of mind not in the least averse from receiving chic invitations, if any were going, but always flavoured with a certain animus against what was grand, rich, fashionable. In due course, when he adopted quite another approach, something always remained beneath the surface of a kind of social resentment.

I think there is nothing mysterious about either standpoint. Waugh was, in his way, an extraordinarily uncomplicated man; so uncomplicated that even in those days—far more so later in life—it was often hard to accept that some of his views and attitudes were serious. That was mistaken. They were perfectly serious to himself; within the limits that, possessing his father's powerful taste for self-dramatization, all Waugh's energies were concentrated on any rôle he was playing, however grotesque or absurd.

This simplicity of approach was particularly true in Waugh's manner of looking at social life. He really did believe in entities like a 'great nobleman', 'poor scholar', 'literary man of modest means'. Of course, in one sense, such stylized concepts may certainly exist, but at close range they usually require a good deal of modification. At the same time their acceptance—allied to gifts like Waugh's—can be by no means a disadvantage to a novelist, clearing the air automatically of extraneous detail that can clog a narrative. Hardy, for instance, is prepared to employ positive lay-figures to simplify telling a story; no less Dickens, a strong influence on Waugh's early style.

The 'high-life' of *Decline and Fall* is mostly depicted from imagination, hearsay, newspaper gossip columns. Later, when Waugh himself had enjoyed a certain amount of first-hand experience of such circles, he was on the whole not much interested in their contradictions and paradoxes. He wished the *beau monde* to remain in the image he had formed, usually showing himself unwilling to listen, if facts were offered that seemed to militate against that image. This taste for stylization is somewhat modified in *The Ordeal of Gilbert Pinfold*, the most searching of Waugh's works, a book unmatched for its combination of funniness and horror.

3

On these pleasant North End Road evenings, Arthur Waugh would tell literary anecdotes at the dinner table; Mrs Waugh (whose quiet exterior suggested much inner firmness of purpose) scarcely speaking at all, slipping out at the first opportunity. When the company moved from the dining room Arthur Waugh might continue to chat for a minute or two, then also retire, probably to work. Waugh and I would sit and talk. I usually stayed until nearly midnight, when a last bus could be caught to the neighbourhood of Piccadilly. Once I missed this bus, and had to walk all the way back to Shepherd Market; a weary trudge that seemed unending even by the time St John's Wood was gained.

One night Waugh asked if I would like to hear the opening chapters of a novel he was writing. (Somerset Maugham remarks somewhere that British authors, unlike French, never read their works aloud to each other. Such is not my own experience, but perhaps they do so only when young.) Waugh's embryonic novel—then called *Picaresque: or the Making of an Englishman*—was the first ten thousand words, scarcely at all altered later, of *Decline and Fall*. The manuscript was written with a pen on double-sheets of blue lined-foolscap, the cipher EW printed at the top of the first page of each double-sheet. There were hardly any alterations in the text.

In his early days Waugh would write all his books straight off, then make one fair copy for the publisher, which was not, I think, typed; though I could not be certain about that. I found this overture extremely funny, but did not in the least guess the *popular* success *Decline and Fall* would eventually achieve. Some months after the reading aloud of these chapters—probably a moment towards the end of the same year—I asked Waugh how the novel was progressing. He replied: 'I've burnt it.'

On the evening of the reading, or another, Waugh gave me an inscribed copy of *P. R. B. An Essay on the Pre-Raphaelite Brotherhood 1847–1854.* Bound in blue-grey boards, printed on handmade paper, slim, elegant, this essay had been specially written for Waugh's close Oxford friend, Alastair Graham, who at that time owned a small printing· press. Graham had issued it privately the previous year. Waugh himself dismissed *P.R.B.* as a mere trifle, but, even if the author clearly needs more room in which to manoeuvre, the instinctive ability of the writing, feeling for words, unusual point of view, are all immediately apparent.

P. R. B. also puts on record for the first time Waugh's lifelong pleasure in mid-Victorian culture. He was proud of his own family con- nexions with the Pre-Raphaelites; Holman Hunt having married succes- sively (then against the law) two Waugh sisters. In the essay Waugh makes the comment that Holman Hunt's *The Awakening Consciousness* (called by a slip *The Awakened Conscience*, a picture by William Henry Hunt, confusingly so titled) 'is, perhaps, the noblest painting by an Englishman'; a startling opinion within the aesthetics of 1926.

At the time simply a spontaneous gift, *P. R. B.* turned out to have bearing on what Waugh was in due course to write for Duckworth's. A month or two earlier, discussing potential biographies that might be commissioned by the firm, Balston had remarked that an up-to-date account of Dante Gabriel Rossetti's life was already overdue. Various names were put forward to undertake that; nothing decided.

In the course of these North End Road meetings with Waugh, it had been arranged that he should come to Henrietta Street to talk over the possibility of authorship. Waugh brought a copy of *P. R. B.* with him as evidence of literacy. Balston, on the strength of the essay, immediately suggested Rossetti as a theme. So far as I can remember, Waugh had no particular plan to deal further with the Pre-Raphaelites—he may even have had some other subject in mind—but the combination of *P. R. B.* and Balston's already existent leanings towards a book about Rossetti, resulted in *Rossetti: His Life and Works* being commissioned in May, 1927.

4

On one of Waugh's visits to Henrietta Street as a future Duckworth author he suggested that we should lunch together at a Soho club he had just joined, The Gargoyle, founded a year or two before with an eye on the intelligentzia; even if Constant Lambert was later to complain that the dance floor on Saturday night was 'packed with the two hundred nastiest people in Chiswick'. I had already heard of The Gargoyle, which was on the top floor of an alley just off Dean Street, but had never been there. In principle a night-club, it was one of respectable kind, drinks not likely to be available 'after hours.'

On the way to The Gargoyle (possibly on its premises) we met a girl Waugh had recently come across at *The Daily Express*, a newspaper on which he was himself employed for a few weeks at about this time; later contributing items for its gossip column. This was Inez Holden, one of several figures belonging to this early stage of my London life, whom I was to meet on and off for forty years or more. A word may be said of her here, because she was an unusual person.

The three of us lunched together under the large picture by Matisse that hung in The Gargoyle's dining room, lending an air of go-ahead culture to the club. I feel pretty sure that Waugh, with his usual generosity, paid for Inez Holden's lunch, though the advance on *Rossetti: His Life and Works* was probably not more than twenty or thirty pounds. Afterwards I was put up for the club, of which—though never a great frequenter—I remained a member for some years. It would have been logical for Waugh to have put me up, Inez Holden to have seconded me, but I have an idea that for some reason the process was vice versa.

The appearance of Inez Holden in later life was sadly altered by some glandular condition. In those days she was very pretty, with the fashionable type of beauty Lambert used to call 'consumptive charm' (he thought her attractive but too *difficile* for involvement), a fragility of feature well suggested in two drawings by Augustus John, though neither a striking likeness.

Inez Holden was a torrential talker, an accomplished mimic, her gossip of a high and fantastical category; excellent company when not—as sometimes in later life—obsessed by some 'story' being run by the papers, of which she was a compulsive reader. At this period she too was trying to find her feet in London. Later she became a writer, erratic, though never without wit and originality. Very much a figure of the Twenties and early Thirties, she moved from High Bohemia to the extreme political Left, possibly as far as Communism. Her later passionate hatred of the Communist Party suggested close knowledge of its methods.

Born Old; Died Young (1932), probably Inez Holden's best book, contains something of a self-portrait; the heroine described as an 'adventuress', daughter ('left homeless and penniless') of an Edwardian beauty. That was more or less her own case (her father a retired cavalryman), and, sometimes desperately poor, she lived fairly dangerously in a rich world of a distinctly older generation. This makes her sound like a *poule de luxe*. She was certainly not that, no one seeming to know (outside the fantasies she projected about herself) whether she allowed these shadowy love affairs to take physical shape.

'There was a period of my life,' she told me years later, 'when I knew only millionaires. That was when I was working on the *Express*. They were always asking me to arrange for them to buy the paper for a halfpenny, instead of a penny.'

For a couple of years after this Gargoyle luncheon I scarcely saw Inez Holden, but in 1929 Duckworth's published her first novel, *Sweet Charlatan*, a manuscript not steered there by me (unconvinced of its merits), nor, I think, by Waugh. She had met Balston somewhere, and brought pressure to bear on a nature altogether unused to adventuresses. It would not be going too far to say that for a time she made hay of him.

After her interlude as a Duckworth's author, I did not see much of her again until the late Thirties. By that time I was married, and we were living at Chester Gate. Inez Holden had rooms in Albany Street, just round the corner. Then the war came, and I have described in the first volume of these Memoirs how she introduced me to George Orwell, to whom she was always greatly devoted.

The story of the row between Orwell and H. G. Wells (another friend of Inez Holden's) has often been told, its climax in Wells's famous note to Orwell saying: 'Read my early works, you shit'; a recommendation many authors must have been tempted to prescribe at one time or another, in just those terms for suspected carpers. The coolness had taken place when Inez Holden was living in Wells's garage. A long time later there had been some public controversy as to the precise circumstances of the row, and, in a letter on the subject to me, written about two years before her death (1974), she said: 'My memory is, I think, phenomenal—really like the horse "Clever Hans". Do you know about him? He could answer almost any question, but did have to tap it out with his hoof.'

5

I spent one or two weekends in Birmingham during the two years Yorke was working in his factory there. He boarded with a family in the manner of an ordinary engineering operative, and seemed happy; more so than when at home, or travelling in America with his father, a journey that at one point interrupted this Birmingham reclusion. Yorke said that he never followed up occasional temptingly frisky invitations to join groups of factory girls roaming the streets after work, though they would sometimes shout after him. My impression is that he was as content during this Birmingham period as I ever knew him to be.

Meanwhile I had involved myself in activities quite other to those suggested by Henrietta Street and The Gargoyle. I did not reveal any hint of these explorations to friends of my own age, who would have regarded them as eccentric to the borderline of lunacy. Partly from an ingrained curiosity about military matters, partly in continuation of the process of de-Oxfordization, I had decided to try out anyway the preliminaries of becoming a Territorial.

My father, without offering much active encouragement, undertook some of the necessary enquiries, which seemed to prompt the claims of the Royal Artillery. I felt that if the Gunners were good enough for Tolstoy, they were good enough for me; in consequence finding myself 'on probation' with a Territorial battery, its Headquarters in a South London suburb, possibly Brixton. To reach there required several changes of bus, followed by a ten minutes walk. Most of the officers (a fair sprinkling of stockbrokers) owned cars, so there was usually someone driving back within range of Shepherd Market.

I used to attend drills twice a week. Those evenings, after a sandwich and glass of beer in the Mess, were spent for the most part in the riding school. Goethe, in his autobiography, observes that an air of brutality seems invariably attached to indoor riding schools, and certainly impelling an iron-mouthed horse round a dusty shed under glaring electric light bulbs can be a thankless, if not humiliating, occupation.

In this particular case the Sergeant-Major in charge could not have been more agreeable. One night he was himself exercising the Commanding Officer's charger. I was not having much success in putting the animal I was riding through its paces, so the Sergeant-Major—philosophically remarking: 'What the eye doesn't see, the heart doesn't grieve'—told me to dismount and try the jump again on the Colonel's mare. It was the first (and last) occasion when I have ever sat a really good mount, and, for someone used to my luck in hacks, it was a striking experience; one I have always valued as giving insight into an otherwise closed world of equestrian enjoyment.

More esoteric mysteries were performed in another outhouse, the upper storeys of which were reached by an external iron staircase like a fire escape. At the top of this stair, a low doorway led into a long dark attic, at the end of which, when suddenly lighted up, appeared a rural scene set on a small stage: fields, woods, rivers, villages, churches, railway lines, a landscape that receded into downs and foothills:

> Into my heart an air that kills
> From yon far country blows:
> What are those blue remembered hills,
> What spires, what farms are those?

This rustic panorama at first appeared to be in preparation for a miniature dramatic performance. In front of the stage were several benches for the audience, at which telephones were installed at intervals. The assembled officers would sit on the benches, one or other taking charge of a telephone.

The Adjutant (or Commanding Officer) would announce: 'A detachment of cavalry (*sic*) is advancing through the trees towards that gully on

26

the left of the railway line', or 'Such-and-such a gun has opened fire from behind the church on the right of the hill.' One of the officers would then be deputed to take action on this information, give orders by telephone as to the placing of HE 106 (high explosive) to be loosed off at the imaginary enemy; the range estimated by holding out a clenched fist. After the order was issued, some hidden agency behind the scenes manipulated wires in such a manner that a small projectile would fall on the spot indicated by the calculations, often a long way from the target, exciting unfavourable comment from the Adjutant.

These exercises in bombardment were stimulating—though a single term's uncomprehended trigonometry might eventually have proved inadequate for the mathematical side of gunnery—and there was a certain sense of moral as well as physical uplift in being taught systematically to ride. On the other hand, thought of a fortnight's camp taken out of a three weeks holiday was daunting; equally, what had not earlier occurred to me, the Battery's highly organized social life off duty; chiefly small dances within the unit, which gave opportunity to wear mess-kit.

This inevitably golf-and-bridge world was not my own, though as a probationer I was able to escape too close immediate involvement. That exclusion clearly could not continue for ever. Incidentally, so strong was the passion for 'dressing up' in the Twenties that some of the Battery dances would be fancy-dress in the same sort of way that 'bohemian' parties were fancy-dress; the men perhaps tacking coloured lapels on to their tailcoats.

Hoping to conceal so far as possible intellectual commitments likely to raise their accustomed barrier, I talked little in Mess, confining myself to the most banal comment and four-letter words. I had been attached to the Battery for about two months when one night an officer turned up I had not yet met. The Adjutant's introduction was: 'This is Powell—he's a Senior Wrangler or something.'

Grasping now that any attempt at seeming something other than an intellectual had been vain—in any case rather tired of the large amount of spare time I was spending on buses travelling to South London—I decided to withdraw. I could not, in the army phrase, 'send in my papers', as I had no papers to send in, but I wrote to the Colonel telling him that requirements had arisen which made it difficult, if not impossible, to devote several evenings a week to some exterior occupation. That was quite true,

Duckworth's having issued a fiat that I should undertake a course of printing at the Holborn Polytechnic.

6

This period was also to initiate the close of my father's career, and the actual 'sending in of papers'. He was now within sight of emergence from the post-war traffic block of promotion, being in line to command one of the two battalions of The Welch Regiment; regimental command a scarcely avoidable rung of the ladder for any infantry officer who hoped to achieve senior rank. My father's health, undermined by dysentery during the war, was not likely to stand up well to a tropical climate (one battalion of each regiment in those days stationed in India), but he was specifically marked out for the 'home' battalion; after command of which certainly he himself looked forward to further ascents.

At the beginning of 1927, unsettled conditions in China led to the dispatch of a British Defence Force to Shanghai. Among the units ordered to the Far East was the home battalion of The Welch. For reasons of economy in trooping routines that meant an indefinite tour of duty overseas for the battalion my father was to command. This unlooked for alteration in the pattern of his future was a shattering blow. Apart from the question of health, a posting out of England would have been exceedingly unsympathetic to my mother.

My father served in China for a short time, fell ill, was brought back to convalesce. He made efforts to find employment other than regimental, but the principle that army personnel must be fit to serve anywhere was rigorously applied (the Financial Branch ever dreading disability pensions), though there was irony in the officer who conveyed to him the necessity of retirement possessing only one arm.

In 1928, a disappointed man, my father left the Service. At first he was not without resource. Having always felt a taste for the Law, he read for the Bar, achieved a Second, went into Chambers. There he found it impossible to make any real adjustment to civilian life. That was probably as much due to his own natural intractability of temperament, as to the unfamiliarities of a new profession after thirty years of army ways.

With retirement, increased leisure, my father's interests in books, the arts generally, seemed to diminish rather than increase. He became bored, depressed, irritable, unfriendly; states from which he rarely found it possible to free himself. Both my parents preferring London to the country, they found a house, 3 Clarence Terrace, in Regent's Park. I used quite often to dine with them after they were established there, but relations with my father were never easy. He would have spells of cheerfulness, but they were always of short duration.

7

Other people have told me they too experienced a monochromatic twelve-month before London had much to offer, then all at once new vistas opened up. How exactly that took place in my own case I have never been able to establish. Suddenly at the same moment there seemed fresh paths to explore. That was, I suppose, in the best Balzac tradition. Even so, efforts to chart London social life in the self-confident matter-of-fact Balzacian manner risk floundering in the sea of misapprehension that beats so hard on latterday annotators of the Twenties. Nevertheless, I shall attempt something of the kind.

Spring and early summer brought through the letter-box a few invitations to débutante dances. Deb dances have often been described, usually disobligingly. At the moment they were acceptable, indeed I could have done with more cards for them. In their most intrinsic form the hard core was made up of two or three hundred girls, whose parents were expected to give a similar dance on the 'coming out' of a daughter. The net for young men was cast far wider, a chance meeting easily resulting in an invitation. At Oxford I had already begun to receive these (emanating from Oxford friends with deb sisters or cousins), perhaps the earliest being forwarded on from Balliol. Sooner or later young men who frequented such dances were likely to get on a 'list', or rather one of the lists, nominal rolls said to vary in eligibility.

This was before the depression, a period when young men wore white gloves as a matter of course; as often as not there was 'taking in' to dinner. Three years later a young man wearing gloves was an elegant exception; to go into dinner on a partner's arm fallen altogether into disuse. At the time it seemed not at all odd that, apart from people already met, an entirely unknown hostess should invite one to a dinner party, where not a soul at the table was previously familiar. That did not happen often—less often than I could have wished—but, even when dinner was not on offer (change into tails effected after a meal at The Chesterfield), a dance could make a tolerable evening.

Deb dances included, of course, girls not débutantes in the strict sense of having been presented at Court that year; the number of 'seasons' at which a girl would appear varying according to taste and temperament. I tended to meet girls I knew at dances only at dances, a watertight compartment of my life. There were exceptions to this rule, for example, the charming Biddulph sisters, Adèle (Dig) and Mary (Miss), cousins of the Yorkes (the former of whom was to marry Henry Yorke), and several more. I continued to go to deb dances, on and off, until 1930, when—at what appears to be the last attended—my future wife, Violet Pakenham, was also present (one of her first), but we failed to meet.

8

Because of their predominantly well-behaved nature (the occasional tight young man, couple in a clinch on a secluded staircase, both on the whole unwonted), deb dances were somewhat derided by young men who received invitations; even more by those who did not. Quite a few young men born into that ambience would never figure at them; Yorke himself, for instance, who long set his face against even learning to dance. For the girls, as I found later, dances were often regarded as exquisite torture, and, even for meeting and marrying, London dances were looked on as possessing none of the prestige (or impulsion towards marriage) attributed to country house parties.

A word should be said of the quite extraordinary disfavour in which marriage was held by the parental generation of that day. This, so far as I know, has never been sufficiently remarked. It would not be difficult for me to name half-a-dozen couples in the deb world, who were prevented— at the very least long obstructed—from getting married; although the parents concerned were not able to offer any of the traditional objections, like shortage of money, moral disapproval, or even simple down-to-earth snobbishness. That attitude seems to have been particularly characteristic of the Twenties, either a hangover from the past, or a kind of post-war neurosis about taking so important a step.

Deliberate thwarting of marriage was all the more extraordinary in the light of surplus girls, who, owing to the casualties of World War I, had not found husbands. An aspect of that last situation was the scarcity, almost non-existence, of young married couples; those there were, associated with the war generation, rather than younger near-contemporaries. In general, whatever their circumstances, people grow up, marry, are at once absorbed into the tail-end of other 'young marrieds'. When the young men and girls of my own vintage married, that was like a new departure in social patterns; and up to a point—in the sense that there was no continuous sequence—it was indeed that.

Like most highly standardized forms of life, the deb world was more complicated than appeared on the surface, providing a microcosm by no means without interest. Where everyone is drilled to behave in much the same manner (as Henry James so often suggests in his novels), individual differences are often more apparent than otherwise. I do not regret (from a writer's point of view) having served my turn there. I fell briefly in love, though not at all in the circumstances described by the Narrator in *A Dance to the Music of Time*.

The current fashion is to condemn novels or plays about small aristocratic societies on grounds that what happens there is without bearing on the doings of the rest of the world. Yet after all, when it comes to general implications of behaviour, Œdipus was king of Thebes; Hamlet, Prince of Denmark; Petronius clearly not at all inhibited from knowing about everyday things, on account of his position as arbiter of elegance at Nero's court.

III

Astolpho's Horn

I was all the time aware that a more invigorating, less staid, world existed, than that to which I possessed a somewhat hand-to-mouth access. Those other parties—in their specifically Late Twenties/Early Thirties sense—burned phosphorescently for a few years only, dying away as randomly as they had flamed into being. To distinguish the essential 'partyishness' (there must be a German word) of the Twenties party from other sempiternal assemblies of people met together for the purpose of drinking, dancing, making sexual contact, is not easy. At the same time Twenties parties (with their brief extension into the Thirties) *were* in some manner different, never renewed later in anything like the same texture. In attempting to assess this difference arises an even greater danger of becoming doctrinaire than in speaking of debs.

For the intellectual—not working that term too hard—were, at the upper end of the scale, the parties of Lady Cunard (whom I never set eyes on until much later) and her like; hostesses whose gatherings were—again not using the term too rigorously—what might be called smart. They were at least formal, mostly for an older generation, though flavoured with a few selected young people. At the lower end of the scale of equally formal parties (white ties and tails much favoured from South Kensington to Hampstead) were those given by, say, publishers and art dealers with an eye to business. Neither of these types, nor many between, was essentially a Twenties party, though some of the same people might be seen at either, or the 'real thing'.

The public expression of the old-fashioned 'artists' party' was the

32

Chelsea Arts Ball at the Albert Hall, held on the last night of the Old Year. This still flourished, much changed from the days when Constant Lambert's parents would attend, with a large group of fellow painters and their wives, everyone dressed in the scrupulously correct costume of a given character at the court of Henry VIII. Since tickets could be bought for the Chelsea Arts, its nature obviously differed from a private party, however loosely organized, but many elements of the private party of a similar sort would be present at the Albert Hall, where things were apt to become rowdy towards dawn.

Bloomsbury (using the label in its strictest sense) was in its way exclusive, not rich enough to entertain very magnificently, but here—anyway at the lower levels of Bloomsbury—the true Twenties party comes into sight. C. J. Hope-Johnstone used to describe a Bloomsbury party he attended, to which two guardsmen (met in the street) had been brought by some guest on his way there. Food had been set before them, said Hope-Johnstone, the Bloomsburies standing round watching fascinated the soldiers in their scarlet tunics; from time to time commenting in their high Bloomsbury voices: '*How they eat!*' The incongruity, touch of homosexuality, intellectuals' astonishment at forms of life other than their own, in combination convey the right period touch.

At Augustus John's studio in Mallord Street, Chelsea, allowing for the marked tang of the host's unusually strong personality, the essential Twenties party is almost reached, especially in the multifariousness of those present: old friends, rich patrons, ornamental models, recently discovered or of long fame.

Nevertheless, the typical Twenties party was likely to be given by host or hostess of far less distinction, probably fairly rich in contrast with guests, though not in any high range of richness, and (as with those who gave expensive Oxford parties) often unknown to many of the invités. Fancy-dress was the rule rather than the exception, though not at all insistently, white ties, black ties, day clothes, probably dotted about here and there. Hostesses were for some reason often well-to-do lesbians; less frequently male homosexuals, whose proficiently organized London community might—indeed certainly would—supply a few representatives, but in general tended to entertain within its own closed circuit.

Most of those present at a 'typical' party would be likely to possess some connexion with the arts, however marginal, but never enough of any one calling to make the assembly a painters' party, an actors' party, an ad-men's party, though several painters would be likely to be present, the stray actor and ad-man. Indeed painters would be more in evidence than writers. There would be occasional musicians; architects; photographers; in the theatrical contingent, the Ballet likely to outnumber the Legitimate. The girls, largely drawn from the all-inclusive (one avoids the word all-embracing) vocation of model—both artists' model, and one who 'modelled' clothes, the latter then quaintly known as mannequins—usually showed an altogether exceptional standard of looks.

Invitations (as with deb dances) would arrive for these parties from people never met—once the barrier of being recognized as the sort of person who 'went to parties' had been passed—and (gate-crashing, in moderation, usually accepted as enlivening the evening) one would sometimes be brought along by a friend. There might be a hundred or more guests, things done in quite a prodigal style. That was particularly true of parties that took place in a vessel called *The Friendship*, a steamer moored in the Thames, kept there apparently for no other purpose.

The age of most of those present would be well under thirty; a few probably in their forties; then perhaps a steep rise to comparatively ancient figures, long established in High Bohemia. Augustus John parties would probably include the practical joker, Horace Cole, by then a shade time-expired; possibly Philip Heseltine (Peter Warlock, the musician), usually involving an altercation; the Marchesa Casati, smiling silently to herself, D'Annunzian eyeballs blazing like searchlights. At routs other than John's, highly stylized figures were to be seen: the academic painter, Stuart Hill, known as Christ-in-corsets; the insatiable raconteur, Harry Melvill ('For people one has had to give themselves moral or social airs is childish,' wrote Wilde, when Melvill cut him); another authentic Nineties relic, Ada Leverson, the Sphinx (still whispering passable epigrams), in huge black hat, tangle of veils, faraway expression, gliding through dimly lit rooms between couples locked in suffocating embrace.

This demi-monde—the designation much more appropriate than usually applied—once penetrated, solved some of the problems of making contact with girls in a manner less formal than that available at dances. One heard stories of debs who could be got to bed, but I should have thought such emancipation belonged, in general, to a somewhat later period, when chaperonage had diminished, the night-club taken a firmer hold. Dances were not an easy jumping-off point for closer intimacies, on account of the manner in which the evening was organized.

At the other kind of party girls expected to have passes made at them, and were well able to look after themselves. Nevertheless, if parties severed one sort of knot, they tied another, a great many of the girls who attended them having to think in terms of young men rich enough to contribute something more to their upkeep than a regular dinner invitation and occasional pair of silk stockings.

2

Like Augustus John and Bloomsbury, the three Sitwells had created a world perceptibly their own, though its affiliations, differing in the case of each individual Sitwell, seemed less immediately recognizable. One of Balston's earliest publishing ambitions was to take over the Sitwells' work; his first capture, Edith Sitwell, whose volume of verse, *Bucolic Comedies*, had been published by Duckworth's as far back as 1923. In the month I began employment with Duckworth's, the firm brought out both Osbert Sitwell's first novel, *Before the Bombardment*, and Sacheverell Sitwell's 'autobiographical fantasia', *All Summer in a Day*.

The triune nature of the family cartel—fatally effective at the time as vehicle of publicity—has not otherwise been advantageous to the Sitwells as individual writers. Their striking physical resemblance, a taste (in at least two) for polemics that was excessive, even for the chronic literary skirmishes of that date, the whole nature of the family's myth and its propagation in their own writings, have in different ways helped to obfuscate the picture for separate consideration.

To say that is in no way to decry all manifestations of subjectivity, flamboyance, fireworks, in intellectual life. The great thing about the Sitwells was that they believed, however idiosyncratically, that the arts were to be enjoyed; not doled out like medicine for the good of people's social or political health. Their phalanx impeded not only straight philistinism (never dormant in any society), but also a wholesale takeover by the pedantic, the doctrinaire, the 'committed'; assailants by whom the arts are also eternally menaced.

Tall fair attentuated courtiers from a mediaeval tapestry, the Sitwells spoke with a clear rich articulation, tones musical, emphasized, to be differentiated from the high speech of Bloomsbury. Edith Sitwell was the first of the family I met; almost certainly dining at Balston's. She got on well with Balston, whom she unremittingly teased. Lacking her brothers' easy flow of conversation, unless in company familiar to her, she could be a little alarming at first, and was never really at ease in large gatherings. With people she knew and liked, no one could be gayer, though controversial topics were even then to be avoided.

At this period, to some extent throughout Edith Sitwell's life (explanation of the biographical potboilers), she was not at all well off. She lived in a tiny flat at St Petersburg (eccentrically written 'St Petersborough' on the street sign) Place, Bayswater, where she would give tea parties; the sitting room on such occasions filled to capacity—and beyond—with guests invited for a thousand incongruous reasons. She used to say that she killed flowers, nourished jewels, the exotic sweeping gowns she wore usually decorated with a *bijouterie* of gigantic topaz or aquamarine.

Notwithstanding the literary rows in which she was so often emmeshed (notably with Wyndham Lewis, who at an earlier stage had executed several admirable portraits of her), Edith Sitwell was a person of the kindest instincts; indeed to a fault, in a manner that could involve her with worthless hangers-on. She was altogether unsuited (though she herself would have strenuously denied that) for the virulent public squabbles in which she found herself forever caught up; scrimmages often her own fault, but really an extraneous part of her existence.

Much later than this period, Dylan Thomas, at one of Edith Sitwell's parties, said: 'If poetry was taken away from Edith she mightn't die, but she'd be bloody sick.' This characteristic uttering, gnomic and earthy, was a fair estimate of the case. Dedication to poetry, poetry alone, made Edith Sitwell in a sense the least complicated of the three. An agonised upbringing had caused her to suffer when young, and, among the writings of the family, hers make pain the most explicit; *Gold Coast Customs* (1929) especially conveying a sense of horror and squalor that recalls Hood.

Edith Sitwell's judgments were always clearcut. Her critical faculties might be arbitrary, they were never narrow. She said of Virginia Woolf and V. Sackville-West: 'I don't like what Virginia writes, but she knows what writing is about—Vita doesn't know what writing is about'. Describing how she herself had refused to dine with some literary bore (I do not remember which), she added: 'After all, I only have one dinner a day.' When a sudden warm friendship sprang up between Siegfried Sassoon (then in his forties, of melancholy saturnine appearance) and Stephen Tennant (at that moment the prettiest of pretty young men), she used to call them The Old Earl and Little Lord Fauntleroy.

3

I first came across Osbert and Sacheverell Sitwell in the office, where the former especially would spend most of the morning or afternoon—sometimes a fair proportion of both—if he had a book to be published. After leaving Balston's room, Osbert Sitwell would gossip, discuss other authors (he could feel competitive about the most insignificant of writers), rag Lewis, who enjoyed Sitwell leg-pulling, however time-wasting. Balston would come in for his share of Sitwell badinage too, but for quite a long time controlled with adroitness their not too easy team; himself producing a *Handlist* (1928) of Sitwell publications up-to-date. Osbert Sitwell thought Gerald Duckworth a *faux-bonhomme*, but at this stage nothing worse than an armed neutrality existed in that quarter.

Although usually complaining of imminent bankruptcy, Osbert Sitwell (by the standards of most youngish writers) lived in fairly sumptuous style at 2 Carlyle Square. This Chelsea house had been shared with his younger brother until 1925, when Sachie Sitwell married Georgia Doble, a Canadian beauty, who took on Sitwell lore with an extraordinary receptivity. Not long before marriage Sachie Sitwell had inherited (from a comparatively distant relation) a house in Northamptonshire, handsome but of manageable size. These circumstances—marriage, a country house, taste for living à la mode (Osbert Sitwell liked the beau monde too, but rather different areas)—had already set the younger Sitwell brother a little apart from the other two.

The Carlyle Square house was crammed with pictures and art objects of every style and every epoch. On a table in the back half of the ground-floor sitting room (a kind of ante-room, where pre-dinner drinks were likely to be served) stood a huge bowl filled to the brim with ever-replenished press-cuttings. The dining room, also on the ground-floor, built out at the back of the house, was reached by a narrow passage, to traverse which in winter Osbert Sitwell would sometimes assume a cloak. Food, usually topped up with some specially bought delicacy, was simple but excellent; wine, flowing always in abundance, sometimes of exotic vintages, never less than first-rate. After dinner the party would ascend to the first floor drawing-room, where no spare inch of wall space remained uncovered by pictures; artefacts and bric-a-brac crowding the room.

Osbert Sitwell—to borrow the phrase of the arch-enemy, Wyndham Lewis—was essentially a personal appearance artist. As a writer he is most gifted at satirical verse. His novels and short stories, full of good ideas, never attain quite sufficient deftness of execution; while the memoirs, *Left Hand, Right Hand!*, unforgettable for the portrait of his father, show an over-elaboration which the author admits himself unwilling to curb.

The 'portraits in verse' of *England Reclaimed* (1928), village people known to Osbert Sitwell as a child, sometimes bring an odd reminder of sequences in novels by Henry Green; not only as affectionate, almost romantically yearning, pictures of a different world, viewed (notwithstanding both writers' efforts to minimize that angle) through aristocratic eyes, but, more essentially, on account of certain parallels in style, arrangement of words. If Henry Green's paragraphs were cut up into short lines like verse, Osbert Sitwell's poetry set continuously as prose, without too much adjustment either might be presented as the alternative art form. I don't think the two ever met one another; if so, only superficially.

Distinction as poet and writer gave appropriate background for Osbert Sitwell's true rôle as wit, dandy, leader of fashion, writer of lively letters to the paper, partisan in literary campaigns and vendettas; one who stubbornly kept the arts before the public eye, by no means a useless function if well contrived. There was something of the Nineties about all this, the tradition of Wilde, shorn of too much aesthetic affectation by Osbert Sitwell's years in the Grenadiers, a regiment in which his brother also served. The Brigade of Guards ambience, not at all conspicuous in either of them, was always there; and, during the second war, Osbert Sitwell confessed to me that 'you never get used to not being saluted'.

Excellent company tête-à-tête, Osbert Sitwell's wit was best adapted to the set-piece with an audience, rather than the kind that instantaneously grasps—then brilliantly caps—the implications of a conversation. He dominated a dinner table with geniality, but essentially as protagonist.

That does not mean that he lacked repartee. On some occasion he and Harold Nicolson were together filling embarkation forms on a Channel crossing.

'What age are you going to put, Osbert?' asked Nicolson.

'What sex are you going to put, Harold?'

4

Like his sister, Osbert Sitwell was by nature very kind; at the same time far better equipped than she, or his younger brother, for the dusty encounters of the arena. In these gladiatorial shows Sachie Sitwell loyally, but perhaps not very profitably, seemed at times carried along at the chariot wheels of the other two. His variety of interests make him the most complex of the three Sitwells, the one who has always reaped least advantage from collective attack, handicapped, rather than sustained, by antecedent family influences thrust upon him.

The sheer luxuriance of Sachie Sitwell's intellectual concerns strikes the imagination: theatrical décor of the past; exotic musical excursions; every aspect of the macabre; a thousand more things too. Almost singlehanded in this country he cleared a path through the jungle of now forgotten prejudice to the long obscured kingdom of the Baroque. The Sitwells have been attacked for dilettantism. It is not remembered that in those days even to admire the Paris School of painting (now looked on as, say, a safe investment for Trade Union Funds) was then the taste of a small minority; while few had heard of Sitwell-promoted masters, at the time wholly unfashionable, like Domenichino, Magnasco, Laroon, Fuseli, Dadd.

Sachie Sitwell's poetry, strongly influenced by the 17th century, remote in feeling, at times a trifle stiff, remains always unique to himself; the minutiae of aesthetic sensation, rather than the poet's relation to other people. The few love poems make one wish for more. Often the lines describe some infinitely delicate state of physical consciousness, the wind's touch of *Gardener's Song* (*The Thirteenth Caesar*, 1924), or (from the same volume) coruscating images of a fantasy Latin America in *The Rio Grande*; later set to music by Constant Lambert, who was also associated with *Façade*; a performance at which Edith Sitwell's poems were declaimed against a background of William Walton's music.

39

The least known of the trio, Sachie Sitwell is perhaps the most gifted, though the goods he offered were always for some reason those not always readily saleable. He remains an enigmatic figure, inwardly withdrawn from life, in spite of having lived much in the world.

5

William Walton, whose musical inspiration Sachie Sitwell first recognized, when both were undergraduates at Oxford, had been taken on by the Sitwells more or less as a member of the family. Willie Walton (now Sir William, OM), quiet, well organized, faintly satirical in manner, also lived at Carlyle Square, and was usually present at any party held there. He was very much one of the household (together with another occupant, Osbert Sitwell's close friend, David Horner), yet also in a curious way somehow separate from it.

Walton (like the poet, Roy Fuller, also with musical affiliations) came from Oldham, Lancashire, and was physically of much the same North Midlands type as that to which the Sitwells themselves belonged. (When visiting Derbyshire, and neighbouring counties, one notices at once in local trains the predominance of this tall fair acquiline race). Walton, as protective colouring, naturally acquired other Sitwell resemblances and tricks of speech. In consequence (so Constant Lambert asserted), foreigners, at musical occasions attended by both Walton and the Sitwell family, would smile at English hypocrisy in pretending that this manifest Sitwell was not a by-blow of their father, Sir George; though, in fact, nothing could be less Sitwellian than Willie Walton on a night out with Lambert or other uninhibited cronies.

Walton had unforeseen abilities as handyman. The Sitwells were fond of describing how a piano had been delivered for him, when alone in the house, which by some superhuman means, Walton had transferred to an upper floor. When questioned as to how that had been effected, he replied: 'I did it with a bit of string.'

At the London Surrealist Exhibition of 1936 (oldest of old hat to anyone with the least claims to avant-gardism), Walton, to rag the whole affair, arrived at the Exhibition with a bloater in a paper bag. This, at a suitable moment, he removed from its covering, and, as a piece of active surrealism, hung on one of the pieces of sculpture. There, so far as I know, the fish remained throughout the run of the show; perhaps returning with the exhibit to whatever gallery or studio was its home.

That the London cosmos secreted a richer mixture than any offered by Oxford was for some reason peculiarly brought home to me at an early dinner-party given by Osbert Sitwell, where—with perhaps one or two more—the guests included Willie Walton, Constant Lambert, David Horner (called by Lambert 'The Captain's Doll', from D. H. Lawrence's short story), Harold Acton, Robert Byron, Evelyn Waugh. Outwardly uproarious, the evening was indefinably out of harmony. It made me feel that Oxford affiliations, as such, were to be looked on as over.

6

After publication of *Before the Bombardment*—in a principle he was to follow on later occasions between the appearance of more solid books—Osbert Sitwell arranged for his next work to be a collaboration: *The People's Album of London Statues* (1928), thirty-two drawings by Nina Hamnett, to which he would provide an Introduction and Commentary.

Nina Hamnett has recorded her own life in two volumes of memoirs, a trifle breathless in tone, but essentially first-hand in what they say about painters, sculptors, writers, nondescript bohemians, met at one time or another in the course of an adventurous career. Her father, an Army Service Corps colonel, cashiered for taking a bribe in South Africa, landed his dependents in fearful straits by this indiscretion, but his daughter's gift for drawing had somehow got her to the Slade; later to Paris, in a luxuriant epoch. The surname (recalling Shakespeare's early departed only son) was indeed a Warwickshire one.

Sickert, whose pupil she had been, wrote in praise of Nina Hamnett's drawing (the painting, never less competent, is not so stylish); Augustus John too, with the literary flourish he loved: 'A slight French accent adorns a perfectly original talent.' Now in her late thirties, short haired, a good figure, rather belligerent manner, Nina Hamnett had become an alcoholic, a condition not affecting her gift, but restricting continuous work to a few months at best; human relationships to equally fragmentary associations.

The Sitwells admired Nina Hamnett's work, Osbert Sitwell (with an unaccustomed seriousness that throws light on himself too) once remarking: 'Of course Nina is the sort of person one couldn't possibly imagine doing a mean thing.' That integrity, founded on an unshakeable, if not always very judicious, confidence in her own myth, together with an undiminished response to life, no less inconsequent, kept her going through the hardest of hard times, to what was inevitably a tragic end.

In the course of delivering the drawings of the London statues to Duckworth's, Nina Hamnett suggested doing a drawing of me too. Her studio was off Fitzroy Street, environs long established as an artists' quarter, by this time looked on as more *sérieux* than Chelsea, latterly much penetrated by the amateur. Though separated from Bloomsbury (where only Paris School or indigenous Bloomsbury painters were recognized) by no more than Tottenham Court Road, the Charlotte Street purlieus constituted a region wholly apart.

Nina Hamnett's studio was one of two on the ground-floor of Thackeray House (some reputed connexion with the novelist), a small dilapidated but not inelegant façade (now no more), among the otherwise undistinguished dwellings of Maple Street. The opposite ground-floor studio belonged to another painter, Adrian Daintrey; a larger one, taking up the whole of the first floor, occupied by an inventor and his mistress. These three studios made up the whole house. As neighbours some sort of a *modus vivendi* had been established, but Nina Hamnett and Adrian Daintrey never cared much for each other. I first met Daintrey there, when the drawing was being undertaken (he also drew me later), and we have remained friends to this day.

7

The Charlotte Street restaurant and pub, which, each in its own kind, dominated the remainder, were the Restaurant de la Tour Eiffel (The Eiffel), at the west end of Percy Street looking north towards Fitzroy Square; The Fitzroy (Kleinfeldt's), on the corner of Charlotte Street and Windmill Street. In Windmill Street also existed a strange establishment, The Windmill, where nocturnal bacon-and-eggs—served by a grave butler-like personage in a tailcoat, whom a duke would have been proud to employ—could be obtained at any hour of the night until dawn.

The celebrated Vicar of Stiffkey (subsequently defrocked, and devoured by circus lions) was said to patronize The Windmill for the entertainment of prostitutes; who in any case provided a proportion of its midnight clientèle. This pub world was peopled by transient shapes, some in due course to make a mark, others disappearing into heaven knows what depths. There were many painters, and it was not long before one encountered Augustus John; based on Chelsea, but spending a good deal of his time in this neighbourhood.

Among the many lesser figures, John Armstrong (unexpectedly a Gunner captain during the war) was then occupied with classical compositions, temples and towers that veered towards Surrealism. He became a stage-designer of some note, and ARA. Armstrong seemed to belong to a race of lank cadaverous kobolds, quiet but genial, and appropriately he was remembered in Hollywood (when I was there ten years later) for a remark made one night looking down on the brightly lighted-up city from the Santa Monica Mountains: 'It would be Hans Andersen, if it wasn't so terribly Grimm.'

John Banting (who executed the décor for Lambert's ballet, *Pomona*), also Surrealist in tone, like Armstrong, resembled a fabulous being too; his shaved head, curious laugh, recalling the madman playing with the piece of rope in the ballet of *The Rake's Progress*. Oddly enough, short lengths of rope often figure in Banting pictures.

These meetings with painters made a strong impression. Pictures, hitherto admired in galleries, amateurishly attempted by oneself and one's friends, now became a reality. As in a vision, the professional necessities of painting were all at once revealed. I don't think there was ever a period when I learnt more in a short time.

8

Intellectuals' pubs, English substitute for the café, can easily become catchments for bores. They also provide a useful medium (if not necessarily the locality) through which almost anyone can get into touch with almost anyone else in the country. Like deb dances, I am glad to have served my turn at their bars. They change little over the years, the atmosphere of the Twenties and Thirties largely preserved in the post-war Forties, renascent

Fifties; possibly not so very different today. In the Twenties, anthropologically speaking, this nomadic society was at its height; pubs themselves really pubs, not smartened up into the pseudo-cocktail lounges many have since become.

The tendency was, I think, for that sort of pub in due course to be more 'literary'. Writers did not much frequent them in those days. One of the Charlotte Street poets was Anna Wickham (I quote from memory: 'My mother was a harlot/My father was a clerk'), known to me only by sight. When she strode into the saloon bar, her severe air, Roundhead cast of feature, broad-brimmed hat, short skirt, grey worsted stockings, suggested Oliver Cromwell dissolving Parliament.

Roy Campbell was another poet who would occasionally appear; to all appearances very farouche. I met him only after the second war, some literary occasion at the Spanish Embassy, when he seemed agreeable enough. A more grotesque vignette of Campbell also belongs to the same post-war period, the prelude to a notorious incident.

Constant Lambert and I were in a Kensington Church Street pub. Suddenly Campbell glanced through the door, evidently looking for someone, then made as if to retire. Lambert, who knew him, called to come in. Campbell shook his head gravely: 'No, I can't stop. I have to go to the Ethical Church to beat up Stephen Spender for insulting the South African Army.' He went off on this bizarre mission. I believe a piquant sequel to whatever happened at the Ethical Church was that Spender, soon after on some public platform, found himself, as fellow poet, presenting Campbell with a medal for the promotion of poetry.

9

The Eiffel was treated almost like a club by those *abonné* there, as more or less notable representatives of the arts, or otherwise looked on as desirable customers by Rudolph Stulik, the proprietor. The restaurant being relatively expensive as a haunt, I never had much to do with Stulik, a Viennese with a brusque manner, who talked Comic Opera broken English. He was very conscious of being a famous restaurateur, on easy terms with the great, but, while naturally preferring his clientèle to be as renowned as possible, nevertheless behaved accommodatingly to the less prosperous in the art world; indeed finally ruined himself by too generous addiction to bohemian life at all levels.

The Eiffel was a favourite background for Augustus John, by this time evolved considerably from the incarnation shown in early photographs of an impetuous young Welshman in exotically-cut tailcoat and Guy Fawkes hat; though he continued to give thought to his clothes, usually a light-coloured suit, shaggy but elegant. If in one of his fairly chronic gloomy moods, John could be gruff, but, melancholy cast for a brief moment aside, he was a good raconteur, ever hospitable, prepared for anything but people who bored him.

The legend of a sort of artist-Silenus, staggering at the head of a bacchanalian throng by Jordaens, if not wholly deniable, was only one of John's avatars. At parties he would lurch forward over good-looking young people of either sex (things stopping there, amorously speaking, where young men were concerned), but he enjoyed quiet times too; good food; good wine; talk about books. His reading was wide, especially in French, a language he spoke fluently.

This literary side of John was perhaps a handicap to his painting; an aspect over-developed, or, like other characteristics, developed in too undisciplined a manner. It is not uncommon for painters to take a keen interest in writing. John did so more than most. His own abilities in that direction are seen to better advantage in letters, or short forays into reminiscence (the piece on Firbank), rather than the full-length of memoirs, at times rather too mannered in effect.

The matter of painters and the 'literary' approach is perhaps illuminated by a glance at Sickert in that sphere. Sickert—largely to tease the Bloomsburies, though in his own work often no less than the truth—used to insist that 'every picture tells a story'. If that proposition is accepted in Sickert's case, it cannot be denied as any less true of certain canvases and frescoes executed by John. The subtraction of 'pure painting' from a Sickert picture leaves, in general, a 'literary' comment at once mordant and witty. The same process, when applicable to a John picture, runs the risk of discovering a residue of the wrong sort of bravura, even downright sentimentality. Any excursion into 'literariness' on the part of painters requires, in addition to the disciplines of painting, those normally imposed on a writer. This fact may sound obvious, but the additional burden, as such, is an aspect often forgotten.

Nevertheless, whatever may be said—and a good deal has been said in recent years—in denigration of John as a painter, a too conscious sense of his own facility, display of cynicism unworthy of the work itself, mere bad drawing, all John's notorious failings, his early gifts as a draughtsman were liable to show themselves, even up to the end.

The complexity of John's character goes some way to explain a lack of fixed purpose which was the root of the trouble, above all a too abandoned romanticism. John never took hold of himself, intellectually speaking, in a manner of which he should have been capable in the light of his own talents. On the one hand, he was a man who could meet anyone on equal terms; on the other, a kind of shyness, an almost startling personal modesty about his own attainments, undermined him, pointing the way to easy self-indulgence.

In those days one used to be warned never to introduce the names of Sickert or Picasso into any conversations with John. Years later—only a year before his death in 1961—he undertook some drawings of me. They were probably the last portrait drawings he executed, because he was then working most of the time on his triptych, *Les Saintes-Maries*. I used to drive over to Fryern for sittings. John would place himself at the end of a long narrow dining-room table. I would be in a chair at the side. On these occasions he would repeatedly bring in the names of both Sickert and Picasso, deriving obvious pleasure from reminiscence about both of them. Sickert he had known well; Picasso once invited John to his studio.

One day I remarked that, passing through Fordingbridge in the car, the girls had seemed pretty. John grunted, but made no comment. Later, Dorelia John brought in his mid-morning whisky. John took it from her.

'He says the girls in Fordingbridge look pretty.'

His wife glared at him.

'You'd better go out and pick one up then.'

By that time John, in his eighties, was very hard of hearing. He sometimes wore a deaf-aid. This caused chronic dissatisfaction. In the midst of an interchange of conversation that had interested him, he would suddenly wrench the appliance from his ear with an exclamation of strangled rage, and throw it to the end of the refectory table. There the deaf-aid would come to rest, its mechanism ticking ominously, like a bomb about to explode, until the close of the sitting.

46

10

Both Augustus John and Wyndham Lewis had painted convincing like-
nesses of Thomas Earp, an indispensable drinking companion of Charlotte
Street. Exactly where he lived supposedly no one seemed to know, but
just round the corner from Fitzroy Square. I don't think anyone was ever
invited there. Rather unexpectedly, Earp was married. His wife, May,
younger than himself by some years, cannot have found domestic life easy.
It was said that she and her sister (subsequently married to Frank Dobson,
the sculptor) had first visited the Café Royal with Augustus John. The
future Mrs Earp was reported to have spoken only once in the course of the
evening, which was to ask the name of a man sitting at a table on the far
side of the room. The answer was of course: 'Tommy Earp'.

Sometimes crimson, sometimes waxen, Earp's large face was set off
under a cloth cap, probably relic of a former Oxford fashion, rather than
claim to a proletarian manner of life. Ineligible for military service in
World War I, he had stayed up at the University, becoming secretary,
sometimes sole member, of every conceivable Oxford club; handing on
in apostolic succession these secretaryships, representing continuous
existence of the clubs themselves, when hostilities came to an end.

Now living modestly (though the Sitwells, who did not like him, alleged
more money than admitted), Earp was reputed to have got through a fair
amount as a young man. He seemed designed by nature for an earlier
epoch, possibly tolerated, even loved, hanger-on of the Samuel Johnson
entourage. His remarks, much bandied about, were uttered in a thin
trembling voice. Working intermittently as an art critic (in spite of
resolute detestation of all pictures about equally), Earp would from time to
time produce a volume of belles-lettres. In youth there had been a book of
poems. His *Who's Who* recorded *Recreations* were: 'as many as possible'.

When drunk, a condition not infrequent, Earp showed little exterior
sign of intoxication—certainly none of exuberance—sooner or later falling
into a stupor. Returning from comparatively far afield one night, he felt
that state coming on, and took refuge under the tarpaulin cover of a Covent
Garden barrow; waking up the following day at an early hour to find that
he had been wheeled to a distant part of London.

Even if not at all outwardly fitted for home life in many of his habits,

47

Earp had his own preferred domestic rhythms. When an affluent friend invited him to luncheon one day, Earp shook his head: 'No—going home to lunch—apple-charlotte'. On another occasion, seeing Earp at midday in a pub, in front of a pint of beer and large hunk of bread-and-cheese, an acquaintance commented: 'I thought you said you were lunching with Lord Ivor Churchill [patron of the arts, brother of the Duke of Marlborough] today?' Earp, in his shaky treble, replied: 'I am—but I believe in being on the safe side.'

On one of these occasional forays into upper-crust life, spending a weekend at some country house, Earp brought with him to read in bed a work entitled *The History of a Pair of Drawers*. He had not foreseen that his bag would be unpacked, this volume set out on the dressing table beside his hair brushes. It was possibly on the same visit that the butler, helping Earp into an overcoat in the hall at departure, slipped his hand underneath the topcoat to adjust the lower part of Earp's jacket, but, missing the jacket's edge, seized the habitually baggy seat of Earp's trousers, jerking them down.

II

C. J. Hope-Johnstone (mentioned in the first volume of these memoirs) would also appear in Charlotte Street from time to time. Although not 'of Bloomsbury' in anything like the strictest sense, Hope-J was accepted in Bloomsbury circles as an equal, for his Cambridge education, learning, eccentricities. He belonged more to the Augustus John world, though not in the least confined to John's court either. Spare, bespectacled, dry in speech, Hope-Johnstone had some of the air of a well turned-out don. Notwithstanding chronic money difficulties—he claimed he could live in fair comfort on £150 a year—he was always prepared to discuss the best tailor, where a man should buy his shirts.

When J first knew him Hope-Johnstone's chief means of support (he no longer edited the *Burlington Magazine*) was picture dealing. He was likely to be in possession of a minor work by some master—a small Gainsborough, say, or a Renoir (in those days to be bought for a couple of hundred pounds)—on which he hoped to make a quick turnover. In excess of that canvas, he probably controlled a working capital of thirty shillings or less

in his pocket. He said: 'A fortune-teller once told me I'd got the temperament of a civil servant—liking for routine, detail, what is meticulously
arranged—yet lived dangerously, always on the brink of an abyss'.

This antithesis of action and character in Hope-J was well put. He
seemed to have read most books, was always familiar with (usually to
demolish) the latest thing in aesthetics or philosophy. He much recommended Rimbaud to me; also Restif de la Bretonne, an author I did not
attempt until years later, nor got on at all well with, beyond noting signs
that Restif had perhaps influenced Stendhal.

Not having read *Les Liaisons Dangereuses* at that time, I never discussed
Laclos with Hope-Johnstone, but I am sure he knew the book well, as he
loved analysing the character of women. Indeed the general view was that
Hope-J preferred theory to practice in that field. Certainly his own
marriage in middle life (to a beautiful dancer) was almost imperceptible, so
quickly ended, and never referred to by himself. He used to say: 'Those
very fair ethereal virginal-looking girls are almost invariably nympho-
maniacs.'

An interesting assertion of Hope-Johnstone's, which I have never
confirmed, was that Wyndham Lewis, in early days, wrote many poems
strongly influenced by Browning. These, he said, had appeared in obscure
magazines. If so, they seem to have been omitted from all studies of Lewis.
It is certainly true, vice versa, that Browning's *Soliloquy of the Spanish
Cloister* has more than a touch of Lewis in its tone.

Hope-Johnstone liked children: they him. At an Augustus John party
I was watching him blow smoke rings from his cigarette for the amusement of one of the sons of Lady Cynthia Asquith (painted by John some
years before), and, after watching the rings slowly floating through the
air, the small boy said: 'Now blow square ones .'

12

The atmosphere of the Eiffel Tower restaurant had points in common with
the Cavendish Hotel in Jermyn Street; emphasis at the former on artists,
rather than the Brigade of Guards; at the latter, the reverse, though both
elements might merge in these drifting scenes of a semi-smart semi-
bohemian world. By the time I arrived in London the name of Rosa

Lewis's hotel had been long familiar from stories told by my father. He regarded the place with a certain amount of awe, as haunt of various dashing contemporaries of his own. I do not know whether he himself ever went there, but imagine he must have crossed the threshold at one time or another. He would hint at orgies, but gave no clue to their nature. I did not like to ask.

I think I first entered The Cavendish with Richard Plunket Greene (an easygoing figure, known through many Oxford connexions), whom I ran into one evening in Jermyn Street. He suggested stepping into the hotel, which were were just passing. Plunket Greene was a friend of Rosa Lewis, but we struck a night when she was absent, accordingly nothing at all going on; all Cavendish life completely dependent on the proprietress.

The atmosphere of The Cavendish, unforgettable, is at the same time not easy to convey. Evelyn Waugh's picture in *Vile Bodies* is pretty close to life in some respects, but, among other things, omits the air of melancholy that hung like a pall over the place. I do not know who first took Waugh there, probably Alastair Graham, very much *ami de la maison*, but Plunket Greene was also a friend of Waugh's, and the introduction may have been owed to him.

At the time of which I speak the hotel was already in its decadence, a silver period, but I suspect that even in more palmy days lightheartedness was always tempered by a touch of something a shade macabre. I never stayed there, which must have been an interesting experience. A small but steady proportion of the clientèle was drawn from people who came up from the country from time to time, and knew nowhere else round the Piccadilly area so 'reasonable' in its terms; remaining totally unaware of the hotel's less prim side.

Rosa Lewis's legend is well known. Renowned in her early days as cook for Edward VII (when Prince of Wales) and his circle (plenty of lesser households too), she was reputed to have been the future monarch's mistress. The story is unconfirmed, and has all the air of myth, but (b. 1867) she gave the impression of considerable beauty in days gone by. She talked that old-fashioned cockney now passed almost as far into oblivion as the speech of the Etruscans.

Tall, stately, white-haired, Rosa Lewis was formidable to a degree. It is often said that she possessed a very aristocratic mien. If she had looked like a rackety duchess, or minor royalty who was no enemy to the bottle, she would have seemed less exceptional in appearance. Rosa Lewis, so it seemed to me, showed far more the utterly unexpected exterior of the statuesque wife of a senior civil servant, or President of the Royal Academy; a lady who had suddenly decided to have the most reckless of nights out, rather than attend a reception at the Guildhall, or Ten Downing Street. Perhaps that is hair-splitting, but social hairs are the most enjoyable ones to split.

People went to The Cavendish fairly late, after 11 o'clock, probably after midnight, when drinks had in general ceased to be procurable in public places. Round the large drawing-room on the first floor (done up in the manner of a somewhat decayed country house, but nice pieces of furniture there, and throughout the hotel) one or two persons—perhaps more—might be sitting. It is impossible to say who these figures would be, or what particular circumstances caused their presence in the room. One thing The Cavendish very decidedly did not represent was a place where anyone who felt so disposed could get a drink 'after hours'. It would have been a very determined man or woman who, if personally unknown to Rosa Lewis, brought that off.

On the other hand, the loiterers to be found in that drawing-room would often defy definition; sometimes appearing themselves scarcely aware why they were there. A couple of pink-faced Guards ensigns would not be unexpected; nor an American, perhaps a couple of Americans, drawn from almost any of the widely varying types of the US, the extreme 'Western' not to be ruled out. Augustus John, sitting drinking alone in the corner, was always a possibility. Then, probably only passing through the room, would be vague individuals, or parties of people, whose presence seemed absolutely inexplicable. They probably belonged to the category mentioned above, guests who liked the hotel as cheap, convenient, central, and had stayed there once a year for decades on visits to London.

13

Rosa Lewis herself tended to wander about her domain, ever restless, passing through the drawing-room from time to time, rather than playing any static part as hostess. She was excellent company if in good form, but had her gloomy moments. 'Lights on all over the house,' she would complain despairingly. 'It'll be the ruin of me. I'm too old now to keep an eye on things. I'm turning the front into shops as quick as I can. That'll bring something in. I'll go bankrupt otherwise.'

Possibly someone might be playing the piano in the corner. A little man in a dinner jacket was strumming jazz one night. After a time he left the piano and came across the room. Rosa Lewis, occupied with her reflections, was lying back in an armchair. Noticing the music had ceased, she looked up sharply.

'Go back and play *Ole Man River*,' she ordered.

The pianist began to protest. He was an American, and obviously played very well. Probably he was a well-known performer.

'Do as I tell you.'

'I'm not going to be treated like a servant.'

'Don't be a bloody fool.'

'I won't be spoken to like that.'

'Don't talk so much. Let's have another bottle of wine. Go back and play *Ole Man River*, and do as you're told.'

He gave in, of course. It had been foolish to rebel. The champagne arrived. It was poured out all round. At The Cavendish 'a bottle of wine' always meant champagne. It was as if champagne was the only wine anyone had ever heard of there. The American obliged again with *Ole Man River*. Rosa Lewis went fast asleep in her armchair. The faithful Edith, Rosa Lewis's lady-in-waiting (who was herself to rule The Cavendish in the years that remained of its existence after the death of the proprietress), appeared in the doorway for a moment, pale, tired, but ever watchful, saw all was well, disappeared again.

The most affluent person present—often American—was in general expected to pay for champagne. He would probably be staying at the hotel, the wine put down on his bill; in any case the legal fiction always observed that drinks were served for hotel residents only. It was by no means unknown for Rosa Lewis herself to 'stand' a bottle, especially if those present were notoriously hard up. There was usually someone on the spot to accept the acting of host as a privilege; more or less so, according to temperament. Rosa Lewis's famous pie—like Frau Sacher's chocolate cake—might be produced at unexpected moments.

As an impecunious young man, the question of being suddenly faced with a bill for a dozen bottles of champagne did not arise, though persons of more mature years, less exiguous means, could feel extremely apprehensive as to such a possibility. This sense of financial anxiety had perhaps something to do with the tense menacing atmosphere of The Cavendish, an oppression that only more beakers of champagne could wash away. As Douglas Byng, incomparable singer of his own comic songs (which brilliantly mirror frivolities of the period), neatly put it:

> The bridegroom's with Rosa,
> She's saying he owes her
> For millions of magnums of Mumm.

It has been asserted that Rosa Lewis was a great snob. The indictment is undeniable if the word—one of many meanings—is used merely in the sense of being interested in the ramifications of aristocratic life: who engaged to whom; who running away with someone else; who blessed with grandchildren; who forced to sell their estates; who resigning from the Brigade of Guards after matrimonial disaster.

On the other hand, Rosa Lewis could not have been less of a snob in the sense that she liked only the grand or successful; nor would she have hesitated for a moment to order from her hotel anyone of whatever rank or station, if bored or otherwise displeased by them. When she found people amusing, or they otherwise took her fancy, neither class, race, colour nor tongue, would create a barrier. She liked the feeling of belonging to a huge family, the sort of gossip too subtle to reach the ears of the professional gossip writer.

In her day she must have been a kind of nanny, a faintly sinister one, to a lot of rich raffish, but perhaps ultimately rather lonely young men, whose photographs in bearskin cap, or frogged military frockcoat, covered the walls of the downstairs office.

Nevertheless, whatever her rôle of nanny to some, Rosa Lewis could feel strong dislike for others. She never forgave Evelyn Waugh for *Vile Bodies,* and would often—for what reason I don't know—vilify the name of Mark Gertler, who would seem an improbable frequenter of The Cavendish. In any case all question of sentimentality should be rigorously excluded from any account of Rosa Lewis and her hotel, both apt to become blurred with nostalgia over the years. An aroma of toughness permeated the place; the fact never forgotten that dissipation must be paid for.

At the same time something exotic about The Cavendish came almost within sight of the non-commercial, so strong was the sense there of existing in a surrealist Alice-through-the-Looking-Glass dimension, where normal life was turned upside down. I made some effort to reproduce certain Cavendish aspects, briefly witnessed at this period (though located elsewhere), in an early novel, *Agents and Patients* (1936), chiefly in connexion with a Frenchman, Comte de M., who was staying in the hotel with his wife, when they were on a visit to London.

The de M.'s, a somewhat Proustian couple, moved in smart opium-smoking Paris circles. At least the Count smoked opium; his wife was, I think, much better behaved. Nina Hamnett, well looked on by Rosa Lewis, with whom she was perfectly capable of holding her own, took Constant Lambert and myself to call on these French friends of hers, whose entourage included a pekinese and a monkey, the monkey constantly warding off sexual attack from the pekinese. The Count, amusing enough when his narcotic was available, could be exceedingly trying—as on a second visit—when opium was in short supply. In calmer moments he would play the guitar, or do newspaper puzzles (which were to win him some enormous prize), while the company drank Pernod, and a clergyman's voice intoned a church service on the radio.

It was possibly after one of these decidedly Firbankian visits to The Cavendish that an American millionaire (cash-registers, Dayton, Ohio) invited Rosa Lewis, Nina Hamnett, and myself, to supper at the Savoy, where he tipped the cloak-room attendant with a five-pound note. Constant Lambert subsequently asserted that, retiring to an upstairs lavatory on his way out of The Cavendish, he had found the monkey—perhaps only refuge from the pesterings of the pekinese—sitting ruminatively on the seat.

IV

Arts and Crafts

I must undoubtedly have met Constant Lambert in the autumn of 1927 (rather than the following spring, as I have suggested elsewhere), possibly in the company of Earp, whom he always found sympathetic. Lambert was within a few months of my own age, and from the start we got on well. His painter father, George Washington Lambert (born in Russia, son of an American engineer of first-generation emigration), was a great admirer of Bronzino, and, as the Bluecoat portrait of his younger son shows, managed to impose a distinctly Bronzino type of looks on his own offspring.

Lambert *père*, whose work—more romantic, less brassy—was somewhat in the manner of William Orpen, lived mostly in Australia. He was quite prosperous as a painter, but took small interest in his family, his wife remaining in England most of the time with her two sons. Mrs Lambert (whom I always found a little daunting) was a most devoted wife and mother, keeping her household going, never deviating in admiration of her husband, in the face of untold worries and difficulties.

The elder son, Maurice Lambert (also musically talented), was a sculptor, relatively academic in style. Tough, bearded, ungregarious, he had a reputation for morosity that might suddenly erupt into rudeness, but I always liked what little I saw of him. (He was at Augustus John's funeral, but, beard removed, I did not recognize him, and we made no contact before he died not long after.) In contrast with his younger brother, Maurice Lambert was devoted to pursuits like boxing and sailing, committed to spheres of physical action, while being at the same time personally inward-looking. Constant Lambert would have rows with his

55

brother, but was fond of him too; liking to compare what he regarded as the extrovert life of a sculptor with that of a musician: 'The amount of work my brother does is limited only by the hour he gets up in the morning. If you speak to him of constipation, he asks you what you mean.'

A story Maurice Lambert used to tell seems worth preservation. A year or two before the period when I met him he had taken a studio from the widow of another sculptor, James Havard Thomas. Havard Thomas's bronze, called Lycidas, used to stand in the forecourt of the Tate Gallery; a young shepherd, naked, conceived in the sculptor's imagination as having just caught sight of nymphs disporting themselves in the stream below.

Havard Thomas was a friend of Norman Douglas, who writes amusingly of him in *Late Harvest* (1946), alleging that he himself suggested the name Lycidas to the sculptor, as vaguely classical, without too close affiliations with any well-known legend. The bronze of this work was in the Tate, but the original wax model for the statue had been consigned to the Manchester Art Gallery.

At Manchester, Maurice Lambert said, embarrassments had arisen because mill-girls, enjoying a Sunday afternoon's stroll through their city's Art Gallery, would playfully snap off the male organ of Lycidas, and bear it away with them. Accordingly, Havard Thomas was required to travel by train to Manchester, with three waxen 'spare parts' in his overcoat pocket; thereby anticipating further spoliation on the lines of the Mutilation of the Hermae.

I used to come across Norman Douglas occasionally in the 1940s, when he was in London, and greatly regret I then did not know of his acquaintance with Havard Thomas. It was a story Douglas would have enjoyed.

2

Good-looking in a boyish but distinguished way, Constant Lambert was already getting a trifle fat, though Christopher Wood's picture (National Portrait Gallery) shows the emaciated figure Lambert had been only a very short time before. With regard to his own weight, a favourite theme with him was the lean, rather than well covered personage, as typical butt of 18th century jocosity. He would defend this standpoint vigorously.

Although his clothes were ordinary, Lambert never looked ordinary. He usually wore an oldish brownish London suit, a shirt of one fairly deep colour, blue or orange without a pattern, a plain tie of another shade; latterly an open collar, if the weather was hot. His habit of hatlessness (followed also by Walton), slightly unconventional at that period, persisted from Christ's Hospital schooldays. Getting into a stiff shirt or 'morning clothes' for conducting, one or other form of 'tails' required most days, was always likely to threaten apoplexy. Lambert tied by hand the bow of white evening ties, but once caught Sir Thomas Beecham standing before the looking-glass of a Covent Garden dressing room, while he adjusted a made-up one; for which, to Lambert's great satisfaction, the famous conductor muttered some sort of rather embarrassed apology, a rare reaction in him.

Soon after we first met, I suggested Lambert should contribute something of musical bearing to a series of essays by young writers (Waugh, Byron, Connolly, Green, *et al*), contemplated at my suggestion by Duckworth's, though never brought to birth. I addressed the letter to 'Constantine Lambert, Esqre.', thinking Constant an abbreviation of the longer name. Lambert used to affirm—the Russian composer, Modest Mussorgsky, always excepted—that no one had ever been given a less appropriate forename than himself. (He was, I think, never christened for moral reasons, his parents being strict atheists.) I am not sure that was absolutely true. In one sense, as things turned out, constancy may not have seemed the most conspicuous trait in Lambert's character. In another, there was a consistency about his life, even his 'love life', that had something of constancy about it.

At this period Lambert was in professional doldrums, though not long before he had been experiencing tempestuous times with Diaghilev. The Russian Ballet—the most popularly recognized aspect of the burst of vitality in the arts that belongs to the first quarter of this century—was still, anyway for the general public, the most quickly grasped expression of all that was most aesthetically exciting and new. Diaghilev, at the height of his fame, was for a variety of reasons anxious to commission a ballet by a British composer. Lambert, only eighteen at the time, had been chosen for that rôle.

Dealings with Diaghilev had been volcanic, reaching a pitch when Lambert, who would not be bullied, threatened to withdraw his music.

One of the reasons for this explosion had been Diaghilev's decision to use Surrealist painters, Max Ernst and Joán Miró, in place of the English artist, Christopher Wood, to whom the work for Lambert's ballet had been in the first instance assigned. This change made Lambert exceedingly angry. Over and above his liking for Wood's designs, Lambert was a personal friend of Wood, for whom (in a quite unhomosexual manner) he had a certain hero-worship.

Wood (whom I met perhaps a couple of times), a talented performer in the *faux-naïf* manner, was good-looking and self-assured. He was the only British artist found acceptable in the Paris *monde* of Picasso and Cocteau, a convenient bisexuality being no handicap in that sphere. Understandably, this professional success as a painter, popularity in other respects with *les deux sexes et autres*, had made Wood more than a little *tête-montée*, causing him to give the outward impression not so much of an artist, as of a young stockbroker, who has made a pile before the age of thirty. The going proved too fierce. Two years later, tensions of life complicated by drugs, Wood, returning from his parents' home, threw himself under a train coming in at Salisbury station platform.

Lambert's row with Diaghilev was eventually patched up, but ever afterwards (according to Osbert Sitwell), when crisis threatened, Diaghilev would beg: 'Surtout—pas de Lambert.' On his side, Lambert bore little ill will, though he always insisted that one of the great impresario's highest claims to fame was in being the only known Russian, of either sex, to restrict himself to only one sex. Lambert would also complain that Diaghilev's habit of greeting a newly arrived guest with the words: 'Will you have one [a] drink?' always got the evening off to a bad start.

3

Intellectually speaking, Lambert moved with perfect ease in the three arts, a facility less generously conferred by nature than might be supposed from the way some people talk. Appreciation of two arts in a discerning fashion is not at all uncommon; where three are claimed, more often than not grasp of the third shows signs of strain. With Lambert there was no strain. Although he himself had scarcely any talent for drawing (beyond playing a creditable game of heads-bodies-and-legs), he had been brought up in close contact with the technicalities of painting and sculpture, always retaining his own equally penetrating line also on any matter that arose which had to do with writing. He had a natural gift for writing, a style individual and fluid, that brisk phraseology so characteristic of those musicians able to express themselves on paper.

Lambert loved discussing painters, Böcklin to Braque, Breughel to Brangwyn, especially enjoying to put forward subjects for Royal Academy pictures in the sententiously forcible manner of Brangwyn—once much imitated—of which two proposed canvases (titles in which perhaps Maurice Lambert too had a hand) were: *Blowing up the Rubber Woman*, and '*Hock or Claret, sir?*': *Annual Dinner of the Rectal Dining Society*. Lambert once described the work of the Russian painter, Pavel Tchelitchev (a great favourite of Edith Sitwell's), as looking like the winning exhibit in the *Daily Mail*'s annual prize for the season's best design in the sand at Margate.

We used to meet fairly regularly, drinking in pubs, going for walks, attending the sort of parties described earlier. Lambert was the first contemporary of mine I found, intellectually speaking, wholly sympathetic. The fact is not easy to explain even to myself. I lack musical sensibilities, and although, when it came to books and pictures, we had tastes in common, we differed greatly too. Lambert (in the taste of that moment) detested the High Renaissance, loving the arts of Asia and Africa. Admirable as the two last can be, I should never wish to surround myself entirely with their artefacts, and, whatever its undeniable excesses, I enjoy the High Renaissance in all its glorification of the individual.

It was, however, Lambert's general approach to the arts (for that matter, in many respects, Daintrey's) which was in such contrast with that of my Oxford generation. With them there seemed always an amateurishness, a narrowness of view, a way of treating the arts as if they were a useful social weapon. Again explanation eludes me, because several of my Oxford contemporaries were gifted enough. The crux was perhaps that the people I knew at Oxford who practised the arts did so with a self-consciousness of which Lambert—and many others I now met—was totally free. This difference of outlook can be gauged by comparing, say, *Enemies of Promise, Pack My Bag, A Little Learning*, with *Music Ho!*; though admittedly all these books were produced by their authors at different ages, with different ends in view.

Richard Shead's biography, *Constant Lambert* (1973), firmly identifies its subject with Moreland in *A Dance to the Music of Time*. Moreland, musician, wit, sometimes exuberant, sometimes melancholy, has the Bronzino-type features already described as Lambert's. There the resemblance fades, invention, imagination, the creative instinct—whatever you like to call it—takes over. If I have been skillful enough to pass on any echo of Lambert's incomparable wit, then Moreland is like him; in other respects, the things that happen to Moreland approximate to the things that happened to Lambert only within the extent that all composers' lives have something in common.

Here and there, as often falls out when writing a novel, a chance bull's eye is registered. For example, until I read Shead's biography, I was ignorant—or had altogether forgotten—that Lambert was specially interested in Chabrier. Perhaps I had inwardly stored that fact away in the manner characteristic of the novelist's latent machinery. To those aware of Lambert's liking for Chabrier's music and personality (subject of Lambert's first published article), Moreland's talk about the French composer must have seemed deliberate, possibly even including snatches of quoted speech. That was not so, and in a dozen ways Lambert's career differs from that assigned to Moreland.

Towards the end of his life especially, the laughter and talk of Lambert's lighthearted moods had an obverse side of periodical grumpiness and ill humour. Even in his palmiest days there were good friends who could stand only limited stretches of the Lambert barrage of ideas, jokes, fantasy, quotations, apt instances, things that had struck him as he walked through London, not because these lacked quality, on the contrary because the mixture was after a while altogether too rich. The world prefers on the whole, if not simple, at least less nourishing conversational fare. As with every known 'good talker' there was also a modicum of repetition. Speaking for myself, I very rarely felt the show had gone on too long, but I could see what others meant when at times they complained.

Lambert was prodigal of his wit. He never dreamt of postponing a joke because the assembled company was not sufficiently important for a witticism to be used on. Another point should be emphasized. Impatient, at times intolerant, Lambert was also an unexpectedly good listener. He did not in the least insist on holding the floor. In fact he liked nothing better than being entertained by the talk of others. He had a mind of extraordinary quickness (equalled, I think, for sheer speed in seeing the drift of a given story, only by my later friend, Alick Dru, met in wartime), beginning to shake with laughter before most anecdotes of any merit were halfway through, simply because he saw how they were going to end.

Lambert himself always disparaged those social milieux—again Oxford of my day comes to mind—where the conventions of a supposedly 'amusing' society disallows any development of a narrative. That was true, for instance, of Sitwell life. In such a world anything like a long story must, by definition, be regarded as a bore. Lambert used to point out that the best, the funniest, stories can rarely be told in a sentence. I should not wish support of this view to be perverted into the appearance of exonerating purveyors of prosy *histoires*, but there is a case for unprosy ones that may require a comparatively extended build-up for their punch-line. The wit of the Twenties, often tempered with self-consciousness and narcissism, even a rather childish buffoonery, was on the whole not well disposed to that view. Iago, on the other hand (even if he may have meant something rather different), remarks that 'wit depends on dilatory time.'

If Lambert possessed a different approach from Oxford contemporaries, he was even less like the group then spoken of as the 'new poets', to whom he was not at all drawn. He used to complain of their metre, rhymes, subject matter, the last of which he epitomized as 'like reading back-numbers of the *New Statesman*'. The fact that several of them were school-masters caused Lambert to picture them as discouraging their pupils from all poetry in traditional style, and (himself quite a performer in complicated verse forms) he produced several squibs on this theme. One began:

> W. H. Auden whips a kiddy on
> His bottom for reciting *Epipsychidion*.

Lambert possessed, I think, a touch of genius. The word is unsatisfactory. One envisages a row of lifeless effigies stretching back in time, mysterious unapproachable beings emitting a suffocating leakage of something that inspires awe; lay-figures carousing in cafés, or lying overcome with despair on truckle-beds in garrets. Another label is required. One tries again. Lambert inwardly inhabited, often outwardly expressed, a universe in which every individual, every action, was instantly appreciated in terms of art. Once more the concept threatens to fall flat. It could be even worse than 'genius', if the words suggest a pompous self-conscious aesthete, laboriously evaluating every trivial experience. Lambert could hardly have been further from that too. All the same, those are perhaps the lines along which to explore him as an entity.

4

That October—the Territorial riding school exchanged for the Holborn Polytechnic—I used to turn up several evenings a week to study printing at Southampton Row. The girls flitting about the Polytechnic corridors seemed to offer exciting suggestions of co-educational student life at some foreign university. I dreamt of all sorts of romantic encounters, fantasies that never throughout the course showed even the remotest sign of taking shape. Instruction in the craft of printing was scarcely more fruitful, Union restrictions limiting guidance to what might easily be picked up, with a little experience and commonsense, while handling books in their nascent state; though at the Polytechnic a pupil's 'copy'—say, layout for a simple title-page—could be set up in Caslon Old Face for practical judgment.

One night, on the way down the passage to my printing class, a male student came hurrying from the opposite direction. He seemed deeply preoccupied. His appearance had the familiarity, coupled with complete improbability, which one associates with dreams. Notwithstanding, identification, however hard to accept, was equally hard to deny. There could be no doubt whatever that here was Evelyn Waugh. We saw each other at the same moment. Mutual astonishment was expressed at meeting in such a place at such a time; reasons compared for finding ourselves at this hour in the corridors of the Holborn Polytechnic. My own explanation was simple enough. When I asked what subject Waugh was studying, his reply was less easily comprehensible.

'Carpentry.'

'Why on earth?'

'Oh, Tolstoy and all that.'

This was the moment when Waugh had decided to give up school-mastering, and earn a living with his hands. Carpentry seems always to have held a fascination for him, over and above an interest in the craftsmanship side of the Pre-Raphaelite Movement. For example, at King's Thursday (the country house in *Decline and Fall*) the 'estate carpenter' is described as holding 'an office hereditary in the family of the original joiner'; while in middle life, when living in a prosperous but hardly grandiose style in Gloucestershire, Waugh would sometimes refer to his own employment of a retainer thus designated.

Waugh was determined to take up cabinet-making as a profession; though invocation of Tolstoy's name (recently suggesting itself to me, too, in the Russian novelist's rôle of artilleryman) obviously implied that writing need not be absolutely barred as a sideline. When our respective classes were over we ate something together at a pub-restaurant in Southampton Row, discussing the progress of Waugh's book on Rossetti, commissioned by Duckworth's earlier that year. Waugh was full of enthusiasm for this latest excursion into manual labour.

Some weeks after the Polytechnic encounter with Waugh, Balston, who for some weeks had been talking about giving a party, finally decided to do so. He was very excited about it. The occasion was to be primarily for the Sitwells, but would also include the less stick-in-the-mud Duckworth authors—and potential authors—seasoned with a small but hardy nucleus of relatively bohemian friends Balston himself had acquired over the years. Among these latter were the artist-illustrator Ethelbert White and his wife, a couple to whom Balston was devoted, but not always equally appreciated at parties, on account of their invariable practice of bringing with them a guitar for renderings of such ballads as *Frankie and Johnnie*, of which they possessed an inexhaustible repertoire. When the news leaked out that the Ethelbert Whites were to be present there was a certain amount of trepidation.

Waugh's Diary seems to refer to Balston's party, but I do not remember him being at the flat. Perhaps (for reasons later apparent) he slipped away early to more seductive commitments. In the event, fears as to the Ethelbert Whites and their guitar, if not groundless, proved over-apprehensive, because, although they ran through their copious stock of ballads—including many bawdy ones—to do so they were confined to Balston's small and austere bedroom.

Among other guests was Robert Byron (recently signed up with Duckworth's for his Mount Athos book, *The Station*), who showed no exceptional behaviour throughout the evening, until it came to going

63

home. The several blocks that made up Artillery Mansions were approached from Victoria Street through a lofty arch that stood above high iron gates. These gates were kept open during the day, but (like the portals of a college) closed at a certain hour of the night; persons coming in and out then using a small side-door. While the rearguard of Balston's departing guests was crossing the courtyard, Byron, letting out a series of blood-curdling war-whoops, rushed at the closed gates and began to climb them at a great rate. Reaching the top, he achieved descent into Victoria Street without impalement.

Even in the Twenties this was not the usual tone of Artillery Mansions residents and guests.

5

Whether or not Waugh attended Balston's party, he and I had not met for some weeks when, probably towards Christmas, we saw each other in the same compartment of a Tube train. Waugh was in the highest of spirits. Before a word could be said on any other subject he made a statement.

'I'm going to be married.'

At first I supposed a joke was intended. Marriage, as already emphasized, was something unthought of among contemporaries at that date, an undertaking well outside the consideration of the possible; or so it seemed to me. The next two years were to demonstrate the fallacious nature of that opinion, but at the moment matrimony was something particularly inconceivable in connexion with Waugh.

'Who to?'

'She's called Evelyn Gardner.'

The name was not wholly unfamiliar owing to a chance meeting in the street not long before with Waugh's elder brother, come across once or twice, always very agreeable. I had run into Alec Waugh one evening in the neighbourhood of Sloane Square. I cannot quote verbatim, but roughly speaking Alec Waugh's words were on this occasion: 'Do you know two delightful girls who live just round the corner from here called Evelyn Gardner and Pansy Pakenham? We're always reading newspaper articles about the Modern Girl putting on too much make-up, drinking too many cocktails, being brassy, bad-mannered, gold-digging, but these two couldn't be nicer, prettier, quieter, more intelligent.'

It was not at all uncommon for Alec Waugh himself to write the sort of article typified, so that he spoke with authority on the subject. I knew the name of Pansy Pakenham from debs who talked of her (though she herself had abandoned the deb world), and also from having been at school with her brothers, Edward, 6th Earl of Longford, and Frank Pakenham (now 7th Earl of Longford), neither of whom I had known more than by sight as schoolboys. This was the first time I had heard of Evelyn Gardner. Alec Waugh had not mentioned either girl as friend of his younger brother's, and (Evelyn Waugh always emphasizing the difference of their lives) I had in no way connected him with this exemplary couple.

Evelyn Gardner, like Pansy Pakenham, had outgrown deb dances. She was the youngest daughter of the 1st Lord Burghclere (deceased without heir to the title some years before), himself illegitimate son of the last Lord Gardner, a family of naval distinction in the past. Evelyn Gardner's mother (*née* Lady Winifred Herbert, daughter of the 4th Earl of Carnarvon) was sister to Lady Margaret Duckworth, wife of Sir George Duckworth, Gerald Duckworth's brother. This Herbert connexion was to be not without all publishing (and other) significance at a later date. Pansy Pakenham, eldest daughter of the 5th Earl of Longford (killed at Gallipoli), worked in an architect's office. She and Evelyn Gardner shared a flat over a tobacconist's shop at the west end of Cliveden Place, a few yards from Sloane Square.

For girls of that sort to set up house together was in those days an unconventional thing to do; in this case made possible by both being not only of age, but possessing a little money of their own. The Dowager Countess of Longford, somewhat autocratic in dealing with her children, having, perforce, agreed initially to her daughter leaving home to work, could only accept the situation.

Lady Longford had also, as it happened, fallen victim to Evelyn Gardner's charm. In this she was by no means alone, though a notable captive on account of her position vis-à-vis the girls' household. Lady Burghclere, no less opposed than Lady Longford to girls leaving home, judged Pansy Pakenham—although the younger of the two—a potentially steadying influence on her own daughter, perpetually being proposed to by young men, none of whom her mother found ideal as a potential son-in-law.

I do not remember the circumstances of my first introduction to Evelyn Gardner by Evelyn Waugh (from the start they were known as 'the two Evelyns')—possibly a brief exchange at The Gargoyle—but, not so very long after the meeting with Waugh on the Underground, I was asked in for a drink at the flat shared with Pansy Pakenham.

6

Waugh was not present when I arrived at Cliveden Place. I think he turned up much later. He was probably busy with his now rapidly expanding professional life (writing once more in the ascendant over carpentry), or making the endless arrangements consequent on an engagement, even an unofficial one; the news, once it broke, that he and Evelyn Gardner were to get married, causing a considerable commotion. The welcoming atmosphere of Cliveden Place bore out all Alec Waugh had implied, and he was probably not far from the truth, given the circumstances, in describing the girls as a unique couple.

The warmth and charm of Evelyn Gardner—who remains a friend to this day—were, on the one hand, in direct contrast with the supposedly brassy traits of that ominous figure, The Modern Girl, while at the same time she seemed in her person to exemplify all thought of as most 'modern'. She possessed the looks and figure of the moment, slight, boyish, an Eton crop; that simplicity of style more often to be found breaking hearts at the rackety parties outlined earlier, than in the ballrooms of Mayfair and Belgravia, however pretty the debs; and (Pansy Pakenham among these) some debs were very pretty indeed.

The only other person present, apart from the two girls, was Henry Lamb. I was familiar with Lamb's painting, particularly his quite famous portrait (in the Tate) of Lytton Strachey, and had just caught a glimpse of the painter himself at the party of Augustus John's where Hope-Johnstone had blown the smoke rings. Indeed, it was Hope-Johnstone who had pointed Lamb out to me.

'They say Lamb has got hold of an aristocratic young girl, and is trying to marry her.' Hope-Johnstone said, adding a disparaging view of Lamb.

The first story was no less than the truth, though not so sinister in realization as import of the words sounded at the time. There was no way of guessing that a future brother-and-sister-in-law, with both of whom I was to have long and happy relations, were thus defined. Lamb and Hope-Johnstone, men with strong likes and dislikes, did not get on at all well.

Henry Lamb was then in his middle forties. Regarded when younger as devastatingly handsome, he was thin, unrelaxed in manner, with a searching air that gave the impression you were expected to prove yourself before he easily accepted you. On varying terms with John himself, Lamb moved to some extent within the John orbit; more so, in fact, than among the Bloomsburies, in spite of Lytton Strachey's passion for him. Indeed Lamb, fairly irascible in temperament, lived a comparatively segregated life at Poole in Dorset. Among his friends was George Kennedy, an amusing and agreeable architect, with certain Bloomsbury affiliations. It was in Kennedy's office that Pansy Pakenham worked, and there she and Lamb met.

Lamb had set out in the first instance on the career of surgeon, a profession for which he showed great promise; a touch of the medical man always remaining with him. During the first war he had won an MC as doctor with a battalion in the field, and by now he had made a name for himself as a painter, earning a respectable if not abounding income. Marriage to a celebrated beauty of the bohemian world had gone wrong many years before, but, long parted from his first wife, Lamb had never bothered to sever the union by law. He was now taking steps to obtain a divorce in order to marry Pansy Pakenham.

The Cliveden Square household at that moment had some of the air of a play: the two charming girls (as sketched by Alec Waugh); the two detrimental but gifted suitors; the very situation come into being most dreaded by the two dowager mammas.

Notwithstanding his relative fame as an artist, a gallant war record, ability to support a wife and family, Henry Lamb, divorced (if he brought that off, not absolutely assured, as the Law then stood), long committed to the bohemian life, more than twenty years older than Pansy Pakenham, could not be looked upon by Lady Longford as ideal *parti* for a pretty and talented daughter of twenty-three; even if the brothers and sisters were keenly in favour of the match, as likely to add an exciting dimension to family life.

In a different manner, Evelyn Waugh, though younger, could be regarded, in the circumstances he found himself, as even less eligible by Lady Burghclere. If Lamb was too old to be immediately acceptable, Waugh, only just twenty-four, was, in the eyes of the parents of those days, too young as aspirant to marriage. Apart from the potential royalties of *Rossetti : His Life and Works* (due to appear in the spring), he possessed no visible means of support, while nothing popularly known of his life was of a nature to inspire confidence in an aristocratic mother-in-law of admittedly straitlaced outlook.

It was, indeed, one of Waugh's most endearing characteristics at this period not to care in the least what anyone thought of his goings-on. To a large extent that contempt for public opinion remained with him throughout, but, the style of his own life altering, those who disapproved of his attitudes in later days, did so for quite other reasons. One need hardly add that, as soon as the engagement became known, rumours of Waugh's supposedly dissipated habits were hurried to Lady Burghclere's ears.

7

The two mothers concerned took the impact of a daughter's engagement in a differing spirit. Lady Longford, who at that time lived, with the rest of the Pakenham family not yet grown up, at North Aston Hall, Oxfordshire, had already met Henry Lamb at tea in the girls' flat. She received a letter one morning from Pansy Pakenham announcing the engagement; containing the added information that Lamb was being brought down to the country to renew their acquaintance.

If Lamb wished to make himself agreeable, no one was more capable of doing so. The second meeting was an unqualified success. All had gone admirably, the engaged couple were just leaving the house, when Lady Longford drew Lamb behind a pillar.

'I have to be father and mother both,' she said. 'It *is* a clean sheet, Mr Lamb?'

Lamb, having absolutely no idea what was meant, was struck dumb for the moment. Lady Longford, like Pilate, did not wait for an answer. She spoke at once of other things. The car drove away.

Afterwards, Lamb would often speculate with his in-laws on the bearing of the question. Illegitimate children? Venereal disease? Forgery? Murder? There the matter rested. The enigma of Lady Longford's enquiry was never solved. No sort of obstruction was offered, and Lamb was soon welcomed by a large circle of new relations, many of whom he was to draw or paint in the years that were to follow.

In connexion with the Lamb/Pakenham wedding (which took place in August, 1928) only one matter made Lady Longford cross—very cross— which was that Waugh (by that time married himself, and contributing items of social gossip to the *Daily Express*) fed in several paragraphs, which were printed in the paper, to the effect that 'the wedding of Lady Pansy Pakenham and Mr Henry Lamb had been almost secret.' It had, of course, been nothing of the kind.

On the other hand, there was truth enough in calling Waugh's marriage to Evelyn Gardner 'secret', since he had experienced with Lady Burghclere no such easy passage as that encountered by Lamb with Lady Longford. There had, indeed, been several unhappy interviews. Waugh told me that on one occasion he called on Lady Burghclere (whom, from the locality of her house in Mayfair, he always referred to as 'the fairy of Green Street') wearing a top-hat and tailcoat, even in those days rare except for weddings and Ascot. I am uncertain whether he chose this turnout for the initial visit to ask her daughter's hand in marriage, or on a subsequent call at the Green Street house, when the match was already meeting with considerable discouragement.

Lady Burghclere was no enemy to intellectual life as such (indeed had herself written several books), but, as mentioned before, she had already raised objection to several other young men as suitors, some of them— from a conventional point of view—more eligible than Waugh; of whom she was reported to have used the phrase *les moeurs atroces*. Accordingly, when the wedding took place in June, 1928, that was without Lady Burghclere's knowledge.

This disapprobation, involving as it did parent and daughter, might not be entirely unexpected, but all sorts of other people, with little or no business to concern themselves about the wisdom or unwisdom of the marriage, expressed their views loudly on the subject. Among those feeling something well short of approval (so Balston revealed) was Gerald Duckworth, who, on the one hand, a sort of uncle by marriage of the bride (his brother having married Lady Burghclere's sister), on the other, publisher designate of the bridegroom, regarded himself as in a position to speak out.

8

Henry Lamb and I got on pretty well at our first meeting, and so things remained until his death in 1960, but after introduction at Cliveden Place I scarcely came across him until early in 1934, the year I married Violet Pakenham, his wife's younger sister.

Lamb, who, as well as being a painter, was a musician of more than ordinary attainment, held opinions very much his own. Witty, unpredictable, fractious, he wrote vigorously articulate letters, especially to people who rubbed him up the wrong way. When William Rothenstein sent what Lamb deemed patronizing criticism from a fellow painter of a recent Lamb picture-show, in which the phrase 'a tendency to tightness' had been used, Lamb sent a letter to Rothenstein in reply, saying that he used to be loose, but nowadays he was always tight.

When he remarried, Lamb threw himself into family life with the same sort of energy and enthusiasm that he brought to everything else he did, behaving as if no one else had ever produced children—at least none like his own—confounding all who had shaken their heads about his reactions to domesticity.

Lamb had many stories of medical, military, and intellectual life that deserved preservation. For example, wounded or sick during the first war, he had been for a time in an army hospital. One day the RAMC officer doing the rounds turned out to be the then bestseller novelist, Warwick Deeping (author, among many other works, of *Sorrell and Son*, describing an ex-officer, a widower, who has to take a job as an hotel porter); Deeping having himself begun life as a doctor. Lamb was lying in bed reading Milton. Deeping, after making routine medical enquiries, looked over Lamb's shoulder at the book. 'Strange old-fashioned stuff,' he said.

After this or another spell in an army hospital, Lamb came up for examination before a medical board. Seeing from the report that he was a fellow medico, the members of the board treated him as a colleague who knew the ropes. Just as everything was over, Lamb leaving the room, one of the board said: 'Perhaps we'd better see your Rhomberg, old boy.' (The Rhomberg Test is a tap below the knee given to register muscular reaction.) Lamb, absent for many months from medical practice, his mind filled with thoughts of painting, music, Milton and his old-fashioned stuff, had forgotten the meaning of Rhomberg. Making a guess, he began to undo his fly-buttons.

In later life, Lamb always retained a tremendous physical wiriness and dexterity. When we were once staying at Coombe Bissett, in Wiltshire, where the Lambs lived after marriage, a pair of stilts were for some reason brought into play. Even supporting myself against a wall, I failed to mount them in a manner to stay upright, much less walk away from the wall. Lamb, then in his sixties, took the stilts, ran a few steps with them, leapt on to the foot-rests, began to perambulate round the garden. He was wearing a soft felt hat with a broadish brim, the crown crushed down to the level of the ribbon. He looked exactly like a stilt-performer—probably Breton— doing a turn at a French fair.

V

Spring Buds and Autumn Leaves

During the three years of my novitiate at Duckworth's, 'learning the business', I did not make much headway in the technicalities that The Complete Publisher should master. The course at the Holborn Polytechnic had expounded no more than the eternal truth that some layouts are more pleasing to the eye than others. Nothing at all methodical was ever done at Henrietta Street in the way of teaching how to 'cast off' a manuscript for dispatch to the printer, nor was I supplied with any sort of classification of specific printers' charges in relation to their varying degrees of competence.

Lewis, not a born instructor—in any case much too busy with immediate problems to give lessons that could be easily understood—would from time to time mutter a few traditional watchwords about typefaces, flourish the wooden rule marked out with 'ems' (the unit for measuring printed matter), but he did not care for the routines of production escaping from his own direct control, and would become a little sulky if even Balston took too close a hand in that field. There was never any question of my 'seeing through the press' any given book from start to finish, including costs, and to do so would certainly have needed more professional knowledge than I ever acquired.

Balston, for his part, would occasionally remark: 'You ought sometimes to get the books [the account books] down and have a look through them.' If I ever attempted to extract 'the books' from the accounting department, every sort of difficulty was put in the way; usually the simple and effective answer that work was being done at that very moment on whatever author's sales I hoped to examine. The accountant himself, a stunted troglodyte, neither young nor particularly obliging, caused concern at about this time by uttering strange animal cries from behind the closed door of the tiny cell where he totted up the royalties, and, long years at Duckworth's having affected his brain, he had to be removed in an ambulance.

No doubt maladroitness at picking up the technicalities of publishing was largely my own fault, an inherent unhandiness at grasping that sort of information. In any case impeding attitudes towards allowing a neophyte to 'learn the business' are probably the universal experience of every young man, whatever his early calling; only those who possess the true vocation emerging at the other end as a satisfactory product. Something of the sort is equally true of the army (regimental level or staff equally), and it is perhaps right that professional competence should be won almost wholly in the face of obstruction. At the same time there can also be no doubt that imaginative superiors are on the whole quicker to assist the needs of the beginner than unimaginative ones.

Early resolution, perhaps never as vigorous as it should have been, to gain prosaic skills, withered away under passive resistance. There were in any case plenty of other things to do. Once I had left invoicing behind, I read MSS, composed ads, interviewed callers (those to be got rid of in no other way), made up the bi-annual illustrated catalogue of new and already published books, designated (in one of Balston's more puckish moods) *Spring Buds* and *Autumn Leaves*.

My own attempts to brighten these booklists with appropriate pictures were not always well received by the public. The juxtaposition of a Modigliani nude (rather emphasized pubic hair) on the page opposite a Staffordshire pottery Venus (grasping her breast with one hand, concealing her sexual parts with the other) particularly provoked letters of disapproval. One householder wrote that, having a 'family of children and young servants', he would be obliged if Duckworth's did not 'deliver their cess at his door'; while a lady living in South Kensington dispatched so vigorous a rebuff that I preserved a copy over the years:

Mrs —— requests that Messrs Duckworth & Co will not waste their money on sending her lists of their publications. She is one of the few remaining who were privileged (and also unfortunate eno') to touch the fringes of civilization—real civilization—and all this modern decadent rubbish wh. *calls itself* advanced, and works of the *un*-intelligentsia wh. has arrogated to *itself* the term intelligentsia—only causes nausea and sadness. It is pathetic to think of such wasted enthusiasm wallowing in the mire instead of rising to the skies. The miasma and fumes they spread cannot be avoided, but we can do our best to breathe between while the purer air of Heaven—a heaven of any sort. There is no originality in their work. It is a poor copy of early strivings after what was out of reach & the modern decadents should be only ashamed of themselves, & you who print their messes, shd sit down and think what you are doing. Are you helping *sincerity, cleanness, happiness? NO.*

Yours faithfully

(Mrs) ——

2

I had first pick at the five hundred or more MSS (once in a way written by pen) that arrived every year, mostly through the post or via agents, a few delivered by hand. Of these perhaps fifty had to be more than cursorily examined; thirty fairly seriously read. It is, of course, not necessary to ingest the whole of a manuscript to know that the reader's firm will not wish to publish the work, but incipient authors find that hard to believe. They will often complain if they receive the parcel back by return of post, or even within a few days of submission. That is why MSS are sat on by publishers for months at a time. Trouble can also be caused by a special demon, who arranges that the reader's report should be accidentally included in the back pages of a rejected manuscript.

So far from treating lightly what is sent to them, publishers are only too anxious to find something to sell; even a few coherent sentences raising hopes in a desert of literary ineptitude. Perhaps things have changed now, more people competent to frame the semblance of a saleable book; thereby increasing the work of the publisher's reader. Most MSS of any merit came through personal contact, or the recommendation of an agent. Much of the reading done was naturally in relation to the firm's existing authors; combined with a certain amount of suggestion for alteration or modification, if the author in question was amenable to such treatment.

This reading and tinkering about with manuscripts is not, I think, to be underestimated in the opportunities such work gives for picking up the rudiments of 'writing'. When some experience in that art has been undergone, it is possible to see, anyway to some extent, how 'good' books are written—the breaking down into elementary essences of the writer's method—but, when you are without the rough-and-ready self-training acquired by writing a book or two yourself, it is possible to read the classics over and over again without being able to see how a great writer brings off effects. On the other hand, the faults of a 'bad' book can immediately spring to the eye, and, in a publisher's office, your job may be to put those faults right. Suggesting such emendations can in due course point to what are more or less general rules, even if rules not easy to define in words; the developing of a kind of instinct applicable as much, say, to *Middlemarch* as to *Ulysses*, though that might not appear on the surface. Critics, competent in other respects, simply because they themselves have never practised (or practised inadequately) the writing of novels, can often show themselves startlingly ignorant of what might be called the logic of a given technique.

Where new blood was in question, my own introductions to the firm included Evelyn Waugh, Robert Byron, the historical biographers Wyndham Ketton-Cremer and Roger Fulford; quite a few more. Duckworth's did not manage to retain all of these. I also pressed the claims of Ronald Firbank, whose novels at this period were all out of print. The directors showed no overwhelming enthusiasm for Firbank, but, in consequence of making enquiries as to where the 'rights' lay, it was disclosed that Firbank had left a sum of £800 to be devoted to guaranteeing the re-publication of his books at some future date.

In the face of this sweetener, Duckworth's agreed to reprint them, choosing to do so in the form of an edition de luxe, limited to one hundred sets, to be called *The Collected Works of Ronald Firbank*, though some of the inferior writing was omitted. The directors—and Lewis—were astonished when this edition was 'oversubscribed' to an extent that showed the booksellers would have accepted at least twice that number at the same price. Duckworth's followed up this limited edition with various cheaper ones; the firm publishing Firbank to this day.

Among manuscripts brought in by me, or marked for special attention, then turned down, were Antonia White's novel about a convent school,

Frost in May, which went to several editions; Christopher Isherwood's *The Memorial* (which came, I think, through an agent); and (among American books of 1933 seeking a publisher in England) Nathanael West's *Miss Lonelyhearts*; the last two noted here for their writers' later celebrity, rather than because either was likely to have proved a bestseller.

3

One or two of the Old Guard of Duckworth authors would turn up at the office from time to time. I never had anything to do with the better known ones. Elinor Glyn, a neat figure, red-haired, smartly dressed, once disappeared through the door of Gerald Duckworth's room, when I was coming up the stairs. Belloc, wearing an Inverness cape, Wellington boots under his trousers, grumpy, bad mannered, would look in from time to time to collect a copy or two of his volumes of comic verse, which the firm still published.

One hot summer afternoon, feet on the desk in front of me, I was reading a manuscript, when the door opened quietly. A tall man, dressed in the deepest black, stood there in silence, clothes and bearing suggesting a clergyman. He smiled—to use an epithet he might well have employed in his own writing—'quizzically'. I withdrew my feet from the desk, but he seemed to expect more than that; indeed instant acknowledgment of something in himself. A further survey convinced me that here was John Galsworthy. He gave off the redolence of boundless vanity, a condition not at all uncommon among authors, in this case more noticeable than usual.

I was about to alert Lewis, bent double at his desk over a sheaf of estimates, which, according to habit, he was examining at a range of about two inches off the paper, but Galsworthy, making the conventional gesture of finger to lips, indicated silence. He was just within sight of Lewis round the corner of the desk, the implication being that by sheer personality Galsworthy would send out rays which would compel Lewis to look up.

We both awaited a respectful burst of recognition. For some reason the magnetism did not work. Galsworthy stood there smiling with benevolent condescension; the smile becoming increasingly fixed, as Lewis continued to ponder the estimates. Finally Galsworthy gave it up as a bad job. He announced his presence abruptly by word of mouth. He was evidently disappointed in Lewis's lack of antennae, where famous writers were concerned. Lewis raised his head to see who had spoken, then, taking in at a glance one of the firm's most lucrative properties, jumped up full of apologies, and hurried the Great Man into the Senior Partner's room.

Galsworthy's novels, even if they retain a certain vitality where portraits of his own uncles are concerned, through lack of any real understanding of human behaviour, fail in their attempt to deal on a wide front with English upper-middle-class life. His stylization of character, near-Marxist moralizings about the wickedness of owning property, by artificial heightening of drama at the expense of reality, both work better on the stage.

Sometimes, one feels, the situations might have been truer if presented in reverse: for example, Irene, in *The Forsyte Saga*, seen as a thoroughly tiresome woman; while the play, *Loyalties* (a hard-up army officer steals the racing winnings of a Jewish fellow-guest at a house party), would have been subtler, possibly likelier, if the Jew had romantically assumed that a brave man could not be a thief; the officer's comrades-in-arms muttered: 'There's always something fishy about these swashbucklers—do you remember that gold cigarette-case that disappeared in the Mess?'

4

Another Duckworth author, though only intermittently, was Ford Madox Ford. As the work of an old acquaintance, Gerald Duckworth was prepared to publish Ford's books from time to time, but they were not popular with Balston, who did not regard their small sales as redeemed by the author's undoubted interest in literary experiment.

Ford's novels usually deal with a similar social level to those of Galsworthy, though Ford is far more aware of the paradoxes of human nature, the necessity, at that moment, of exploring new forms of writing. An immense self-pity—in general an almost essential adjunct of the bestseller —infected Ford adversely as a serious novelist, while at the same time for some reason never boosting his sales. His misunderstandings and sentimentalities on the subject of English life (half-German himself, he very nearly opted for German nationality just before 1914) make him always in some degree a foreigner, marvelling at an England that never was.

Much canvassed as an underrated writer, Ford undoubtedly brought off something in the war tetralogy, which shows signs of brilliance in the treatment of the earlier sequences. Notwithstanding that, when, late in our lives, Cyril Connolly, a Ford fan, gave me *The Good Soldier* (one of Ford's best constructed novels, and written with great attack), he failed to convert me.

At Duckworth's I remember reading the typescript of a novel by Ford, which began about a man who had fought in the Carlist War. I think this never appeared—anyway as the story then stood—in print, but another Ford novel, placed at the period of the Hundred Days, was being discussed at a moment when I was about to spend a day or two's holiday in Paris, and it was arranged that I should get in touch with him.

Ford invited me to luncheon at a favourite restaurant of his, the Brasserie Lipp in the Boulevard Saint-Germain. He was then in his middle fifties, walrus moustache, puffy face, half-open mouth. I saw what the novelist, Mary Butts, meant, when she had said: 'It's extraordinary what a fuss is always being made about who is to get into bed with old Ford', but he seemed amiable enough in a somewhat bufferish genre. Drinking in those days either what was probably too much, or scarcely anything at all, I refused a pre-luncheon apéritif. Ford was surprised. He said: 'You're going to be a very cheap young man to entertain.' I don't remember being in the least grateful for this hospitality, though Ford was chronically hard-up (no doubt he signed the bill), and, as representative of his publisher, I might reasonably have been expected to do the paying myself.

5

Duckworth's, an impecunious firm, were, in fact, not at all forthcoming in allowing expenses for entertaining authors (though Balston certainly did a good deal of that himself in his flat), and it never occurred to me that quite often it would have been reasonable for my employers to shell out for meals and drinks produced by myself to get some promising writer on the hook. The only occasion when I remember being specifically told that the firm would pay, if I took someone out to dinner, was in the case of Hilda Harrison, former girl-friend of Herbert Asquith (1st Earl of Oxford and Asquith); the Liberal Prime Minister having deliberately written a sequence of chatty letters to this lady to provide some sort of a small dowry for her after his own death.

A friend of a slightly older Oxford generation, Alan Harris (who just missed a Balliol Fellowship, and later himself worked at Duckworth's), produced Mrs Harrison, who was then seeking a publisher for the Asquith letters. I gave her dinner at the Savoy Grill. She looked the part in every respect; reddish hair; evasive manner; air of carrying within her bosom all sorts of state secrets. Unfortunately, after these *billets doux* reached Henrietta Street, disagreement about terms resulted in their appearing under the imprint of another publisher.

Duckworth's used occasionally to make a little on the side by issuing books 'on commission', that is to say paid for by the author. One of these, a novel, accepted rather unwillingly as not quite up to the firm's standard (called *Impetuous Betty*, one reviewer wrote: 'There is humour as well as pathos in a tale that never flags in the telling') confounded everyone by selling quite well.

At about this moment three unusually well-off young men decided almost simultaneously that they wanted their poems to appear in book-form. Duckworth's was prepared to oblige. Lambert suggested that these separate volumes of verse should be reprinted as an omnibus under the title *Poor Poems by Rich Poets*.

6

A somewhat bizarre work which I was responsible for Duckworth's publishing—not without some trepidation on Balston's part—was *Tiger-Woman* (1929), the autobiography of Betty May; a title highly coloured, if not wholly indefensible, as designation for the author, one of the many professional artists' models from time to time making an appearance in the Charlotte Street pubs. Betty May dated back to pre-1914 Café Royal days (when she must have been very young), and had been represented on canvas by many painters, though best known for the bronze portrait-head by Jacob Epstein.

Even allowing for a good deal of journalistic exaggeration, Betty May must have experienced fairly hair-raising adventures in various under-worlds of one kind or another. For some time she had been anxious to have certain newspaper articles that had appeared about these experiences several years before (bestowing the sobriquet 'Tiger-Woman') cobbled into a book. A young journalist with whom she was then living was prepared to take this job on.

Betty May, as it happened, linked up with a story much talked of during my first Oxford year (though at that time I never heard her name connected with it), which had involved the magician, Aleister Crowley (familiar to me by repute from childhood), and an undergraduate of St John's College, Frederick Charles (renamed by himself Raoul) Loveday.

Loveday, an early member of The Hypocrites Club (which gave him a certain additional interest), like the Scholar Gypsy—though with far more baneful results—had abandoned Oxford halls to learn the secrets of Crowley's magic lore. In the first instance he had met Crowley in London, but, soon after an association between them had been struck up, the Mage moved to Sicily, where he established an abbey (in fact, a whitewashed farmhouse of characteristic local type) at Cefalù. There, having first married Betty May, Loveday followed him. While engaged in practising the magical arts, Loveday died at Cefalù; quite how and why, no one seemed to know. That happened in 1922, the year before I came up to Balliol.

The earlier forms of the Loveday myth had centred on a projected undergraduate expedition to rescue this Oxford friend from Crowley's clutches. I think the party was to have included Alfred Duggan and several other members of The Hypocrites. By the time the story was retailed to me Loveday himself had died the previous year; Crowley been ejected from Sicily by the Italian authorities. Nevertheless the circumstances were remembered for their sinister climax.

When, not without some difficulty, Betty May managed to get back to England, she sold to the press a fairly lurid account ('ghosted', of course) of her Cefalù experiences. The routines of daily life at Crowley's abbey sound thoroughly unpleasant, making the official expulsion of the magician not in the least unreasonable. Among other disagreeable ceremonies, Loveday had been required to sacrifice a cat by decapitation, then ritually drink the animal's blood. This cannot have been good for anyone's health, but—in spite of digestive consequences of such an act, and rumours that he had been strangled by Crowley—Loveday's end seems to have been brought about by the banal indiscretion of quenching thirst by water from a polluted mountain stream.

7

Betty May, who described herself as of East London costermonger origin, looked like a gipsy, the two elements not at all incompatible. With her hair tied up in a coloured handkerchief, she would not have seemed in the least out of place telling fortunes at a fair. I believe she did undertake a little soothsaying when in the mood. The remarkable modelling of her features, exotic formations somewhat oriental in suggestion, had appealed to Epstein in sculptural terms, but, when asked if she might dedicate the book to him, he refused in a cross letter.

In spite of a reputation for turbulence, Betty May, diffident in conversation, articulating with the utmost refinement, always behaved with complete decorum on the few occasions I met her. Most of the arrangements about the book were made by correspondence with the 'ghost', and, when Betty May herself once came to the office to arrange about illustrations, so far from behaving in a tigerish manner, she was overcome with terror in dealing with Lewis.

Lewis himself, paralysed with shyness at the sight of this figure from the fortune-telling booth on the pier, had taken refuge in a flood of publishing technicalities, uttered in the severe tone that merely meant he was ill at ease. When I saw Betty May down the stairs to the front door, she said: 'Please, please, never, *never*, make me talk to that *thin* man again. I fear him. I *fear* him!' Used as she was to artists, gangsters, magicians, drug-fiends, Lewis had proved altogether too much for her.

> I fear thee, ancient Mariner!
> I fear thy skinny hand!
> And thou art long, and lank, and brown,
> As is the ribbed sea-sand.

8

Since everything said in *Tiger-Woman* about Crowley had appeared years before in the newspaper articles, when no legal action had been taken, trouble about libel—an aspect of statements about himself in which Crowley always took keen interest—was not much feared. At some stage, however, whether before or after publication, I do not remember, Crowley telephoned to the office, inviting me to lunch with him at Simpson's in The Strand. I had never met him in person, but his celebrated near-cockney accent grated at once on the ear, as familiar from stories.

'You will recognize me from the fact that I am *not* wearing a rose in my buttonhole.'

The ring of the old-time music-hall comedian in this observation was much Crowley's style. On the way to Simpson's I wondered whether I should be met in the lobby by a thaumaturge in priestly robes, received with the ritual salutation: 'Do what thou wilt shall be the whole of the Law'; if so, whether politeness required the correct response: 'Love is the Law, Love under Will.'

(In this connexion, Hope-Johnstone told how, at a period of his life when he saw Crowley quite often, the Magician had remarked: 'Hope-J, I'd very much like you to greet me with a phrase from the Book of the Law whenever we meet.' Hope-Johnstone, examining this curious compilation of Crowley's, came on the sentence: 'Curse them, Curse them, Curse them!', which henceforward he always made a point of using at future encounters.)

The reality at Simpson's was less dramatic. Instead of a necromantic figure, sonorous invocation, a big weary-looking man rose from one of the seats and held out his hand. He was quietly, almost shabbily, dressed in a dark brown suit and grey Homburg hat. When he removed the hat the unusual formation of his bald and shaven skull was revealed; so shaped as to give the impression that he was wearing a false top to his head like a clown's.

This Grock-like appearance was not at all unbefitting the steady flow of ponderous gags delivered in the rasping intonation. Crowley's ancestral origins included more than one dissenting sect (Quaker, Plymouth Brethren), and I wondered whether his cadences preserved the traditional 'snuffling' speech ascribed to the Roundheads. There was much that was absurd about him; at the same time it seems false to assert—as some did— that his absurdity transcended all sense of being sinister. If the word has any meaning, Crowley was sinister, intensely sinister, both in exterior and manner.

Sylvia Gough, a raffish South African beauty of the first war period, once remarked: 'Crowley, you've got such a kind face.' The countenance that had thus struck her was dull yellow in complexion, the features strangely caught together within the midst of a large elliptical area, like those of a horrible baby, the skin of porous texture, much mottled, perhaps from persistent use of drugs required for magical experiment.

We lunched off Simpson's traditional saddle of mutton, Crowley drinking a glass of milk, his guest a pint of beer. He began to complain at once about Betty May's book (which suggests it must have been published by then), though not at all violently, almost as if he expected nothing in the way of response. Crowley kept up this monologue for some little time, then gradually moved away from Betty May, her inaccuracies and vulgarities of phrase, to more general consideration of the hard life of a mage, its difficulties and disappointments, especially in relation to the unkindnesses and backbiting of fellow magicians.

Crowley was full of resentment at the injustice with which the world had treated him. His demeanour suggested that of a general relieved of his command for dropping shells into his own trenches; a mixture of explanation, apology, defiance, self-pity. Throughout luncheon it was never quite clear what he had really hoped to gain from our meeting; perhaps merely hungering for a new listener. I heard him out, and, though no conclusions were reached, we parted on good terms. I did not mention that my mother had met him with friends years before, an experience she had not at all enjoyed.

9

Subsequent brushes with Crowley may be dealt with here and now. Several years after this period, Nina Hamnett, who had known Crowley for a long time both in Paris and London, produced a volume of memoirs. What was said of him there might have been thought well within his own accepted terms of self-reference, but he brought a libel action against the publishers. Had Crowley won that case (which he spectacularly failed to do), he would certainly have instituted another suit regarding *Tiger-Woman* against Duckworth's. Accordingly, I was sent to court to observe the proceedings.

Betty May, one of the witnesses for the defence, was effective in the box as an innocent young wife, who, on her honeymoon, had been trapped into enduring the aberrations of behaviour then taking place at Cefalù. Crowley, on the other hand, giving evidence on his own account, was altogether futile. He seemed unable to make up his mind whether to attempt a fusillade of witty sallies in the manner of Wilde (a method to which Crowley's music-hall humour was not well adapted), or grovel before the judge, who had made plain from the start that he was not at all keen on magic or magicians. Crowley's combination of facetiousness and humility could hardly have made a worse impression.

An increased element of knockabout was added to the proceedings by the stage-Irish accent of Counsel for the Defence.

'Mr Crowley, is ut thrue that ye crucified a toad on therr basilisk's abode?'

To counteract cross-questioning in that vein, Crowley's Counsel read out a poem of inordinate length, written by his client as a young man, each verse of which terminated with the lines:

> Ashes to ashes, dust to dust,
> So let it be, in God we trust.

It was of no avail. The reiterated moral sentiment of the refrain did not establish in the mind of judge or jury any conviction of Crowley's innate goodness. On the contrary, the case was not argued to an end, the foreman of the jury sending up a note to the judge expressing their view that Crowley was a man impossible to libel. Much of the evidence had certainly pointed to that conclusion.

Crowley is perhaps seen at his best writing comic verse: the clerihew about the painter, Giovanni de'Bazzi, which (however misleading as to Italian pronunciation) ended with the lines:

> They called him Sodoma,
> Which was not a misnomer.

or his limerick:

> The obscene and obese Mrs Besant
> Once accosted an innocent peasant,
> Who said: 'Of a surety
> I shall tell Krishnamurti,
> When results will be more than unpleasant.'

Our tête-à-tête luncheon at Simpson's was the only occasion when I met Crowley in the flesh (perhaps one should say The Beast 666 incarnate), but about a year after the publication of *Tiger-Woman* (and before the libel case) a letter headed with a Berlin address, written in Crowley's hand, arrived at the office:

My dear Powell,
    I am the beautiful German girl for whose love the infamous Aleister Crowley committed suicide . . .

The gist of this not always very lucid communication seemed to be that Duckworth's was offered 'the story of our elopement'—entitled *My Hymen*—for an advance of £500 on a 15% royalty. The signature, a woman's name, was followed by the words: '"Blue Eyes" only to Horace Cole.'

At about this time Duckworth's (at my suggestion) launched a 'Hundred Years Series' (Wyndham Lloyd wrote *A Hundred Years of Medicine*), and I had dealings with my father's army friend, Major-General J. F. C. 'Boney' Fuller, who contributed to this project *War and Western Civilization, 1832–1932*. Years earlier, the General had been an admirer of Crowley—indeed published a eulogy, *The Star in the West*, which suggested the world had waited ten thousand years for such a messiah— but these former enthusiasms (not to mention Crowley's recent letter) seemed better unresurrected.

Crowley, though acquaintance remained unrenewed, made a final appearance, during the first period of my married life, when we lived in Great Ormond Street. Unless an hallucination, Crowley's tall figure would from time to time stride past the Children's Hospital just opposite our flat. Hatless, heavily bespectacled, he was dressed in green plus fours, as for golf. Some days, too, a large bald skull could be seen, highlighted over a table, through the window of a Great Ormond Street ground-floor room, where Crowley was playing chess with a friend. Beyond the silent chess-players, an open door on the far side of the house gave on to a garden, revealing a fig tree; appropriate background for a magician, from the fig's wonted place in myth and symbolism.

10

Soon after I joined the firm, Duckworth's took over the books of William Gerhardi (later Gerhardie), including *The Polyglots* (1925), an outstanding novel, particularly in the rare gift of making child characters come to life.

I never had more personal contact with Gerhardi than to meet for a moment or two in the office, but through him Duckworth's also published several books by his close friend, Hugh Kingsmill, whom I met for the first time at this period, but did not know at all well until many years later. I did not much take to Kingsmill at the outset (though our contacts were of the slightest), but greatly liked him on meeting again in the 1940s, when he was literary editor of the *New English Review*.

Kingsmill's books (Duckworth's published, among others, *After Puritanism, Matthew Arnold*) never quite do justice to him as wit and critic. His journalism was composed with care, but he was too lazy to write at book length. Although in revolt against Victorianism, Kingsmill (b. 1889) remained very much a Victorian himself in the complacency of his judgments. In his own field he possessed powerful attack, founded on exceptional familiarity with certain standard writers: Shakespeare; Boswell's Johnson; Wordsworth; Tennyson; Dickens; a few more. These he knew almost by heart. He was not at all interested in authors who fell outside his chosen scope. For example (except in direct connexion with Shakespeare) he seemed scarcely to have heard of Ben Jonson, and I doubt if there was a single Greek, Latin, Continental writer, except Cervantes, whose name meant much to him. He had a passion for the novels of Stanley Weyman, which, it has to be admitted, reflected in some degree Kingsmill's own view of history.

Good talk, however, is not a matter of pedantic accuracy. The very opinions that might lay Kingsmill open to criticism on paper were often the most illuminating when spoken extempore. From the limited number of writers he had canonized, he could keep up a flow of brilliant and apposite quotation. He was anti-Nineties, anti-Kipling, most of all anti-Freud and anti-Jung. This aversion for psychoanalysis—then thought of as very much the latest thing—gave him unclouded judgments that could be a refreshing corrective to fashionable pretentiousness.

In one sense flying counter to any suspicion of imposed psychology, Kingsmill himself regarded all writing as strictly subjective. He would scarcely bother to listen to any discussion of *Hamlet* which did not accept the Prince of Denmark as more or less exact projection of Shakespeare—anyway Shakespeare at a given moment of his life—and always insisted that an author who embarked on biography did so at the price of almost total self-identification with his subject. This approach, like the expert knowledge of a few writers and contempt for psychoanalytical theories, could be effective in producing new aspects of investigation—for instance, Kingsmill on Dickens—but, however ingenious and entertaining, the method had its flaws; also at times recoiling on the operator of such tests.

One of Kingsmill's literary categories (adapted from Horace Walpole) was the 'inspired imbecile', the writer whose books do not stand up to 'serious' examination, perhaps are not even intended to do so, but remain alive, readable, even poetic. Kingsmill put the Sherlock Holmes stories in this class, a useful one, critically speaking. He was always adept at defending his own critical position. He had, for example, expressed dislike on some occasion for the weekly articles the novelist, Charles Morgan, was then writing for a Sunday paper. I asked Kingsmill what he would say if, the following Sunday, Morgan's piece was devoted to praise of a Kingsmill book. 'In that case,' said Kingsmill, 'I should consider the whole question of Morgan's status as critic reopened on an entirely new basis, bearing in mind the fresh evidence to be considered.'

A favourite saying of Kingsmill's was that *No Exit* always means *Exit*. There is a certain truth in this view, as most people must have discovered, but, in his own style of setting about things, Kingsmill was apt to carry to extremes the principles of this paradoxical conviction. As a writer he never quite made the mark he should, but, in spite of existing in a state of acute financial crisis, he managed somehow to keep himself and a family afloat, while never in the smallest degree deviating from his own rule of living.

Kingsmill's vision of the world is well illustrated by a remark he made on hearing my account of an investiture at the Czechoslovak Embassy at the end of the second war. I had been awarded a decoration for work as military liaison officer with the Czechoslovak forces in Great Britain, and, when the ceremony was at an end, refreshments handed round, the occasion became a party. One of the British generals, who had been honoured, hung the riband of his Grand Cross across the chest of our elder son, then aged six. In the relaxed atmosphere of what had become an ordinary social gathering, the sparkling stars and crosses seemed reasonably appropriate on the uniforms of the soldiers, however threadbare the khaki; on the shiny lounge suits of one or two senior civil servants from the War Office, who were also decorated, they looked more than a little strange. I described to Kingsmill this incongruous scene. He said: 'I always think moments like that are when the poetry of life has gone wrong.'

87

VI

Spare Men

After our first meeting, Adrian Daintrey and I used often to see each other in those early London years; and have continued to do so, on and off, ever since; except for the war period, when he was serving as Camouflage Officer on a Corps Headquarters in Persia. Daintrey, who has done several drawings of me at one time or another, is one of the few artists of my acquaintance who possess a perfectly coherent remembrance of the moment when the visible world woke for them in painter's terms. He was coming back from school; on the station platform at Earl's Court the colours and shapes of the goods in a cigarette kiosk suddenly came to life as a pictorial conception.

Without being in any way part of the Augustus John entourage, Daintrey was on easy terms with John, something of an authority on the older painter's varying moods. Even when first encountered, Daintrey had set out on a pattern of life—one on the whole more characteristic of painters than of writers or even musicians—that veered between the pinnacles of the beau monde, and social circumstances of a far more down-to-earth order. At both ends of the scale, Daintrey (a notable admirer of women in their many forms of attraction) has always been a master of spoken reminiscence, on that subject and many others. He has written memoirs (illustrated by his own drawings), but more fantastic experiences than any told there have sometimes come his way, reserved for the ears of friends.

At some fairly early stage of our acquaintance, probably one Easter, Daintrey and I arranged to spend a few days' holiday at Le Havre, a port

88

firmly set in painters' country: Fécamp; Étretat; Harfleur; Honfleur; Trouville; coast saturated with memories of Isabey, Bonington, Corot, Courbet, Boudin, the Impressionists. We were to travel over by night boat.

The trip opened inauspiciously, Daintrey mislaying the tickets, and our having to buy a second lot; the original ones turning up on the top layer of his suitcase, when opened on arrival at our fairly seedy hotel. I have an idea we recovered some sort of a rebate in due course on the tickets, but a certain strain was put on resources. Worse in that line was to follow.

Outside Honfleur was a spot Daintrey had read about called La Ferme Saint-Simeon, where it was said you could get a meal. This farm had been associated in the past with Corot, Courbet, later painters. We crossed by paddle-steamer to the then enchanting little town of Honfleur, lying on the other side of the bay from Le Havre. The Ferme Saint-Simeon was reported to lie between the Trouville road and the sea.

Daintrey was fairly vague about who had frequented the farm. It turned out later that Courbet, Boudin, Jongkind, had all of them eaten there, though I am not sure whether they had, like Monet and Bazille, been lodgers. The owner, la mère Toutin, used to cook lunch for the last two artists, who made a practice of getting up at five and painting until eight in the evening. Bazille (killed in the Franco-Prussian War), a lesser painter with some good points, is said to have introduced Cézanne to Monet, Renoir, and Sisley. In short, the Ferme Saint-Simeon was something of a monument to painting, especially Impressionism.

When we arrived on the doorstep, it was at once clear that the farm had been smartened up since la mère Toutin's day. The shutters were tinted a bright shade of chrome yellow. That in itself should have been a warning. Daintrey (always a fancier of automobiles and aircraft, he and I once went to watch the Schneider Cup flown) remarked on a striking Delage outside, parked with several other vehicles no less impressive. More sagacious tourists, their minds less cluttered with *les maîtres d'autrefois*, would have taken warning from these smart cars, the yellow shutters, above all the fact that no menu was posted up outside the door.

If the exterior of the Ferme Saint-Simeon suggested steep charges to the more wary, that was even more apparent within, where a central table was piled high with expensive-looking sea-foods. We were shown to a place, handed menus. They were written on parchment, framed in leather.

These we studied with sinking hearts. There was a long pause. Daintrey said: 'You ought never to have allowed me to come here.'

I suppose luncheon at the Ferme Saint-Simeon was a shade under ten times what we had expected to pay. The best to be said for the situation was that—in the tradition of la mère Toutin—the cuisine remained first-rate; setting us up, gastronomically speaking, for the rest of a highly enjoyable, if latterly more economical, trip.

2

In his memoirs, Daintrey, the least political of men, mentions my name in connexion with a matter perhaps worth brief expansion here. In 1935, the year after I married, he had a studio in Oakley Street, Chelsea. In the same house lived a young man from the Foreign Office called Donald Maclean. Finding Maclean very agreeable, Daintrey asked me to meet him.

So far as I can remember, Daintrey's account of Maclean approximately ran: 'Donald's not a bit like what people imagine someone in the Foreign Office to be. He's always very shabbily dressed, and is more or less a Communist. Apparently he was walking back from Whitehall the other evening with von Ribbentrop [recently appointed by Hitler German Ambassador to the Court of St James's], and made Ribbentrop absolutely furious by stopping in the street to buy a copy of *The Daily Worker* [the current name of the Communist Party's official newspaper] from a man selling them on the kerb.'

When the meeting with Maclean took place at Oakley Street—there were just the three of us at the studio—I did not at all share Daintrey's view of this Foreign Office young man. He seemed to me vain, pompous, and in his own particular way, notably snobbish. These are no doubt venial enough imperfections in themselves, but, in Maclean's case, so it seemed to me, was an emanation of shiftiness positively creepy. I reported these reactions at home, so am on record in the matter. There was no reason to see Maclean again. I forgot about him until the later 1940s.

By the time Maclean reappeared, to a small extent, in our lives (an occasional meeting at dinner-parties or in a club), he had become quite a talked-of personality. His drunkenness and violence were referred to with awe as example of what you could not only get away with, as member of the country's diplomatic corps, but actually turn to good account in augmenting your reputation as a rising man. I can vouch for the fact that Maclean broke a colleague's leg, because the leg was in plaster when we first met, but only hearsay reported the wrecking of a flat belonging to a female member of the US Embassy in Cairo.

Such antics belonged, of course, to Maclean's lighter moments. In a more serious vein, he was reputed to decline invitations to official dinners (which after all he was paid to attend) from moral objection to expenditure of that sort in a country with Egypt's low standard of living. Maclean's superiors (blind to political affiliations that Daintrey, a painter without the least interest in politics, had noticed as far back as 1935) not only took these whims in their stride, but showed themselves positively impressed by such humanitarianism.

On the several occasions when I met Maclean on his return to London— though we got on perfectly well—I saw no reason to change my earlier opinion of him. He still struck me as inordinately conceited, unreliable, drunken, bisexual, yet remaining in his own way a typical civil servant; the *fonctionnaire* who wishes to be 'different', a not unfamiliar category, carried to its logical conclusions; the complete reversal of conventional behaviour, while remaining in conventional circles. That was, of course, only the exterior.

> During his office treason was no crime,
> The sons of Belial had a glorious time.

At the moment of the Maclean/Burgess decampment (1951), we were in France. The French press was understandably elated by such a story about 'English diplomats', especially the homosexual angle; while even in England the couple were written of as if they belonged to the same official level. Such was, of course, far from the case. Maclean, however protracted his wild oats, was an authentic member of the Foreign Service, who had passed the required examinations, was supposedly destined for a routine career, ending as an ambassador. The same was by no means true of his confrère, Guy Burgess, of whom a word may also be said in passing.

Burgess, taken on as a temporary wartime governmental employee, was well known in London as a notorious scallywag, to whom no wholly baked person, among those set in authority, would ever have dreamt of entrusting the smallest responsibility, or access to secrets of even a low grade classification. In fact, if Maclean is the supreme exemplar of the civil servant who wants to be 'different', Burgess is equally representative of the manner in which official bodies (noticeable, too, in the army) lack as a rule the faintest idea of what an individual is 'like'.

In London circles of a kind that could not possibly be censured as puritanical—even fastidious, about sexual goings-on—Burgess was regarded as a man to steer clear of. Indeed, it might be said of him, as Churchill is alleged to have remarked of the Labour MP, Tom Driberg (later created life-peer as Lord Bradwell): 'He has the unenviable reputation of being the only man in this House who has brought buggery into disrepute.'

When the row broke, my impression was that I had never met Burgess in person. That proved a mistake; the fact emerging long after. I was sorting out some letters written to Violet in the early months of the war (she was out of London expecting a baby), and came across one of these (dated 4 October, 1939), which said: 'I had dinner with the so-and-so's the other night . . . after dinner an absolutely nauseating character called Guy Burgess came in, a BBC fairy of the fat go-getting sort.'

Perhaps it is scarcely necessary to add that this encounter with Burgess took place in the house of a distinguished member of the Treasury.

3

The Varda Bookshop (of which I spoke in the first volume of these Memoirs) was at 189 High Holborn; its sign (painted by Edward Wadsworth) hanging outside, simply announcing in the idiom of the Twenties, without definite article or capitals, *varda bookshop*. The business was still (1928) being conducted by the beautiful and stormy Varda, who had appropriated the surname of her Greek husband, Janko Varda, Surrealist painter and designer of ingenious artefacts.

I probably met Varda through the fact of Lambert living in a flat above the shop, but she had first manifested herself by writing to me at Duckworth's (at the suggestion of some common acquaintance), putting up a project for translating *Le Diable au Corps* (1923), the first of the two novels written before his early death by Jean Cocteau's protégé, Raymond Radiguet. Nothing came of this proposal, nor later of a novel Varda herself wrote (called *Faces*, always referred to by its author as *Faeces*), which had a few poetic moments, but not much construction.

Varda, whom I was to know for years (until the terrible devils of self-destruction took their final revenge, when her life seemed at last well ordered), was both a beauty, and a personality not to be disregarded. Her taste for strife caused trouble in the lives of a lot of men, several women, at one time or another, but, when in good form, no one could be wittier, or show greater appreciation of wit in others. She was unfortunately incapable of finding tolerable any known pattern of existence. She would racket round London; retire in complete solitude to a country cottage. Neither simple nor complex paradigms of life suited her, nor were effective in casting the devils out.

Notwithstanding that, Varda could be wonderfully funny about her own troubles; other things too, but desperation with life was her accustomed theme. She was, indeed, unique in her kind. One of her favourite stories was of a former charwoman of hers, who had remarked to a subsequent employer: 'That Mrs Varda wore herself out thinking of others.'

4

Lambert was pretty comfortably situated at the Varda Bookshop flat (always decorated with a vase of flowers unless he was acutely hard up), but, at an early stage of our knowing each other, would complain that he had been kept awake until a late hour by Varda's friends carousing in her sitting-room, especially by prolonged singing of 'The Hole in the Elephant's Bottom.' The names Lambert cited as causing a disturbance with this chorus were those of John Heygate and Bobby Roberts. Roberts I had not heard of till then; Heygate, familar by sight from having been only a year senior to me at Balliol (where we had scarcely met), I had never come across at that time in London.

Bobby (in fact, Cecil A.) Roberts was an acquaintance of Evelyn Waugh's at about this period (often mentioned in the Waugh Diaries), but I don't think Waugh had ever spoken of Roberts to me. He was a figure to crop up often, usually in farcical circumstances, during the next twenty or thirty years; and, of course, like most persons of his sort, must have fought against a desperately melancholy side, though that was rarely if ever revealed.

Although far from military in background or outlook, Roberts had been to school at Wellington, where the poet-journalist, J. C. Squire (then editing *The London Mercury*, a fairly stodgy literary monthly), had come to lecture. Even as a boy Roberts clearly possessed a measure of that devious persuasiveness that distinguished him later, because, after hearing how much Roberts loved books and poetry, Squire, in an unguarded moment, offered him, when he left at the end of the term, a job on the staff of *The Mercury*.

Roberts—who would gaze benevolently through huge spectacles set in a moonlike face, while he recounted some startling act committed in his cups—proved competent to cope with the work on a literary monthly only so far as the heavy drinking was concerned, a *sine qua non* among Squire's entourage. Squire, a man who had kept afloat by dexterous manipulation of his own talents, grasping the extent of his mistake, unloaded this still outwardly plausible assistant on to the BBC. The Corporation, come only recently into being, was then established at Savoy Hill, just south of The Strand. Among several other young men working there, inimical to the prudish overlordship of Sir John Reith (later Lord Reith), was Heygate. I don't know which arrived at the BBC first, but Heygate and Roberts soon became friends.

Although a little of his company went a long way, Roberts was a richly comic figure, and, as I have suggested, possessed also an element of tragedy. He always wore the same suit (a restrained Glen Urquhart check), which never seemed to grow any older; Heygate attributing the suit's apparent agelessness to the care Roberts expended on it; however drunk always remembering to fold coat and trousers before he himself passed out. After a few drinks Roberts would indulge in protracted monologues, usually devoted to the meaninglessness of life. His undoubted success with women was assigned by many of his friends to the fact that the objects of his desire found less trouble in going to bed with him, than in sitting up all night listening to an inexhaustible flow of Joycean streams of consciousness.

At a certain stage of intoxication Roberts would become a compulsive telephoner. Attending a party in a house where there was a nursery, a fellow guest, who knew about this fever for telephoning, found a toy telephone (reasonably like the actual instrument), and put it within reach of Roberts. When in due course the lust for telephoning descended upon him, Roberts seized the toy telephone (these were pre-automatic days), and tried to 'get through' to the exchange. He made many complaints about the London Telephone Service, but this kept him out of mischief for the rest of the evening.

5

One night I was with Roberts and some others at a fairly seedy night-club, The Blue Lantern, in Ham Yard just behind the Piccadilly end of Shaftesbury Avenue. Like The Gargoyle, though at a lower level, The Blue Lantern could claim a faintly intellectual tinge. On this occasion a party at the next table included Tallulah Bankhead, then at the height of her fame as embodiment of the Twenties, an unusual star to appear in that place.

Tallulah Bankhead was on the right; the table on the left dominated by a man with one of those peculiarly resonant voices, who for some reason was telling a long story about the sterling qualities of his mother. Customers are said to visit brothels largely to talk about their wives and children; perhaps some night-club habitués find the atmosphere congenial for working off their Œdipus Complex. Halfway through this undoubtedly rather tedious narrative, Tallulah Bankhead, who seemed bored with her own companions, suddenly turned away from them, leant forward with elbows on my knees, projecting herself towards the man reminiscing about his mother.

'Do tell me whom you're speaking of?' she asked.

The mum's boy looked startled by the question from such a source, though it was put in the most formal tone.

'I was talking about my mother, as a matter of fact.'

'Oh, I see,' said Tallulah Bankhead. 'I thought you *must* be describing Sybil Thorndike.'

Having never shared the almost universal admiration for Sybil Thorndike as an actress, I enjoyed this exchange. Tallulah Bankhead levered herself off my knees. As she straightened herself, this seemed an opportunity not to be missed.

'Will you dance?'

She looked me up and down.

'Do you dance well?'

'Very badly.'

'In that case I will.'

She moved with incredible lightness, holding her was like holding nothing at all, a contact with thistledown, which at the same time controlled my own steps, as she glided across the floor. The story, I'm afraid, ends there. It was not the start of a great romance. We never met again, but the impression remained of much fun and charm, as well as a very decided toughness. The period flavour of the incident must excuse its triviality.

6

At a somewhat later stage of acquaintance with Bobby Roberts, he was appointed assistant-manager at Sadler's Wells (built by Lilian Baylis to present opera, ballet, the drama, on the site of the old 18th century theatre there, a stage in north London to work in conjunction with the Old Vic on the south bank), where, as 'front of house', Roberts, in a dinner jacket, relatively sober, was to be seen every evening. He undertook this job at first with enthusiasm, and would sometimes hand out free tickets for the show.

This high standard of conduct was hard to maintain, and a day came when it was clear to his friends that Roberts was in no state to attend the Theatre, undertake his 'front of house' duties. An excuse must be found, that quickly, to propitiate the formidable Miss Baylis, who ruled Sadler's Wells and the Old Vic as a dual despotism, absolute in character. If Roberts did not turn up, he would certainly get the sack.

Then some man of genius remembered that the date was the 11th of August, the day before grouse-shooting opened on 'The Twelfth'. Roberts had probably never discharged a shot-gun at a bird in his life, but Miss Baylis was nevertheless asked by telephone 'if it was all right for Mr Roberts not to come to the Theatre that night, as he wanted to sit up late cleaning his guns.' This plea (which might be held to imply an overnight journey to Scotland, brief blaze away at the grouse, return for duty the following evening), although one of the most fantastic that can ever have been offered in comparable circumstances, was at once accepted.

'Front of House' at Sadler's Wells included the concession of hiring out camp-stools for use of those who would queue for hours outside the Theatre to buy seats in the pit. Much later, after he had left the job at Sadler's Wells, Roberts retained dominion over these camp-stools (possibly available at other theatres too), an increment brought to an end, I think, only by the outbreak of war in 1939.

In due course finding himself in the Public Relations Branch of the RAF, Roberts was posted to India and Ceylon. There, as usual, difficulties arose with those higher up. One night, travelling down the subcontinent to Colombo in a railway sleeping-compartment from Madras, Roberts was assailed by a Pinfold-like hallucination that his Commanding Officer—with whom he had often been in trouble—was repeating a complaint already made: 'Roberts, you are sycophantic.' This was not to be endured. Roberts, opening what he took to be the office door behind him, backed out to the plains of the Carnatic. Although the express was travelling at 50 m.p.h., he was discovered some hours later, hardly at all damaged, but so great was his persecution mania when he returned to the Colombo office that he habitually arrived each morning by way of the fire escape.

After demobilization (as squadron-leader), Roberts geared himself once more to theatrical life. This seems to have been to some extent undertaken in the provinces. I lost touch with him. Then he rang up at eleven o'clock one morning, and tried to explain something. It had to do with the Belgrade Theatre in Coventry. The voice was indistinct, trailing away, then ceasing altogether, before I could learn what was happening to him. That was in the middle 1950s, the last time we spoke together. While writing these Memoirs I heard to my regret that Bobby Roberts was no more.

7

After marriage, the Evelyn Waughs moved into a maisonette in Canonbury Square, Islington, where (in another house on the south side) George Orwell was to occupy a flat twenty years later. In those days Islington had no particular connotation for writers. Painters were sometimes to be found there—and in Camden Town—Sickert and others, years before, having established the beauties of the North London landscape. For anyone with a taste for going to parties, especially smartish parties, the district could not be called handy.

It has often been suggested that, after his first marriage foundered, Waugh turned to social life as consolation. Undoubtedly certain social objectives became more outwardly explicit after matrimonial disaster, but I think the process of change that took place was only hastened by the parting of ways. A transformation of some sort was inevitable, both in the light of Waugh's energetic ambitious character, an early success that necessarily, and suddenly, widened the scope of his life. The old Waugh—in my view—was already fading into the past that night we met on the Tube, when he said: 'I'm going to be married.' It was gone for ever, such is my belief, by the time he moved into Canonbury Square.

There can be few persons, whatever their place in life, who, as their own situation changes, expanding or contracting, have not shed a few early friends, or been shed by them. As an example of this process, Waugh was very positively no exception. Indeed, even before marriage, his Diaries reveal a fairly steady sloughing off of acquaintances who had become uncongenial; sometimes a jettisoning that no one could look on as unreasonable. On settling down as a married man, he made no secret that he wanted his life in some ways to alter, expressing a desire to know 'only the intelligent and the smart'; even in those days highly amorphous concepts, and an ambition hard to satisfy in its very simplicity of definition.

The Waughs' Islington flat, looking out on to a wide quiet 19th century square, was transformed by the hand of Evelyn Gardner (so it seems simplest still to call her), a light but accomplished touch, which then and later made every place she inhabited comfortable and attractive. Brought up in an aristocratic world, she was perfectly prepared to accept that world's most notable characteristic (as remarked in the very different case of Rosa Lewis), its vast panorama of relationships, but, so far as she herself was concerned, she wanted to diminish, rather than increase, those aspects of aristocratic life that become tedious if taken too seriously.

In short, Evelyn Gardner liked to enjoy now and then what was conventionally offered by her former background, without burdening herself with too much of its ironmongery. Waugh, on the other hand, so far as could be managed on a limited—if expanding—income, was not in the least averse from taking up the Smart Man's Burden.

From the start there was much hospitality at the Waughs' flat. Among those who reappeared in my life, if he can be said previously to have figured there at all before, was John Heygate. It was at Canonbury Square that Heygate and I effectively met; for, when Alfred Duggan, visiting his younger brother, had brought Heygate over from Oxford to Eton, I had not at all demurred at Hubert Duggan's complaint about the dullness of his elder brother's Oxford acquaintances. When Heygate turned up at the Waughs', on the other hand, he seemed a different person. We became friends almost at once.

8

John Heygate's father (younger brother of a baronet, to whom Heygate himself was heir, though never on good terms with his uncle) had retired as an Eton housemaster just before I arrived at the school. Heygate's mother, a woman of rather uncomfortably dominating personality, having lost an eldest son in childhood, doted on this younger one, though barely agreeable to her daughter. She was proud of her descent from John Evelyn, the diarist, and Heygate was nearly named 'Evelyn' after this distinguished ancestor; something which would have added additional confusion to future events.

As a young man, Heygate *père* had gained a reputation for such oppressive social correctness of demeanour and dress that Edwardian society had coined the verb 'to heygate' or 'do a heygate' (see, for example, the letters of Julian Grenfell, the war poet), meaning to act in a manner uncompromisingly conventional, bordering on the priggish. In principle, Heygate got on well with his schoolmasterly father (rather less well with his adoring imperious mother), but, while approving the relative fame implied by existence of the term 'to heygate', did not himself at all follow that rule of life.

Tall, good-looking, with an easy rather lounging carriage, John Heygate, so far as outward appearance was in question, tended to be well dressed, as the word was popularly used, with the addition of some slight eccentricity in colour or cut. He had been through the routine of deb dances, and, so to speak, come out the other end. It was perhaps strange that he had never run across Evelyn Gardner at any of these dances, as they (and Waugh) were much the same age, though for a girl that implied a slightly earlier vintage. Waugh was very much taken with Heygate—whom he knew through Bobby Roberts—in the early days of Canonbury Square.

In a piece of self-analysis that illustrates his own brand of wit, Heygate

99

used to say that his tragedy was that stupid people thought him intelligent; intelligent people found him stupid. This drastic definition of a personal predicament was not without all acuteness in its attempt to pinpoint relations with others. At Eton (notwithstanding the prestige of Sixth Form) he had undoubtedly been regarded as a dimmish figure; at Oxford never emerging, either at Balliol or outside the College, in any easily identifiable undergraduate world. Heygate would laugh about his father's ineffectual efforts to turn him into a country gentleman by a gift of guns, but, at Salt Grass, the seaside house near Keyhaven, opposite the Isle of Wight, to which his parents had retired, he was prepared to enjoy routine social life among New Forest neighbours, and liked solitary sailing on the Solent.

Heygate himself would often refer to his own lack of sparkle at school and university, for which he was inclined to blame—an element not to be denied—the stuffiness of his family. Release from inhibitions imposed by parents seems to have been brought about at the age of twenty-three, when, just down from Oxford, in preparation for the Diplomatic Service, he was sent to Germany for three months to learn the language.

The Diplomatic Service was never attained, but Heidelberg always remained the great romantic experience of Heygate's life, fundamentally affecting him for good or ill. He lived with the family of a former Prussian cavalry officer, impoverished by the war, and post-blockade Germany— the Germany from which arose the legend that ultimately brought Hitler to power—made an impression that was never effaced, nor even modified, in Heygate's mind. Although not himself a member of Heidelberg University, he knew many Heidelberg students, and shared with them a warm companionship, which allowed watching student duels, and taking part in much student beer drinking. There were also sentimental passages, if frustrated ones, with German girls. He learnt to speak German tolerably well, and always felt at ease in the country, which he loved to visit.

After this Heidelberg idyll (possibly on failing the Diplomatic Service examination), Heygate experienced some sort of breakdown (called by him 'when I was mad'), which had included the illusion that everyone round him in a London club was talking German. His account of this condition (like Roberts falling out of the train in India) conveyed something strikingly like the hallucinations of Evelyn Waugh's alter ego, Gilbert Pinfold, when Pinfold heard voices addressing him from the void. Certainly, in all three cases, a good deal had been drunk at an earlier stage.

'I like dramatizing my work,' Heygate used to say, and seemed quite happy in the news department of the BBC. At school he had painted competent watercolour landscapes, but would have been utterly remote from any such activities as those of the Eton Society of Arts, or other relatively aggressive forms of intellectual life. In London, he would go to an occasional picture show, read the book of the moment, but at this period was in no way committed to any of the arts, certainly having no particular ambition to 'write'.

Heygate drank a good deal without being an alcoholic, even if at moments he was within hail of that condition, notably at the time of the breakdown. He had a flat in Cornwall Gardens, South Kensington, when a homosexual man-servant was employed (merely by chance, not for erotic reasons), who disapproved so strongly of Heygate's drinking that he planned a practical illustration of the harm alcohol can do. He came into Heygate's sitting room holding a tumbler of neat whisky in one hand, a piece of liver in the other. Dropping the liver dramatically into the whisky, he paused for a moment while the meat shrivelled up. 'That,' he exclaimed, 'is what is happening to your liver all the time you drink as you do.' Heygate, who was undoubtedly startled by this action, reported himself as replying: 'What a shameful waste of liver and whisky.'

Agreeably successful with women, Heygate remained well short of being anything like a professional womanizer. He rather enjoyed admitting to hypochondria (which remained with him throughout life), and suffered from occasional black moods, when he was fairly unapproachable; these last rare in those early days. None of his friends guessed how deep-seated was a neuroticism that began to take a grip in middle life; eventually, after frequent bouts of melancholia, precipitating his own end. On the contrary, Heygate then seemed to most of his friends—among them myself—a man who had solved many of the pedestrian problems some contemporaries were still unable to face.

9

If Lambert, intellectually speaking, came as a refreshing draught after Oxford self-consciousness about the arts, Heygate, in quite another manner, offered a different freedom of movement in his acceptance, if not on its most obvious terms, of everyday life. That was an attitude equally unOxonian. He was familiar with the conventional social world (the snobbish social world, if you like), aware of its amenities, but quite undazzled by them. If grand invitations came his way, he did not refuse them; they were never pursued for their own sake.

In short, Heygate took life as it came; an ideal 'spare man', who could be produced anywhere, high or low, easygoing, often witty (though that might not be guessed from his books), a generous host, prepared for any sort of adventure, with any sort of people. That was, of course, observing him on the surface, which is how one meets most people; an aspect often unjustly deprecated, as if of no account.

Heygate to some extent revolutionized my London existence; among other things (though that was later) inciting me to save up, and buy a car (one of the first £100 models), which materially affected my way of life. He was stimulating in the sense of providing something that had not been there before. Intellectual vagaries did not surprise him, nor did a humdrum point of view. Most of the people I knew, even at this early stage, seemed committed to one path, from which they were already unwilling to stray. I myself did not feel at all like that. All kinds of different things appeared to possess advantageous, disadvantageous, sides. I was not at all inclined to settle down to any of them exclusively. For a writer, there is something to be said for this point of view, though one not particularly adapted to getting on in a material way.

Quite soon after we met, Heygate and I arranged to make a trip together in his car, which was to take us to Berlin the following summer. He gave a glowing picture of the charms of Germany, a country I had caught a glimpse of only once; on the way back from Finland with my parents, briefly passing through Hamburg at the moment of the election which gave Hindenburg the chancellorship; a period when the country was still scarcely recovered from the war.

10

Much myth has circulated on the subject of Duckworth's failing to publish Evelyn Waugh's first novel, *Decline and Fall*, offered to the firm as next book under contract, after *Rossetti: His Life and Works*. Some of these legends appear to have emanated from Balston himself, when, in latter days, as one of the weavers of sagas in the Garrick Club, he would rehearse the tale to fellow members, who may well have heard it before, in any case not greatly interested. At least one version that gained some acceptance, which has no basis whatever in fact, was that Gerald Duckworth turned down Waugh's novel out of hand, while Balston was taking a holiday abroad.

In its pristine state, when *Decline and Fall* (for which several other titles were canvassed) arrived at the office, the manuscript contained a sprinkling of phrases, mostly in the dialogue, to be regarded in those days as falling into an equivocal category. At that time, where an 'outspoken' book was concerned, the publisher ran not only risk of prosecution—often on absurd grounds—which might result in a heavy fine, even imprisonment, at best landing the firm in heavy legal expenses, but also, at an unofficial level, the additional censorship exercised by booksellers and librarians, unwilling to stock a volume that might upset their customers, or even their own often delicate moral susceptibilities.

When I first worked at Duckworth's, the typist-secretary was a provincial bookseller's daughter. She instanced a case where her father had refused to market a new novel in which (to define an area of the human body) the word 'bottom' had occurred. Such scruples set an exacting standard. However broad-minded a publisher might be, the battle was lost from the start, if retailers and circulating libraries would not even accept copies of books they deemed improper.

Evelyn Waugh, brought up from birth in the shadow of the publishing trade and its traditions, was well aware of these obstructions, notwithstanding his impish side, and the conviction he shared with every other serious writer of the day, that literary censorship should be resisted so far as possible. At the same time, Waugh (prepared even to alter the ending of his novel, *A Handful of Dust*, for serial publication) held extremely practical views on encouraging sales. He was not an amateur writer with no workaday grasp of the situation, nor a fanatic, determined to charge the authorities head-on.

When demur was made at Duckworth's about some of the things he had written in *Decline and Fall*, Waugh did not, as sometimes implied, immediately walk out. On the contrary, had not a special problem arisen, tactful handling would probably have resulted in mutual agreement about a small amount of discreet trimming before publication. This unlooked for complication was vested in Gerald Duckworth himself as semi-uncle of Evelyn Gardner.

Not particularly well disposed towards Waugh from the start as a writer, Gerald Duckworth liked even less the prospect of having him as a semi-nephew. It might very well be urged that Waugh's marriage, even to a semi-niece, was no business of his. That was not the way Gerald Duckworth looked at the matter. In short, *Decline and Fall* gave an excellent opportunity to be awkward. Waugh might be an already published Duckworth author; that did not prevent him from being an undesirable character to have in the family. People like himself, who had always feared the worst—such was Gerald Duckworth's stance—were now proved quite right. Here was Waugh, a blatant adventurer, not only married by stealth to his publisher's semi-niece, but trying to foist on the firm an obscene novel.

Balston, for his part, not at all opposed to a touch of impropriety, at the same time suffering chronic fear of sexual scandal, found himself between the Scylla of losing a promising young writer, and the Charybdis of having a stand-up row with his partner, regarding a matter about which he himself harboured mixed feelings; while his adversary held the comparatively trump card of protesting that this connexion by marriage added family insult to business injury.

Accordingly, Balston set about doing what he could to arrange a satisfactory compromise. He went through the manuscript of *Decline and Fall*, marking everything he judged risky; Waugh showing himself perfectly prepared to await the result of this picking over. In the event, fussed by the circumstances, Balston may well have lost his head, queried more than was necessary, but even so, without Gerald Duckworth's specialized intrusion, some sort of agreement could almost certainly have been reached. As it was, Waugh considered the suggestions, then turned them down.

One of the classical situations of the publishing business is the process of a publisher requesting certain alterations in a book, the author refusing to make these; afterwards agreeing to do so for a subsequent publisher. Waugh, as he records in the foreword to the reset edition of *Decline and Fall* (1962), took the manuscript up the street to his father's firm, Chapman & Hall (a publishing house certainly, in principle, no less stodgy than Duckworth's), where they too demanded certain excisions. These were made.

The 1962 Edition of *Decline and Fall* replaced words and phrases removed or altered for Chapman & Hall. In his brief preface Waugh implies that the chief emendation was the Welsh station-master pimping for his sister-in-law, rather than his sister. Those with the curiosity to compare the two texts will find about a dozen other changes to indicate Chapman & Hall's determination to be on the safe side: 'Boiler-room', for example, takes the place of 'lavatory' (where the boys smoked illicit cigars); the comment, 'because women you do not like', is omitted in relation to Grimes; nor is Grimes's marriage allowed to be qualified by 'nothing happened'. These alterations give some idea of a publisher's fears in those days. There are more on the same lines. The difference between them and Balston's recommendations cannot have been very great. Nevertheless, severance was probably inevitable in the light of Gerald Duckworth's feelings about Waugh's first marriage. He did not live to see the second one; also to a Gerald Duckworth semi-niece.

From this time on, Chapman & Hall published Waugh's novels; Duckworth's, his travel books. The first of these travel books was to be Waugh's next work to appear. The Waughs were to take a cruise, free of charge, in a Norwegian ship touring the Mediterranean. In return for this trip Waugh was to write a book giving publicity to these holiday cruises. The prospect was additionally acceptable, because at the outset of married life, Evelyn Gardner had not been at all well; a combination of physical illness and nervous exhaustion. It was hoped that the voyage, which was to begin in January, last about three months, would set her health right again.

VII

Set Books

In the spring of 1929 I moved from Shepherd Market. This change of scene was chiefly due to the demolitions that had begun to take place there. The leases of the two separate halves of Carrington House were both a few years longer than those of the rest of the street; or any rate their owners were unwilling to be bribed or bullied into giving up their homes earlier than necessary. After devastation had begun, it was pleaded by those responsible that the structure of the Williamsons' house might be threatened by the work in progress. Accordingly, the authorities insisted that a thick wooden stanchion should be set up in the centre of my sitting room—where space to manoeuvre was already, to say the least, limited—in order to support the ceiling, should it show signs of descent. This and other supposed precautions—if more than the traditional harassment of persons trying to preserve ancient or historic buildings—were shown to be altogether superfluous when Carrington House was finally reduced to rubble; its innate solidarity causing exceptional labour to the demolishers.

I bore these inflictions for some time, but eventually dust and the stanchion, especially the stanchion, forced a decision to seek somewhere else to live. I regretted parting from Mrs Williamson, who had been so kind, thought me so crazy; and I have felt ever after that I never showed myself grateful enough to her. Other accommodation in Mayfair was likely to be too expensive, the district in any case only intermittently convenient for the life I found myself living. Piccadilly was certainly halfway house between those two vital centres, Chelsea and Bloomsbury (Lambert used to say that the best years of his life had been spent shuttling backwards and forwards from them on buses 19 and 22), but I had begun to think of emigration to Bloomsbury, even if that located Chelsea (apt to be a centre for girls) yet further away than before. Besides, even without the stanchion, my Carrington House sitting room, still less the bedroom, could hardly be called 'a good place to write'.

In those days it was possible to rent an unfurnished two-room flat, kitchen and bath, for £100 a year; a few pounds more if there were some special 'feature', like outlook on to a square. I set about acquiring a few bits of furniture. My mother said she would give me a divan bed. My grandmother died at about this moment, and, from the dissolution of The Elms, my father ceded some kitchen chairs, washstands, bamboo tables, much prayed-on oriental rugs.

I moved into the first flat inspected, the self-contained basement of 33 Tavistock Square, Bloomsbury, three rooms for £110 a year. I did not require three rooms—in fact never really had all three properly in commission at the same moment—using the front one as sitting room, ringing the changes on the other two. There was a little garden-yard at the back, but for some reason I never made any effort to develop its possibilities; nor did I do any serious cooking in the small kitchen; both omissions now inexplicable to me. In one of the flats of the house above lived Thomas Burke, poet of London's Chinatown, whose mild exterior did not suggest the title of one of his works, *Limehouse Nights*. We never met.

2

Once settled in Tavistock Square, I began to get my life into better order, if one can ever be said to make any headway in that process. Plans to write a novel, never in practice advancing in the least at Carrington House, had in any case been held up by work on another book, which, quite fortuitously—indeed, rather pointlessly—I had taken on. This was the editing of a volume published by Duckworth's under the title *Barnard Letters* (1928), a collection of late 18th century and early 19th century correspondence, preserved by a family of that name.

I had come across the Barnards (Anglo-Irish, by then living in Kent) through Eton friends. The son, a soldier serving in India, was my contemporary, though I had never known him at all well. There were two pretty daughters, who, on some occasions when I was taken to their house in the country, spoke of these Letters, which the family hoped one day to get published. I asked to see them, and in due course Duckworth's took them on. After going through the collection several times, the simplest solution to the problem of editing seemed to do that myself. I was not paid, beyond Duckworth's putting up ten pounds as entrance fee for membership of the London Library.

I am now a little shocked at the lighthearted manner in which I accepted a job for which I had no special qualifications, such as knowledge of place or period, but the book was quite well received, when published, and may have been useful practice in routine research. *Barnard Letters* out of the way, the basement more or less habitable, I took a firm hold on the question of what sort of a novel was to be written—an extension of that enigma—in what style?

At Carrington House I had reached the third or fourth page of what now seems to have been a try-out for my third novel, *From a View to a Death* (1933); an embryo that never showed any sign of maturing. I also started up a diary. Diary keeping, a subtle and peculiar art at its higher levels (Boswell, Amiel, Kilvert), requires, even for quite pedestrian regular entries, a particular sense of personal motivation. I found difficulty in being brief, pithy, certain of what should be recorded. The instinctive diarist feels none of these things. There may also be dangers for the novelist in making too immediate factual notes of what should possibly be allowed to simmer for the time beneath the surface, emerging as fantasies of the imagination.

After a lifetime of work a novelist can possibly be 'written out'. Before that, if any talent exists, there is never lack of material, as such, only energy to handle what is on offer. At the age of twenty-three that fact is hard to grasp. In any case available material is then inevitably undigested, its intensely subjective nature quite likely to be embarrassing for immediate publication; while at any age it is easy to overlook the truth that every-thing—literally everything—can go towards a novel's creation; all be said, even without the freedom of exact expression recently come to be allowed. These aspects of novel-writing are easy to forget. They should never be lost sight of by any novelist.

In those days there were plenty of people to recommend abstention from writing, especially novel-writing, until you were thirty—forty—fifty.

Something can be said for deferment; something against. The chief objection to delay is loss of a kind of lyricism—and energy—that disappears with increased age. Deeper qualities no doubt take the place of that lyrical element, they never quite match it. I can, for instance, remember at odd moments (on buses, and so on) jotting down on the backs of envelopes scraps of dialogue, dramatic situations, types of character, none of which had relation to any specific book; aspects of writing a novel that in middle life have to be hammered out only by hard work. These unchannelled forces given to youth are not to be wholly disregarded when they bubble up.

The novel I planned was to express in contemporary terms all sorts of feelings about life and love. These themes, as first conceived, were to have a background of dances and country houses, as well as the parties, nightclubs, pubs, which, with a modicum of office life, eventually provided most of the scenario. In the event, the deb side, proving unassimilable within the scope of seventy-five thousand words, was cut out. The original design for my first novel was, in other words, not without resemblance to the initial framework of the later twelve-volume sequence, *A Dance to the Music of Time*; and, allowing for inexperience, the treatment is perhaps less different from the long novel than has sometimes been suggested by critics. Abrupt dialogue certainly predominates, but comparatively elaborate description and commentary are also to be found in the early work. For better or worse, I don't think much fundamental change of approach took place.

3

The year 1928 was an *annus mirabilis* of books that made an impact. It was then, for example, that *The Enormous Room* (1922) by E. E. Cummings reached England. Cummings was the man who opened my eyes to a new sort of writing, putting out of date the style of authors like Norman Douglas and Aldous Huxley. *The Enormous Room* (Cummings's confinement by the French on account of a friend writing indiscreet letters, while both were serving with an American ambulance unit, before the US came into the war) received an unfriendly notice in the *Times Literary Supplement*, which made me pretty sure—the *TLS* being what it was in those days—that I should like the book. This turned out a correct guess; incidentally highlighting an aspect of unfavourable notices to be borne in mind both by writers dispirited at receiving them and reviewers hoping to do damage.

Ernest Hemingway's *The Sun Also Rises* had appeared in England as *Fiesta* in 1927. I had read the novel with a fair amount of enjoyment as a picture of American expatriate Paris life, but without noticing anything revolutionary about the method; by no means a triumph of critical perception on my own part. Then someone spoke of Hemingway's style (whether in praise or blame, I'm not sure), and I read the book again.

Perhaps rereading *Fiesta* had been stimulated by a brief meeting with Duff Twysden (model for its heroine, Brett, Lady Ashley), because I do not recall more than mild interest at being brought face to face with what was then a much favoured brand of heroine in novels of the period, the lost lady. Boyish in appearance, emaciatedly thin, decidedly battered, Lady Twysden (by then possibly married to the young American with whom she was travelling through London on the way back to the States) seemed a type from the bar of a Surrey golf club, rather than what I supposed appropriate to Montparnasse. After a second reading I should have paid more attention.

If E. E. Cummings, rather than Hemingway, was the revelation in throwing overboard a good deal of Edwardian literary débris, Hemingway systematized a treatment of dialogue in a manner now scarcely possible to appreciate, so much has the Hemingway usage taken the place of what went before. It was an approach explored by Firbank (influenced, it seems to me, by Hardy's renderings of Wessex peasant talk), the naturalistic vocable, banal, even inane; purposeless exchanges that are their own purpose, on account (especially in Firbank) of an undercurrent of innuendo and irony.

Hemingway apprehends that a novelist does not have to make a narra-tive-or-character point in every phrase he writes, ramming this doctrine home so mercilessly that, with other of his principles, imitators often failed to understand that aimless dialogue was not an end in itself. Hemingway's own ear for dialogue, whatever its eventual aberrations, is shown by the perfection of his 'British' idiom; so much so that, when Mike Campbell speaks of 'shells' of a revolver, rather than cartridges, the reader is prepared to believe that was because Campbell had so much associated with Americans. It should, of course, be recognized that Hemingway's dialogue at its best is a brilliant representation of 'naturalism', not necessarily 'how people really talk'.

Rather surprisingly (*The Great Gatsby* was published in England 1926), I did not hear of Scott Fitzgerald until recommended by Connolly six or seven years later. It had not occurred to me to question Ford about contemporary American writing when I lunched with him in Paris, though he was then editing *The Transatlantic Review*, and, in his own person, linked the world of James and Conrad with that of Joyce and Stein. My impression is that, in any case, Ford, who always attributed indifferent sales to the inefficiency of his publisher of the moment, kept conversation firmly on to himself, and a history of English Literature which he said he was currently writing, and might have possibilities for Duckworth's.

4

On returning from Paris on that occasion, I undertook the breach of the law required from anyone who hoped to keep up in literary circles, by smuggling back a copy of *Ulysses* (9th printing, May 1927), a work I had first read of in some highbrow magazine in School Library; later done no more than glance through. The purchase was made at the avant-garde bookshop, Shakespeare and Co, run by Sylvia Beach, who also pressed on me *Pomes Penyeach*.

Joyce's verses underline his need for severe stylistic curbs to exorcize the sentimentality and musty prose that sometimes crop up in *Portrait of the Artist* ('singing . . . to her who leaned beside the mantelpiece a dainty song of the Elizabethans, a sad and sweet loath to depart'), although the earlier book is arguably the better one.

Under both brilliance and pedantry, *Ulysses* has a conventional plot, and it would be interesting to see Joyce considered, not primarily as an innovator, but merely among others figures in the mainstream of traditional Irish writers (e.g. Mangan), both in the material he produced and his own way of life. I was impressed by many of the 'naturalistic' passages in *Ulysses* (the Martello Tower, buying milk from the old woman, Mr Deasy paying the wages of Stephen Dedalus, the funeral), but did not find Joyce in general at all a tempting model.

Wyndham Lewis's *Tarr* (1918, revised 1928) was another matter. Hitherto I had thought of Lewis as a Vorticist painter. Now his luminous brutal prose, blocked in with a painter's eye, was at once immensely exciting. On the first round, I accepted *Tarr* at Lewis's own estimation as a deliberate gesture in writing a novel of a new sort—which up to a point *Tarr* undoubtedly was—not noticing Dostoevskian borrowings; the 'privileged' manner with which Tarr himself is treated by the author; the haphazard change of gear in the narrative, all at once removed from the hero's point of view.

These things can grate a little on later readings; nevertheless—together with several of the short stories collected in *The Wild Body* (1927)—for instance, *Bestre, The Death of the Ankou*—*Tarr* remains for me Lewis's most striking work as a writer. Its characters (belonging of course to a pre-war Montparnasse) were a good antidote to those of *The Sun Also Rises*; though *Tarr*'s opening sentence—splendidly poetic, however satirically spoken—would be equally appropriate to the Hemingway novel: 'Paris hints of sacrifice.'

5

When no more manuscripts remained to be reported on, all current book production in the pipeline—sometimes simply when other occupations palled—I used to read the less ephemeral file copies on the shelves of the room at Duckworth's where I worked. Among other writers, those shelves introduced Henry James.

In 1898, Duckworth's had published *In the Cage* (not much more than a short story about a woman post-office clerk's preoccupation with a love-affair conducted by telegram), my first James, which stimulated getting *The Awkward Age* and *The Turn of the Screw* out of the London Library. These last two remain my preference, together with certain snapshots, like Waymarsh (*The Ambassadors*) mooning about half-dressed in his hotel bedroom at Chester.

James, with an exceptional eye for situations (*The Golden Bowl*), unmatched as example of a novelist capable of dealing in his own particular way with any subject, however unmentionable at that day, is at the same time too niggling, too full of inhibitions, for me to regard myself as a Jamesian. At the same time James must be given the credit for forcing, almost singlehanded, the English novel into the status of a work of art; together with the sometimes forgotten corollary, that all works of art require an effort at the receiving end.

I was early familiar with Joseph Conrad, because my father had bought a secondhand set of Conrad's Collected Works (which I think he scarcely read) at some auction-room. In those days I liked several (such as *Romance*) which I am no longer able to read, but only much later took in the innovatory nature of certain Conrad techniques. A strong influence on Fitzgerald, Conrad also gives a foretaste (*The Arrow of Gold*) of Hemingway's strengthening effect by repetition of a word ('And everything was bright and hard, the air was hard, the light was hard, the ground under our feet was hard').

Jamesian influences are not happy in Conrad's dialogue, especially in love scenes (*The Arrow of Gold, Victory*). In the latter area one suspects also Continental models, not of the first class, read in early life. Nevertheless, if naturalism is the aim (which of course it need not be), Conrad, oddly enough, laid down a precept I came across about this time, in one of his autobiographical books, that I found very helpful: that characters in a novel, shown as engaged in conversation, should not be represented as replying to each other's questions.

Conrad's complicated feelings about women (up to date tackled by no biographer with any conviction) sometimes, by their unresolved romanticism, mar the novels. The extent of his technical virtuosity is of a kind to be easily missed on first reading. Lambert was an admirer (particularly of *The Secret Agent*), but, on the not uncommon though really indefensible grounds that he 'did not like books about the sea', Yorke was no Conradian.

6

A file copy, too, probably first put me on to the plays of Strindberg (whose second wife's night club, The Golden Calf, was still in those days sometimes talked of by its former frequenters). Lambert recommended Strindberg's autobiographical writings, perhaps less well known in this country than they should be: the rows with his first somewhat lesbian wife; the cold supper she gave him, while specially bought cutlets were cooked for the dog; his own attempt at suicide, when Strindberg took a lot of sleeping tablets, splashed about naked in an icy sea, climbed a tree, beneath which he awoke the following morning in glowing health. Strindberg must by no means be looked on solely as a dramatist. He is very conscious of the importance to be attached to the coincidences of life, things that happen all the time, yet seem to be magic. As a dramatist, Ibsen, gripping too on discovery, never exercised quite the same attraction.

7

An uncharacteristic pre-war Duckworth venture among the file copies was Robert Burton's *The Anatomy of Melancholy* (first issued 1621) in a three-volume edition. There are worse places to read about Melancholy than a publisher's office. Although a long book, I got through *The Anatomy* in a comparatively short time.

I have never developed the habit of making at all copious notes for use in potential books, but had already (1927) begun to jot down occasional ideas, quotations, scraps of dialogue (invented or overheard), viable names for characters in a novel; all sorts of odds and ends of that kind. They were inscribed in an octavo 'dummy', one of those volumes of bound blank pages made up by the binder for publishers to check the correct size of a book's paper-wrapper. To this day these notes take up only about a hundred pages. One of the earliest entries is a longish passage from Burton, which begins 'I hear new news every day', and ends 'one runs, another rides, wrangles, laughs, weeps, &c.'

For the novel I was then trying to write, *The Anatomy of Melancholy* soon suggested a title (I don't think *Afternoon Men* ever had an earlier name), and its epigraph: '. . . as if they had heard the enchanted horne of Astolpho, that English duke in Ariosto, which never sounded but all his auditors were mad, and for fear ready to make away with themselves . . . they are a company of giddy-heads, afternoon men.'

On the principle that the Narrator of *A Dance to the Music of Time* should be a man who had shared some (though not necessarily all) of my own experiences, he is represented as writing a book about Robert Burton (1577–1640), therefore undertaking researches that would have something in common with my own work, when engaged on a biography of John Aubrey (1626–1697); historical research having a particular bearing on a writer's life, with which no other literary activities are exactly comparable. The passage from Burton entered in the notebook (with several others, and quoted more fully) occurs in the closing sequences of the twelve-volumes; Burton—quite by chance—spanning the opening of my first novel to the ending of my last.

8

Yorke and I had shared the discovery of Proust at Oxford, where we spent a good deal of time discussing *À la recherche*, of which I read the first half as an undergraduate; finishing the remaining volumes on coming to London. I followed that up by attempting to improve a not very extensive knowledge of other French writers, beginning with Flaubert. *Madame Bovary* required a certain effort to get through. I have always preferred *L'Éducation Sentimentale*, although, notwithstanding the great to-do made about Flaubert's technique, its treatment (for example, in relation to time sequences) is perhaps not above all criticism.

I found longueurs too in *Le Rouge et le Noir* and *La Chartreuse de Parme*, though Stendhal was soon to establish a firm grip. The *Chartreuse*, vigorous in its opening, still remains obscure to me after two hundred pages. The unfinished *Lucien Leuwen* would be my choice among Stendhal novels. It is the Diaries and autobiographical works (among which *De l'Amour* should be included) that I find absorbing; notably *La Vie de Henry Brulard*, Stendhal's account of growing up in a French provincial town at the time of the Revolution. *Henry Brulard* can be amusingly contrasted with Jane Austen's not dissimilar level of English provincial life of much the same date.

In due course Stendhal took hold with sufficient force to cause contemplation of writing a book about him. This project, carried far enough to assemble a few notes, was in the end whittled down to representing the Narrator of *What's Become of Waring* (1939) as at work on a study to be called *Stendhal: and Some Reflexions on Violence*.

This title at once recalls George Sorel's *Réflections sur la violence* (1908), a book I had probably read about somewhere, the phrase—as such phrases do—sticking in my head. I knew nothing of Sorel or his views. On becoming aware of this duplication—in order not to confuse the issue—I altered the Narrator of *Waring*'s projected study to *Stendhal: and Some Thoughts on Violence*. I now rather regret the change, also my then ignorance of Sorel, an interesting figure of his period, who believed (as things came about, more than a little mistakenly) that, in the political world, violence was on the way out. A comparison of Sorel's opinions with Stendhal's would have made a convincing subject for a book.

Balzac arrived for me only in middle-age, then wholeheartedly. Proust, a great admirer of *La Comédie Humaine*, observes somewhere that Balzac is vulgarer than life itself, and there can be no doubt that the dedicated Balzacian must accept not only a torrent of vulgarity, but, in matters of situation and behaviour, a great deal of improbability too. Never mind. Balzac's improbabilities do not prevent many of his least likely climaxes from being also the best ones. Besides—something never to be forgotten—with all novelists the reader has to put up with something.

Balzac is supreme example of the great truth invoked earlier, that a novelist can use anything for material, say anything in his (or her) own way. As a young man, I doubt whether I could have got much out of the *Comédie Humaine*. At that age I was preoccupied with 'naturalistic' writing—a will o' the wisp, like most other hard and fast literary concepts, because human beings are rarely 'naturalistic'—and, underneath the theatricality, stylization, of Balzac's method, I should probably not have recognized his grasp of human motive, sense of conflict, knowledge of life.

9

More immediate Continental benefactions came, not from the French, but from the Russians; though from neither of the two most prominent Muscovite performers. Tolstoy, with all his genius, has never been an all transcending idol of mine (not least for his ludicrous views on Shakespeare), and I remained comparatively lukewarm towards Dostoevski (whom I now incline to put top of the league, Russia or elsewhere), until David Magarshack's translation in the 1950s of *The Devils* (*The Possessed*), *The Idiot*, *The Brothers Karamazov*.

These novels are lined up here in my own order of preference, in spite of many favourite passages in *The Idiot* and *The Brothers*: notably old Karamazov, requested by the Elder in the monastery to speak in a less affected manner, be his 'natural self', replying: 'You must not let me be my natural self—it's too great a risk!' Dostoevski's characters and situations have one of the qualities I prize highest in a novelist, the ability to be at once grotesque yet classical, funny and at the same time terrifying. It seems incredible, having once discovered the Russians, that I should take so long to appreciate Dostoevski.

At Oxford I had not been able to get on with Turgenev. Now I saw his virtues: his ability to draw 'nice' girls; the way he sets out the Russian political predicament. *Smoke* was the novel I found most sympathetic. Goncharov's *Oblomov* (translated 1929) also gave pleasure, perhaps pointing the way to Gogol, whom I think I read later. *Dead Souls* is, of course, a far richer work than *Oblomov*, though both tail off disappointingly towards their close. Gogol and Surtees have something in common, Chichikov's tour of country houses comparable with that of Mr Sponge.

There was, however, a more overwhelming Russian revelation than any of these, also owed to the year 1928, when a new translation appeared of Lermontov's *A Hero of Our Time* (1840). I had vaguely heard of this Russian classic (probably only from recent reviews), when I picked up a quickly sold-off circulating library copy, which still contains its stamped label (only two or three entries) on the back cover. This edition (there must be at least half-a-dozen translations now available in English) included a serviceable introduction by the Russian critic, D. S. Mirsky.

As with *The Sun Also Rises*, more than one reading—in fact three—was required for *A Hero of Our Time* to mesmerize me. At Lermontov's first impact I could not in the least understand why this disjointed collection of short stories, loosely linked only by the appearance in different rôles of the 'hero', Pechorin—bored, heartless, Byronic—should be regarded as one of Russia's seminal works. Admittedly there was nothing in Russian literature earlier, except Pushkin (who does not get over in English translation), but later came so much that seemed infinitely more powerful.

Notwithstanding this feeling of being let down, something about the book caused me to read it again—and immediately. On the second reading I found myself better disposed, even a trifle haunted by some of the incidents, though still far from being persuaded. Again I applied myself to *A Hero of Our Time*. The third reading convinced me that here was a writer, and a book, in a very high class indeed; an opinion I strongly maintain.

The clearcut nature of Lermontov's prose (as it appears in a good translation) is unsurpassed, particularly if thought of in the context of its period. It is known that (had he not been killed at the age of twenty-six in a duel, foreshadowed in the novel, prophesied in one of his poems), Lermontov was planning a much longer work, somewhat on the lines of *War and Peace*. One has little doubt of his ability to do so. Tolstoy (*Sevastopol*) learnt much from *A Hero of Our Time*, and, if Stavrogin has more than a touch of Steerforth, Dostoevski certainly had an eye also on Pechorin. Painters and writers who operate on a vast scale are inevitably the most impressive creators; they are not necessarily always the more accomplished artists.

10

In European literature there is perhaps no more subtly moving episode to illuminate the brittleness of friendship (dealt with by novelists much less than love) than the chance reunion, in the mountains of the Caucasus, between Pechorin and Maxim Maxemich, 'the old captain', whose surname we never learn. Four years earlier these two had been the only officers in an isolated fort, a lonely outpost to which Pechorin had been relegated as penalty for duelling.

There Pechorin had kidnapped a beautiful Circassian girl; loved her; tired of her; finally seen her stabbed to death by a former wooer of her own race. Maxim Maxemich, a middle-aged bachelor, his days long occupied in sober military routine, witnesses happenings undreamt of, yet dimly appreciated by him, for their high romance and dire tragedy.

By chance Pechorin, travelling for pleasure to Persia, crosses the path of 'the old captain' again. Maxim Maxemich, still undertaking colourless military duties, is overcome with excitement at meeting once more this dazzling former comrade-in-arms. When he turns up, Pechorin is amiable but distant; firmly refusing to delay his journey for a mere chat about old times. Lermontov's skill consists in suggesting that there was nothing particularly unreasonable in Pechorin's attitude; yet its coldness brings tears he can hardly hide to the eyes of Maxim Maxemich.

If, as it seems, Lermontov projects one side of himself in Pechorin, he perhaps satirizes another in Grushnitski, the pompous officer-cadet,

1. AP, about 1927/1928

2. Shepherd Market, Carrington House (9 Shepherd Street) on corner, AP's
rooms marked X

3. The house in the background (next to the pillared building) later became Duckworth's offices in Henrietta Street—from Hogarth's *Morning*

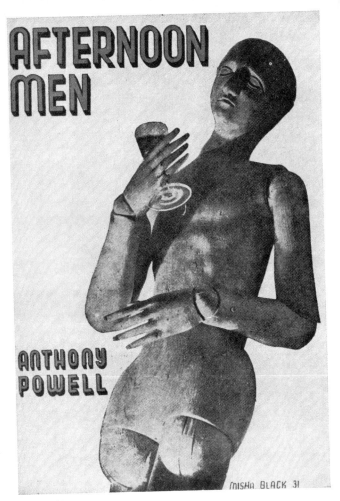

4. Misha Black's jacket for
Afternoon Men

5. Adrian Daintrey, about 1935

6. Constant Lambert, about 1928

7. Evelyn Gardner, about 1935

8. AP—drawing by Nina Hamnett, 1927

9. AP—drawing by Adrian Daintrey, 1931

10. Pansy Pakenham, about 1935

11. Henry Lamb, about 1935

12. AP in his Morris Minor

13. John Heygate, about 1937

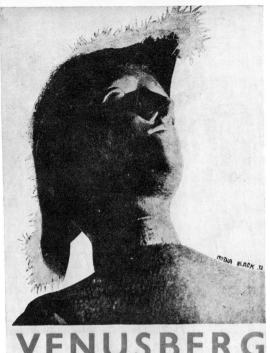

14. Misha Black's jacket for *Venusberg*

15. Misha Black's jacket for *From a View to a Death*

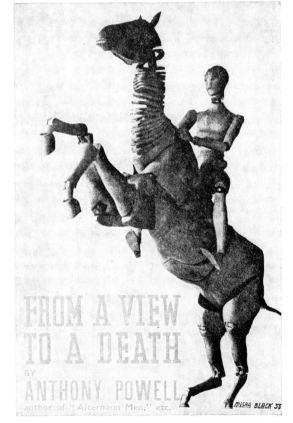

16. AP—drawing in sanguine by Augustus John, 1960

17. Edward Burra and William Chappell at Toulon, 1930

18. William Chappell and Irene Hodgkins at Toulon

19. AP at Toulon

20. Augustus John at Fryern, 1960

21. Sir Osbert Sitwell at Renishaw, 1941

22. Sir Sacheverell Sitwell at The Chantry, 197(

23. Evelyn Waugh at The Chantry, 1964

24. Gerald Reitlinger at Woodgate

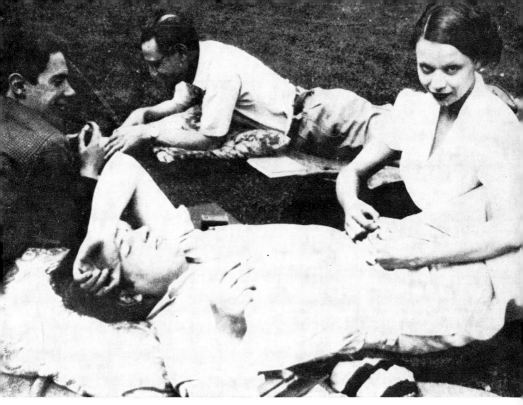

25. *Background* AP and Gerald Reitlinger
Foreground Constant and Flo Lambert at Woodgate

26. Flo Lambert

27. Basil Hambrough and Gerald Reitlinger

28. Hambrough in uniform, 1939

convalescing from a campaign wound at one of those resorts in the Caucasus, where the military come on leave; civilian families, as at Bath or Tunbridge Wells, take the waters. Grushnitski falls in love with a Moscow débutante—vainly, since he is in no position to aspire to the hand of a young princess—and Pechorin, just for the fun of the thing, intervenes; breaks the girl's heart (insulting her in the Valmont manner); killing Grushnitski (represented as behaving treacherously) in a duel.

II

D. S. Mirsky, writer of the Introduction to this edition of *A Hero of Our Time*, prince, former officer of the Imperial Guard, Lecturer in Russian at King's College London, could in those days often be seen striding through Bloomsbury on his way home or to professional duties. Tall, bearded, bespectacled, swinging a walking stick, Mirsky was rather a striking figure. He added a note of distinction to Gower Street and its sombre passers-by. Then he disappeared from that neighbourhood. Mirsky, making his peace with the régime, had returned to Russia.

In 1936, not long after I married, we decided to spend a holiday in the USSR. It was—though we did not know that—the last season of InTourist trips, before Stalin, whose purges had already begun, closed them down. In Moscow, as shortly before in London, Mirsky was to be seen striding through the streets; on one occasion, drinking Russian champagne with friends in the café of the National Hotel. He looked just the same; somehow not quite like the rest of the people in Moscow, any more than he had looked like the rest of the people in London.

Perhaps that singularity alone was considered sufficient reason for including Mirsky in the immolations that began increasingly to take place, until they became one of the great slaughters in the history of the world. It was said—I don't know with how much truth—that Mirsky had also written of Pushkin in a manner to affront a recent change of the Party Line.

I saw Diaghilev's ballet, *Thamar* (décor by Bakst), on its revival, in the 1930s, then unaware that a poem by Lermontov had provided the theme; the Circassian queen, Tamara, credited with taking lovers only for the pleasure of killing them once mutual passion was at an end. Thamar had ruled in the central Caucasus, west of the Terek River, where the mountains merge with the steppe and the Caspian Sea; the region of the outpost in which Pechorin and Maxim Maxemich had been quartered.

When, some forty years after first coming on *A Hero of Our Time*, I found myself among the western spurs of the range, we were far away from that end of the Caucasus, but here it was easy to picture pleasure trips from Pyatigorsk, the watering place where Grushnitski had fallen romantically in love; Pechorin decided to spoil that romance. Pechorin had accompanied the little princess on rides through just such country as this, before the whole incident had been closed by the mountain duel.

It was easy to understand why the Greeks (of whom a few still remain in Trans-Caucasia) associated Prometheus with this mountainous land, focus for much else of their myth. Streaks of sunlight, penetrating the leaves of the forest, brilliantly lighted up an extraordinary kaleidoscope of variations on the colour green. We sat in the woods picnicking, drinking a bottle of Turkish wine brought from the ship. Round about were wild strawberries for dessert.

12

While speaking of books that left a mark, I should mention one that came much later, in fact not long before the outbreak of the second war, by which time I had already written five novels myself. The *Satyricon* of Petronius, a name long familiar, was still unread, until, in a manner that seems to have become endemic with favourite works, I picked up a copy in a secondhand bookshop.

It was the first English translation, 'Made English' in 1694 by 'Mr Burnaby of the Middle-Temple, and another Hand': *The Satyr of Titus Petronius Arbiter, a Roman Knight, with its Fragments recover'd at Belgrade.* The edition (undated), an inexpensive one, rebound also inexpensively but with an eye to style, has only the 17th century publisher's imprint, with head-and-tail pieces of sub-Beardsley design. The 'fragments recover'd at Belgrade' (the text in one place says Buda) was fictitious, a recent forgery in William Burnaby's day, too trivial to affect the rest of the *Satyricon*, especially that masterpiece of characterization and racy dialogue, Trimalchio's Feast.

After a few pages of Petronius I was captivated by the genius of Nero's more intellectual Brummell (forced to suicide on falling from favour); the writer of what can reasonably be looked on as the first modern novel. The *Satyricon*, possibly unfinished, seems designed for reading aloud. Most of it is lost, what remains scarcely half the length of a thriller; the intention apparently a narrative of half-a-million words, say (though otherwise so different), Malory's *Morte Darthur*.

In the picaresque adventures of the *Satyricon*, the pure imaginative vision of the novelist (possibly reinforced by portraits drawn from life) is directed to the world round about the author in a manner that, even at its most grotesque, is never less than convincing; all of it to be easily equated with what is happening today. Petronius, so far as I was concerned, was probably the last writer to help form a taste still open to development.

VIII

Trips in Space and Time

The move to Tavistock Square required some sort of house-warming. In any case a project had occasionally been discussed that one day Lambert and I should work off various social obligations (his largely musical) by giving a party together. The new flat, with its three rooms and back yard, was suitable for that, but nothing was done until the end of June. By that time various things were taking shape in the worlds round about both of us, one of which was foreshadowed by a remark made by Lambert on a Sunday when we were lunching together. 'I have the most boring afternoon ahead of me you can imagine,' he said. 'I have to go and play the piano to a Russian female pianist, who lives in St John's Wood. Can you think of anything one less wants to do on a Sunday afternoon?' I expressed conventional sympathy. He went off on his mission, which I thought no more about.

At our next meeting, quite soon after that lunch, Lambert was in a state of some excitement. He said: 'You never know what's going to happen in this life. You remember the dreary prospect ahead of me in St John's Wood? I arrived on the doorstep of the Russian's flat, and the door was opened by the most beautiful creature you ever saw in the world.'

This superlative, in Lambert's terms, essentially implied the features of Africa or Asia, rather than Europe, even if not necessarily a beauty belonging by birth to one or other of the first two named continents. Where ideal good looks were in question, no Nordic types were permitted in Lambert's canon; particularly not blondes. There had been examples of this rule being broken, but in principle it was a rigid one.

Lambert was too stricken to convey any detailed description of the vision that had opened the door, beyond invoking the name of Florence Mills, the star of *Blackbirds*. This famous musical, recently played in London, had been a great hit, its cast invited everywhere; so much so, that Evelyn Waugh, on issuing a minor invitation, would add: 'It's not a party—there won't be a black man.' On being pressed to reveal more, Lambert enlarged further to the extent of suggesting that the genre of beauty was perhaps Javanese or Malayan, rather than African or Creole.

I asked if he had made a date. Lambert was a little put out in having to admit that he had attempted no assignation. He said that he was determined to do so on his next visit to the flat; the Russian lady's stock having steeply risen.

Most of one's friends (not to mention oneself) suffered from these *coups de foudre*, some (Daintrey, for example) in a more or less permanent state of declension from the sight of some desirable phantom. I did not take Lambert's romantic experience in St John's Wood too seriously at the time, but, perhaps as much as a month or more later, remembering about the exquisite Javanese, made some casual enquiry as to whether he had seen her again. Lambert, though his manner might have been thought in the smallest degree furtive, seemed to have forgotten about her too. I attributed what could have been a touch of embarrassment at my question to regret at having allowed himself to speak of the encounter at all; which, on reconsideration, had probably proved to threaten too many complications of one sort or another, if followed through. There for the moment the matter rested.

2

In about May, the Waughs returned from the Mediterranean. So far from the trip having set Evelyn Gardner on her feet again, she had fallen ill—seriously ill—while abroad. When Waugh, renewing publishing contacts, brought her with him to Henrietta Street, she still looked rather pale, even if in good spirits. Waugh himself seemed in the best of form, full of plans about future books. That, at least, was how things appeared to me. Probably the two of them dined with Balston a day or two later. If I were present, I remember nothing of the dinner party. I did, however, note a comment of Balston's, made either after this visit to the office, or subsequent to an evening spent by the Waughs at his flat.

Balston remarked that he thought the marriage was showing signs of strain. I don't recall how he put that—probably less bluntly than the phrase sounds on paper—but certainly he expressed some such opinion. In general Balston was not specially intuitive, but, as a middle-aged man, he had undoubtedly noticed indications of matrimonial tension not apparent to myself. I attribute this lack of insight on my own part in some degree to the already mentioned unfamiliarity of my generation with the whole condition of young marriage. There were also few, if any, of the Waughs' friends in England—certainly not I—who grasped how exceedingly ill Evelyn Gardner had been in the course of the cruise.

Owing to the shortage of young married couples, marriage going wrong was naturally even more mysterious than marriage as such, itself curious enough. In bohemian circles there existed, of course, quite an assortment of ladies, most of them in their late twenties or early thirties, who, having kicked free from wartime or immediately post-war marriages, were now operating on alimony or their wits; but these *garçonnes* (an essential type of the period), floating on a sea of 'affairs' that most of them, at least outwardly, showed little or no sign of wishing to make permanent, seemed hardly to have really married at all.

One might by now be used to friends (or oneself) having love passages that went better or worse; emotional rows; dramatic reconciliations; changes of mood; scenes that meant little worse than a distressing evening; even if in some cases final severance, a restart on both sides. Those were all within an area more or less accepted as temporary. The break-up of a marriage (soon to become familiar enough) was something of which no one I knew was at all cognisant, an entirely new phenomenon; notwithstanding marriage being so often portrayed in novels as a thorny path.

In short, Balston recognized danger signals imperceptible to myself, or, if noticed, regarded as unimportant from this particular operation of the *Zeitgeist*. The signals in question were perhaps equally misunderstood by the Waughs themselves. Balston's comment seems worth recording, not for itself, but in the light of future events.

Almost immediately after coming back to London, Waugh went off to an hotel in the west country to write *Labels* (1930), the travel book dealing with the cruise. Segregation was his habit when working on a book, but this the first occasion when, as a married man, he had followed the practice. Evelyn Gardner remained in London, where, after their comparatively long absence, she began to reassemble friends at the Islington flat. Among those who returned to the hospitality of Canonbury Square were John Heygate and myself.

By that time Heygate and I had arranged that our holidays should coincide in July, when the trip by car to Berlin was to be undertaken. We were seeing a good deal of each other, and, within the group of friends known to all three of us, we now saw a good deal of Evelyn Gardner. Towards the end of June, I dined with Balston. The other guests were Rose Macaulay, Evelyn Gardner, Heygate, an obscure male Duckworth author, whom I remember being furiously disapproving of Firbank. There had been a party on the *Friendship* the night before, where Heygate (more resolute than I) had stayed till dawn. In consequence, such was his fatigue at Balston's dinner table, that, quite quietly like a child, he went to sleep between courses.

I record this dinner party, Heygate's unconventional behaviour at it, for two reasons: first, because Balston, a man quite peculiarly prone to fear of scandal, would never have dreamt of inviting Evelyn Gardner and John Heygate together had he seen anything approaching a threat to the Waugh marriage; secondly, because the ludicrous incident of Heygate slumbering in his chair at dinner displays the lighthearted atmosphere at this stage. Balston, having had no particular affection for Heygate *père* at Eton, was pleased, rather than the reverse, by that very correct man's son showing such fine disregard for Heygatian standards of correctness at the dinner table.

3

In the same week as Balston's dinner party (a week that had already included a deb dance and the *Friendship* party) Lambert and I gave our cocktail party at Tavistock Square. This accretion of social engagements, suggesting remarkable energy now, was no doubt normal enough at the time. The Tavistock Square party began at six o'clock; in the event, lasting until three in the morning.

When the list of guests had been drawn up, there had been no question on Lambert's side of inviting the vision of the St John's Wood piano-playing afternoon. That caused no surprise to me, as the incident was ostensibly closed. It was only some eighteen months later that friends, attending concerts where he was conducting, began to ask who might be the exotic beauty, sometimes to be seen in the audience, sometimes waiting for the conductor in the foyer at the end of the performance.

The Waughs turned up at Tavistock Square separately, neither staying long, nor seeming greatly to enjoy what they saw of the party; Evelyn Gardner having a brisk disagreement with Heygate. This was the first public occasion when there was a sense of something being wrong between the Waughs. Quite how wrong I did not even then take in. Heygate, one of the first to arrive at the party, was present until the most final moment of its extended revels.

That weekend both the Waughs and I stayed at Salt Grass, the Heygate house on the Hampshire coast. From the undercurrents at Tavistock Square it should perhaps have been clear that a fairly serious situation was blowing up. At the time, Waugh away from home except for weekends, there seemed nothing very extraordinary in Heygate, or anyone else, seeing something of Evelyn Gardner, when she was on her own in London; entertaining both husband and wife, when both were available for a weekend together in the country. That was no doubt a naive point of view, but one all three parties shared in the first instance.

During the Salt Grass weekend, neither of the Heygate parents was particularly easy; Heygate *père* schoolmasterish to a degree; his wife fond of laying down the law on all subjects. I remember no special tensions throughout the visit, though Waugh subsequently complained of Mrs Heygate's snobbishness; particularly in drawing attention to the fact that 'dukes are mentioned in the Bible'.

4

Heygate and I set out for Germany a fortnight later. We slept in a field on the way to the coast (I don't remember where we crossed the sea), once in a way spending a night in the open after arrival on the other side. It might be thought that a lot of conversation was devoted to the embroilment in which Heygate now undoubtedly found himself, but in fact we hardly spoke of that at all. I knew no more than that a tricky situation existed. How deeply those involved were committed, what each proposed to do about it, were subjects not at all discussed, and I was in the dark as to the larger issues.

Germany, in the summer of 1929, seemed on the surface all that was most free and easy. This relaxed atmosphere was in general attributed by British tourists to what they regarded as healthy reaction from German attitudes that had certainly played a part in launching the first war. Few people in England were aware of the sinister vapours seething beneath the surface. That ignorance did not equally persist—as has sometimes been alleged later—after Hitler came to power. When Hitler arrived many persons in Great Britain saw at once that the international situation had become very dangerous indeed. The change of balance was still to come.

The notion of a lighthearted welcoming Germany was not, in fact, an impression peculiar to that particular moment. It seems precisely the response Germany aroused, in spite of a parallel reputation for militaristic regimentation, at the turn of the century, when—just as Hitler was waiting in the wings during the Twenties—the Kaiser, in the Nineties, had already begun his sabre-rattling. This conviction, that German good-fellowship was the most outstanding Teutonic characteristic, is, for instance, especially noticeable, when the author of *Three Men in a Boat* (1889), Jerome K. Jerome, wrote *Three Men on the Bummel* (1900), an outburst of praise celebrating German jollity during a holiday spent there.

That, too, was just how North Germany seemed when Heygate and I drove towards Berlin. There was one row with a motor-bicyclist, an ugly unpleasant youth, who probably ended in the SS; otherwise to be British was an immediate reason for popularity wherever one went. Gallons of beer were drunk. If there were a pool in the village it was taken for granted you could bathe there. The *Wandervögel*, primitive hippies (if cleaner and better looking), wandered about strumming their guitars and singing senti-mental songs. At a wayside café-restaurant, where we lunched or paused for a drink, stood one of those slot machines that give electric shocks to test the endurance of the handle's holder; the force of electricity registered on a graduated scale at the back. Linked hand in hand with the proprietor, Heygate and I tried out this instrument of torture. Unwilling to seem less able than a German to tolerate high voltage, even if electrocution was in sight, we set up a local record.

In the light of Heygate's never more than irrational and undecided leanings towards National Socialism (sentiments with their foundation in happy if confused memories of Old Heidelberg, congenital ineptitudes where anything in the nature of politics was concerned, a temperament that was far from stable), it might be thought that he held forth about Hitler, but I have no recollection of Hitler's name being mentioned during the trip. I remember Stahlhelm marches, Communist marches, but no Nazi marches, and, on this visit, not even many Brownshirts in the streets. It was, however, true that Heygate—as he told me later, after Hitler had made an unpleasant stir in the world—had carried with him on a former holiday (in Bavaria, I think) a letter written by some British journalist of his acquaintance beginning: 'Dear Hitler, this is to introduce John Heygate, a young Englishman interested in your movement'; a presentation he had never bothered to use.

Berlin was then at the height of its Isherwood phase: top-booted tarts equipped with riding-switches; transvestite bars and nightclubs; naked cabarets ('Zweite Klasse', sagely warned the porter at our hotel, by no means first-class itself, of this last form of entertainment, and he was right); all the sexual freedoms that now seem so humdrum. Nevertheless, infested with prostitutes of both sexes, beggars, pimps, freaks, eye-glassed duel-scarred ex-officers, this macabre city presented a monstrous vision of life, the cast peopling the cartoons of George Grosz, the artist who has memorialized for ever the Berlin of that epoch.

After the *boîtes de nuit* of West Berlin, the art galleries, museums, Potsdam's feast of Baroque, we moved southward: Dresden; Nuremberg; Munich; economy becoming necessary after a fortnight consumed of the three weeks' holiday. The Berlin hotel, though central, had been on the squalid side; at Munich, the Goldner Löwe, in the old quarter of the city, took its guests straight back to the Middle Ages so far as accommodation was concerned.

Munich was the first destination to which it had been arranged that mail should be forwarded poste-restante. After establishing ourselves at the Goldner Löwe, we went to see if any letters were to be collected. There were, indeed, letters; a pile of them; cables, too, addressed to both of us. The first I opened read: *Instruct Heygate return immediately Waugh.* Heygate's own communications were no less pressing. It was clear that our trip together was at an end. The blow had fallen; crisis come.

I now see the Tavistock Square party as something of a showdown. To what extent Waugh himself later recognized that juncture as such, I do not know. Certainly he did not do so at the time. Nevertheless he put the occasion to some extent on record (with not unreasonable acerbity in the light of the circumstances) as prototype of one of these infinitely dim items of social news, from a 'murky underworld of nonentities', which, in descent towards suicide by putting his head in the gas-oven, the gossip-columnist of *Vile Bodies* used to write up for his newspaper—'cocktail parties given in basement flats by spotty announcers of the BBC'.

Taking the car, Heygate set out the following morning from Munich, heading for whichever port was to ship him back to England. During the week of holiday that remained to me I made my way by train from Munich to Frankfurt; Frankfurt to Cologne. On one of these journeys, the train very full, I had to travel standing in the corridor. A friendly young German, with a girl, got into conversation—no doubt wanting to practise English, but such amiability was a common experience at the time—and insisted on standing me ham-and-eggs in the restaurant-car. I think he and his girl only drank beer. I mentioned the Berlin night-clubs. He shook his head. 'The shadow of life,' he said.

5

That year several more friends were married; the Evelyn Waughs the first couple known to me—though by no means the last—to be divorced. The place the Waugh divorce was to take in the mythology of the period was at the time not at all to be foreseen. The older generation, in principle discouraging marriage, found in divorce (especially this divorce) complete justification of that attitude. A few worldly persons expressed the view that it had been incautious to leave a young lively newly married wife (only recently recovered from a grave illness) in a comparatively out-of-the-way flat all the week, but on the whole those who had inveighed against the marriage, inveighed equally against separation as inexpiable.

In short, then and later, a good deal of humbug was talked on the subject. I have no doubt whatever that it is, in general, far better to remain married when at all possible, but during the next few years plenty of other marriages were to break up. If this one was to come adrift, that was surely better taking place when there were no children, giving opportunity for both parties to build—as they did—new lives. Waugh's second marriage was successful, but no one reading his Diaries could doubt that an exceptional staying-power was required in any woman who remained married to him.

The inevitable consequence of the circumstances in which I now found myself—committed to Heygate by the trip to Germany, in any case by being by then a friend of Evelyn Gardner's—was that I saw no more of Waugh for some years. No immediate awkwardness took place, partly because Waugh himself was often abroad during the period following the divorce; partly because he had largely ceased to inhabit the sort of world in which we had formerly met. No doubt my own paths were changing too. I was less aware of that at the time than on looking back. Even after I was married (1934), I don't think I came across Waugh more than a couple of times; when we dined on one occasion with the Connollys'; at a party of Alice (Astor) von Hofmannsthal's.

Waugh's irascibilities have been much dwelt on. He took the termination of his first marriage very hard. In a less vengeful character than he, to sever all social contacts with one who had perforce remained Heygate's friend—indeed close friend—would not be unexpected; equally, to avoid all mention in print of a fellow writer who found himself in that position. On the contrary, so far from adopting any sort of professional boycott, Waugh (in an article not mainly about books) went out of his way to write enthusiastically of my third novel, *From a View to a Death*, when it appeared in 1933.

6

The manner in which Waugh and I were again to become associated may be described out of chronological order, the better to appreciate those coincidental juxtapositions that are such a feature of human experience. In 1937, he married as second wife Laura Herbert; through the Herbert connexion, half first-cousin of Evelyn Gardner. Four years later than that, I found myself working at the War Office with Alick Dru, who, in 1943, had married Gabriel Herbert, Laura Herbert's sister.

By that time Dru, as well as military colleague, had become a personal friend. Authority on Kierkegaard (whose *Journals* he translated), Dru had many brilliant qualities, of which I hope to write in a later volume of these Memoirs. At the moment he is introduced merely to explain the manner in which Waugh reappeared on my horizon; and, oddly enough, also to round off what has further to be said here of Rosa Lewis and The Cavendish.

In the days when we first knew each other in London, Waugh, not caring in the least what details he broadcast about his private life, told me things of a fairly intimate kind, but I am sure that he would have revealed them no less to almost anyone else he found momentarily sympathetic; the point being that we were never close friends in the sense in which young men sometimes deeply confide in each other. I think Waugh was perhaps not temperamentally given to friendships of that kind. I may be wrong about that.

Nevertheless, in those days, and in middle life, we always got on well together, though on terms that would never have sustained the sort of behaviour that, in certain moods, Waugh, especially in his latter years, would impose on friends far closer to him than myself. He always delighted in teasing, to which I was as much exposed as anyone else, but, in my own experience, there was never a moment when he attempted to display the savage disagreeableness of which he was at moments so regrettably capable.

After his move from Gloucestershire to Somerset, Waugh lived about fifty miles away from us. He would sometimes arrive without warning on a visit; and at least on one occasion we did the same, looking in on the way to dine with one of his neighbours. For example, one morning while working I heard a car arrive at the door about midday, then go away. This turned out to be the Waughs, accompanied by one child. Waugh (who did not drive a car) was to lunch in our neighbourhood with friends, a house where his wife would deliver him; then take more of the Waugh children out from school for the afternoon, putting the one with them on the train to London. Meanwhile, we were to collect Waugh himself from his luncheon at about three o'clock. His wife would return to us for tea. The two of them would then go home.

All fell out according to plan, but after tea it became clear that the Waughs had nothing ahead of them. They stayed for dinner, leaving about eleven o'clock that night. I record this episode simply because eight hours

on end, without warning, can impose a certain strain on almost any conversation with the same company, let alone someone as cantankerous as
Waugh. Nothing worse took place than a fairly sharp argument (brought
up by Waugh, then abandoned by him) as to what members of what clubs
were homosexual. He had been under the mistaken impression that no
names could be quoted from his own. There is not any particular point in
this story, except to show, in the light of a good deal of evidence to suggest
the contrary, that Waugh was perfectly capable of spending an afternoon
and evening without making a scene.

On another occasion—only about eighteen months before his own
death—we met him at Paddington on a train travelling west. Like ourselves
he was on his way home. We suggested he should detrain at our station,
dine, spend the night. This he did, ringing up his home (though usually an
unwilling telephoner) with a message that he had been kidnapped. The
evening was an enjoyable one. Again, Waugh is presented so rarely in an
easygoing state that the incident seems worth recalling.

7

In November, 1965, at a country wedding, we found ourselves in the
queue to greet bride and bridegroom with Waugh, his wife, one of their
daughters. Waugh did not look at all well. For some time he had been too
fat to be in good health; now he seemed at the same time portly, yet
wasted. He walked in a very shaky manner. One could never be sure
such staggerings were not the pretence of being an old man that he had
begun in middle-age, together with the ear-trumpet, but, if the ear-trumpet
itself remained always something of a game, the deafness and unsteadiness
on his feet were now genuine enough.

'Do you think there's any whisky?' he asked at once.

'I'd forgotten you drank whisky.'

That was true enough. A great consumer of wine, especially port,
Waugh's favourite spirit had always seemed gin, drunk with Italian
vermouth, or orange; though no doubt a whisky-and-soda last thing.

'One must at an affair like this. I'll have a look round the house.'

He broke off from the queue; reappearing a minute or two later, before
we had anything like reached the newly married couple.

'I'd very much like your opinion on two decanters I've found. I'm not sure either is whisky. My sense of smell isn't what it used to be.'

He led me through the back parts of the house into a kind of scullery. On a tray, with a bottle of barley water, stood two all but empty decanters. Whatever they contained could have dated back some days, if not weeks. It was evident they had been put out of the way for the party that was taking place. I diagnosed port residues in each case. Waugh sighed.

'Just what I thought myself.'

We returned to the queue. The main part of the reception was taking place in a marquee, to reach which a ramp had been placed, leading down to the tent from the higher level of the lawn. The slope, though perceptible, was not a specially steep one.

We happened to leave the party at the same moment as the Waughs. Laura Waugh went first, Waugh following, holding his daughter's arm for support. Suddenly, from sheer physical weakness, he could not manage the ascent. His daughter had to call for her mother to return and help. Together they got him up the ramp. This was the first time I grasped quite how bad was his state of health by that stage.

At the top of the slope the three of them paused. Waugh smiled as we passed, making a faint gesture of his hand to say goodbye. That was the last time I saw him. He died about five months later.

8

I had heard nothing of Rosa Lewis, nor her hotel, for a long time, when in 1941, in Piccadilly, by chance I ran into a former fellow-student of an army course we had both attended. I was, I think, by then actually employed at the War Office; he passing through London on the way to a new army posting.

On the course, I had exchanged an occasional word with this quiet slightly eccentric lieutenant, like myself rather old to be of subaltern rank, but we had not known each other at all well. At our meeting in the street, almost his first words were: 'You know, I felt I simply must have a woman before taking on this new job, so I went to see Rosa, who made all sorts of difficulties, said she didn't do much in that line now, was interested in other things, but I absolutely insisted, so in the end Rosa said: "Well, all right, I'll try and get Ivy Peters to meet you in the bar of The Dorchester tomorrow", and I'm hoping everything's fixed.'

I can't imagine why the middle-aged lieutenant unburdened himself to me in this way about his sexual needs, as we had never discussed that sort of thing, nor why he had instantly assumed that I should know who 'Rosa' was. I never discovered the reason for this candour, because he went on to speak of military matters, but, by an extraordinary chance (never to be accepted in a novel), passing The Dorchester in a bus or taxi the following evening, I saw him passing through its doors. I hope all went well. The curious thing was that I was again to hear the name of Ivy Peters (as I have fictitiously called the lady in question) pronounced by Rosa Lewis herself in my own house.

This house, 1 Chester Gate, Regent's Park, was somewhat knocked about during the blitz, but, by 1945, in a sufficient state of repair for us to live there again. The Drus at one moment came to live at Chester Gate too. Gabriel Dru's brother, Auberon Herbert, unable to get himself accepted by the British forces owing to his low medical category, had, with considerable enterprise, managed to join the Polish army in the ranks; somewhat assisted in this endeavour by the fact of Alick Dru, like myself, being Liaison Officer with Polish GHQ in London.

In due course Auberon Herbert was commissioned by the Poles as an officer, and it was probably to celebrate this promotion that he gave a party at The Cavendish, where since his Oxford days he had been on good terms with Rosa Lewis. This party naturally included many Polish friends and their wives, transforming the very English Cavendish into an unaccustomedly Slavonic scene.

By this stage of the war, now in her late seventies, Rosa Lewis herself wore army badges from shoulder to waist. Characteristically, she insisted that an American 'torch singer', staying in the hotel, should join the party, and give renderings of two then popular numbers, 'Clang, clang, clang, went the trolley' and 'Oh, mother, buy me that.' She sang the second song strolling round the room, pausing before a minute Polish major to emphasize the words: 'He's just six feet of paradise.' Rosa Lewis said: 'I knew you'd like her.' Some of the Polish ladies looked less certain.

As sequel to this party, Auberon Herbert arranged for Rosa Lewis to lunch at Chester Gate. Violet was away (lying up for the birth of our second son), but Gabriel Dru cooked luncheon, and there was probably

Algerian wine, one bottle of which, with luck, could be procured most weeks. Only the two Drus, Auberon Herbert, and I, were present.

At first it was like entertaining any elderly lady of the Edwardian zenith, who had begun to feel her age a little; a flood of civilities about the eternal wartime topic, the difficulties of getting hold of food and drink. Then, beginning to warm up at the table, Rosa Lewis set off on a monologue in her old style, in the midst of which she touched on the fascinating subject of 'Lewis', her butler husband, whose personal history was long lost in the mists of time.

'I took The Cavendish on because I was sorry for him.' she said. 'After he went bankrupt, that was.'

Unfortunately, in the course of a fairly long peroration, the name 'Lewis' turned almost imperceptibly into 'Lois'; that is to say Lois Sturt (by then deceased), formerly wife of Evan Morgan (2nd Viscount Tredegar), both of these two last well known at the bohemian end of the beau monde. With the new name Rosa Lewis's narrative swerved, too, in a new direction. The anecdote, which had begun about her husband, became dovetailed into a story about Lois Sturt.

I tried to get conversation back on to the right lines, but it was no good. The subject had changed irretrievably. An attempt to salvage in tranquillity some of what had already been said about Lewis was later equally unsuccessful; impossible to distinguish for certain where Lewis ended, Lois began. Potentially absorbing information was lost forever. 'Somebody ought to write it all down properly,' said Rosa Lewis. 'After what that man put in *Vile Bodies*.'

I feel pretty sure she did not know, at best had long forgotten, that Evelyn Waugh had a sister-in-law, two brothers-in-law, present sitting at the table.

'People repeat all sorts of bad things about me,' she said. 'They never remember all the good I've done. You don't know how much I've helped some of these young men. Look at the way Jack Fordingbridge wanted to marry Ivy Peters. He wanted to *marry* her. Set on it, he was. The Duke was almost off his head about his son and heir. I introduced Fordingbridge to Frieda Brown, and he dropped Ivy Peters like a hot potato. People forget all the good I've done.'

In spite of the apparent paradox in such an illustration of the virtuous deeds a society indifferent to moral values allows to pass unregarded, it was probably true that Rosa Lewis, not at all malevolent in the manner of many of her power-loving kind, had played a comparatively beneficent rôle in that and similar entanglements. The vignette of the middle-aged lieutenant on his way to his assignation with the seductive Ivy Peters—who might have become a duchess—added a piquant footnote to the story.

9

The confusion of 'Lewis' and 'Lois' is a good example of the 'time-travelling' in which Rosa Lewis would indulge during her declining years. Before offering another instance, which involved myself, I shall say a word about the wartime Cavendish as seen through the eyes of J. O. Mahoney, the American painter, who also experienced Rosa Lewis's time-travelling, and—in a volume in which painters have already played a considerable part—should in any case be recorded.

When, in the 1960s, I was staying with Arthur and Rosemary Mizener in Ithaca, upstate New York, they took me to see Mahoney, an old friend of theirs, at his house above the town. Like Mizener (biographer of Scott Fitzgerald and Ford Madox Ford), Mahoney (some of whose pictures have affinities with the work of John Armstrong, mentioned earlier) was a member of Cornell University's Faculty.

Mahoney's house, outwardly austere, indeed almost like a military strongpoint set on the edge of a strategic hill, had been built by him above the lake by which the town of Ithaca lies. Entering this mountain fort through a narrow hall, in which several life-size classical statues elbow each other for room, the visitor proceeds into a huge studio-salon, the walls decorated by the painter himself. Mahoney, where landscape and still-life are concerned, an able artist in the Thirties tradition, is also a brilliant pasticheur, especially in the manner of the American Folk Primitive. The murals he has executed here, including *trompe-l'oeil* curtains in 18th century chinoiserie, are set off by elaborate candelabra, an immense porcelain panelled baroque stove; no doubt deliberately, half the room left unfinished, filled with all the disorder of a working *atelier*.

The studio opens on to a broad terrace, built out in a curve, looking down over the lake a hundred feet or more below. High on its pedestal, in the centre of the parapet round this terrace, stands a massive bust of

Abraham Lincoln. From the great President's forehead sprout the antlers of a Landseerian stag. Beside the presidential bust, set to revolve on a swivel, an old-fashioned brass telescope, of some size too, commands the town of Ithaca, revealing much that is invisible to the naked eye; one day, Mahoney hopes, perhaps a murder taking place.

Meanwhile, from within the house, sounds the voice of Mahoney's mynah bird, Rover (depicted in some of its master's folk-style paintings):

'My name's Rover, what's yours?'

A warning follows.

'Don't forget that I'm a mynah.'

10

I have invoked *chez* Mahoney partly to indicate that its owner was not at all inadequately equipped to wend his way along the Alice-through-the-Looking-Glass corridors of The Cavendish, where, while serving with the US Eighth Air Force in Great Britain, he was accustomed to spend his leaves. What has already been said about Rosa Lewis's time-travelling no doubt explains why she always addressed John Owen Mahoney as 'Ambrose Clark'; as to the identity of whom I can at present offer no clue. Mahoney says that Ambrose Clark appears to have been a figure of whom she had strongly approved in the distant past, reincarnating him in the body of Mahoney himself; thereby (in a manner to which I shall return) so to speak raising Ambrose Clark from the dead.

In consequence of the blitz, the glass had long vanished from Mahoney's bedroom windows at The Cavendish, where he looked on to Jermyn Street, though some protection was afforded by thick 19th century embroidered Japanese curtains. For a long time no water had run from the taps of his bath, which was also filled with plaster from the ceiling, when a landmine was dropped in the mews behind the hotel, shattering all the windows and furniture on the south side. Rosa Lewis would sit in the capaciously hooded porter's-chair in the hall, greeting returning guests with the words: 'Jerry has been very naughty tonight, very naughty indeed.'

On some of these Cavendish leaves Mahoney shared a double suite with a friend on leave from the US Army of the Pacific. One night he was awakened in the small hours by the bedroom light being switched on. Rosa Lewis stood in the doorway. She surveyed the two beds.

'I hoped it would be different,' she said.

The light went off again. The door closed. Mahoney returned to sleep. Regarding the point she had sought to ascertain, Rosa Lewis's doctrine was clearly expressed. She used to say: 'I don't mind the boys doing it, if they do it with their own class, but I won't have the girls doing it, because they've nothing to do it with.'

On this, or perhaps a subsequent occasion when the war was at an end, Mahoney's friend (member of a well-to-do American family of some note) was passing through the hall of The Cavendish *en civil* one afternoon. Rosa Lewis confronted him.

'Have you come about the drains?'

'I'm staying here. You know me well. I'm—'

He mentioned his name.

'Then why are you wearing a brown hat?'

II

The duplication of J. O. Mahoney with Ambrose Clark foreshadowed another Rosa Lewis confusion of identities, which was eventually traced. The war, if not over, was quickly drawing to a close, when, on the way back to work after lunch one afternoon, I saw her approaching from the far end of Jermyn Street. She was smiling to herself. I saluted as we came level. Rosa Lewis stopped me. 'Well, *you're* a ghost from the past,' she said, though certainly she had no idea who I was even after a name was given. We talked for a minute or two.

'Come in and have a drink this evening,' she said.

I got away from the War Office soon after seven, and went along to The Cavendish. Four or five persons, male and female, none known to me, were in Rosa Lewis's downstairs sitting room. I was the only one in uniform. The others, youngish, belonged to the unplaceable Cavendish category spoken of earlier. Since our afternoon chat Rosa Lewis herself had moved a considerable distance along the road of vagueness. I told her my name again, why I had turned up. She seemed quite happy about that; something upon which one could not wholly rely after such a chance invitation. A 'bottle of wine' no longer a practical proposition, I was handed a stiff whisky. Then Rosa Lewis took my arm and introduced me round the room.

'This is Bimbash Stewart,' she said.

At first I thought a joke was intended. The designation, attracting by its exoticism, conveyed nothing. Then, when several more persons arrived, she repeated the name to each one of them, apparently in all seriousness, no more than her usual air of moving in a dream. After a while, deciding the party was not my sort, I said goodbye, and slipped away.

12

Not much less than a dozen years later (possibly in a book to be reviewed) I came across the name Bimbash Stewart again. He was described in a note as an 'Edwardian man about town.' This tantalizing piece of information was a spur to further enquiries These revealed that Henry King Stewart (1861–1907), an officer in the British Army, had also served in the rank of bimbashi (captain, commander) with the Egyptian forces. On retirement he had become a King's Messenger.

Then, quite by chance, an incisive picture of Bimbash Stewart was drawn for me by Lady Diana Cooper. He had lived in a flat, she said, just opposite her parents' house in Arlington Street, Piccadilly. Clearly that address had been convenient for The Cavendish. Bimbash Stewart used to sport a black fur cap, said Lady Diana, and his life was believed to be full of romantic undercurrents. As a child, she added, she had been madly in love with him; when he died in the flat over the way, for some time wearing a chain round her neck as reminder to pray for him.

All this might be gratifying to self-esteem, but, even in uniform, I cannot flatter myself that the resemblance to Bimbash Stewart can ever have been a very close one. Mine must have been one of those arbitrary identifications brought into being to invest the rooms of The Cavendish with relics of the old days. Nevertheless, it was pleasant to feel that one had found some sort of a niche, even if an incongruously shared one, in Rosa Lewis's vast tapestry of memory; rather like becoming an element in that larger consciousness, which some think awaits us when individual existence fades.

On the subject of mortality, as on all other matters, Rosa Lewis had few illusions. After suffering a severe illness not very long before final abdication of her reign over The Cavendish, she is reported to have remarked: 'I've seen the Gates of Heaven and the Gates of Hell—and they're both bloody.'

IX

Science and Miscellaneous

In the London Library, works devoted to the subject of Love are classified under the heading *Science and Miscellaneous*; an indication, if any were necessary, that, however fully investigated over the centuries, the nature of love remains not only unsettling, but also unsettled; as likely to be miscellaneous, as in the smallest degree scientific. The word, anyway in English, has to accommodate a host of meanings: the deepest devotion; the chance adventure; the passionate affair; the *amitié amoureuse*; noble gestures, vulgar banalities, distasteful acts, all jumbled together.

Faced with the emotion in its different forms, individuals behave in such different ways that one becomes distrustful of reminiscences the texture of which seems too neatly woven. Alfred Duggan used to say that he could not enjoy certain 19th century novels, unless he pretended to himself that hero and heroine could 'only do it once'; otherwise their afflictions and anxieties made no sense. On the other hand, Dolly Wilde (whom I barely knew, but had much of her Uncle Oscar's wit, with some slight physical resemblance too) took a more Chaucerian view of the emotion, when told she was a trifle fatter, replying: 'It must be requited love.'

A case could certainly be made for the narrative of love relationships being at least as interesting when the persons concerned do not go to bed with each other, as when they do, and, in any case, when you are young, all such relationships—for both sexes—are largely an attempt to find out what sort of a person you are. Unless a writer possesses a gift for handling 'Confessions'—and plenty of evidence exists to show how rare that gift is—it seems to me that the novel, rather than documentation, lends itself to the more subtle analysis of Love.

Just as I have no turn for diary-keeping—perhaps for the same interior reasons—I should be unable, even had I wished to do so, to undertake the emotional chronicling of these early London years. Their annals would in any case run serious risk of straining the patience of the reader. Besides, writing about love affairs (unless as high tragedy) is almost always apt to make them sound too easy, too carefree, too ideal, which they rarely show themselves to be. A suggestion of the contemporary scene is, however, required to set the tone where Love was concerned.

2

Not long after I moved to Tavistock Square, I was taken by John Heygate to a party in Chelsea, to which he had been invited by some little piece, met casually in a similar milieu a few nights before. It turned out to be a fairly unstimulating gathering (with slightly lesbian undertones), and, Heygate having already left, I was preparing to go home too. I was hanging about in an almost empty outer room, when a girl came through the door from the hall. She stood there for a moment inspecting what could be seen of the mainstream of the party, which was taking place in the room beyond. She looked as if she were a little unwilling to join it.

Small, dark, elegant, this girl was of ravishing prettiness, the looks then most fashionable, though at the same time somehow not at all those of a fashion magazine. I don't think she was twenty. I spoke to her, and we talked for a minute or two. She said she was not going to stay at the party, because almost immediately she had to move on somewhere else, but, mentioning her own name, she asked me to look in at her flat (which was in the King's Road) on a date a day or two later that week. She added an unexpected comment: 'I'll tell them you're my new young man.' I did not know who 'they' might be, but this was a promising opening.

When I made enquiries (probably from Lambert) as to who this, almost literally, enchanting new acquantance might be, I was—as it turned out very reasonably—greeted with considerable amusement at confessing to such naively ambitious enthusiasms. This girl (with her younger sister, or half-sister, at that moment abroad) turned out to be one of the reigning beauties of the already touched on party-world. 'Modelling' clothes, doing odd jobs on the edges of the arts, the two sisters were quite famous figures, the name of each associated with men somewhat older than myself and decidedly richer.

Quite a long time later than this moment, Osbert Sitwell—without, I think, knowing that I had been at all concerned in that quarter—told me that Cyril Connolly and Peter Quennell, walking home through Chelsea one night, had passed beneath the flat (most of the time scene of a minor party), to which I had been invited for a drink. Quennell remarked: 'At the top of that house, Cyril, live the two prettiest girls in London, and you will never meet either of them.'

I cannot endorse the truth of this story, nor, if true, whether or not the prediction was fulfilled. It was certainly a fact that Connolly (then doing his stint as secretary to the American expatriate man of letters, Logan Pearsall Smith) did not frequent the sort of parties where the two girls in question were likely to appear. More material to my own interests at that moment was Lambert's comment that Quennell used to call them (from Villiers de l'Isle Adam's story in *Contes Cruels*) 'Les Demoiselles de Bienfilatre.'

That nickname was, of course, a gross libel, the situation being far from parallel, but for me this caustic pleasantry carried an undeniable sting in the tail. The Bienfilatre sisters of Villiers's short story are two little professional Paris tarts, pretty, elegant, demure, devoted to each other, models of behaviour to their clients and colleagues. Suddenly they separate from their shared household. It appears that one has been deeply shocked by the conduct of the other. Her sister has committed the unpardonable offence of falling in love without mercenary motive. The renegade Bienfilatre is taken ill. In spite of the shame she has brought on the family, the other goes to see her. On her deathbed the lovelorn Bienfilatre manages, with her last breath, to gasp out that honour is saved—her lover has paid up.

Once you have decided that you are in love (unless an accomplished trafficker in that element) the whole situation is likely to change vis-à-vis the other person, not only for yourself, but for her too. It is the difference of the recruit and the Recruiting Sergeant; before taking the shilling; afterwards in barracks. I was for some time an ineffective admirer of the girl I met that night. Even a year or more later, that condition was probably what caused Cecil Beaton—negotiating at Henrietta Street about Duckworth's publication of his *Book of Beauty* (1930), an album restricting itself and its photographs to beauties of only a well publicized order—to note in his diary that he had dealt at the office with a 'young man of Dickensian gloom.'

Painful as love can be, I cannot pretend to have abandoned all attempt at finding consolation. In fact that very situation became largely the theme of my first novel.

3

The Eiffel was often treated as a kind of night-club. Lambert and I, after dinner together one night at some much cheaper restaurant, decided to end the evening in Percy Street. It was fairly late when we arrived, practically the only remaining diners being Augustus John and Irène Dean Paul. Lady Dean Paul (whom I did not know), pianist and composer, being of Polish origins, used for professional purposes the name Poldowski (in its masculine form), though sometimes called familiarly Poldowska by friends like Lambert. She was mother of another acknowledged beauty of the party-world, Brenda Dean Paul, of sad memory, who finally succumbed to the drugs that ruined her life; though not before appropriately playing the lead in Firbank's one play, *The Princess Zoubaroff*, when briefly staged (not long before Brenda Dean Paul's death) at a small theatre in Leicester Square in 1952.

John at once invited Lambert and myself to his table. A further bottle of hock (staple wine of The Eiffel) was ordered. While we drank it, John rambling on about the Welsh princes and their bards, Lady Dean Paul produced from her handbag a box of pills. Holding this up, she praised them in the highest terms as sovereign remedy against the hangover, a menace that undoubtedly threatened all four of us the following morning. 'These pills,' she said, 'have a basis of rubber, which makes them particularly efficacious.'

I cannot recall why rubber was such an advantage, but Lady Dean Paul greatly emphasised that component, taking one of the pills herself, and handing the box round. John, a man of deep experience at that sort of level, shook his head, and continued on the subject of the Bards. I accepted one of the pills. Lambert, who always threw himself heartily into all he did, took two.

I record with shame what followed. The moment the pill was in my mouth I knew I did not like it. By that time the table had been cleared, and there seemed no way of getting rid of it. I was more than a little overawed by the company in which I found myself, and perhaps had drunk too much to grasp that the obvious solution of the problem was to conceal the pill in my handkerchief. I think one must in any case have been intended to reject the rubber residue. Noticing a pot of French mustard remained on the table I slipped the rubber bullet unobtrusively within, ramming it down with the spoon, when no one was looking. Lambert consumed both pills—presumably rubber and all—in his usual manner.

The following morning, Sunday, I was woken by the telephone. I suppose the hour was about half-past nine or ten. It was Lambert.

'I'm telephoning from the bog,' he said. 'I've been sitting here since five or six this morning.'

He sighed.

'What's happened?'

'Those devilish pills Poldowska gave us.'

Then I remembered. I was not feeling particularly well myself, but I had at least refrained from rubber pills. I admitted—a Dostoevskian confession—the disgraceful thing I had done.

'Don't spread the story,' I cravenly added.

'I won't,' said Lambert. 'I shan't spread the mustard either—now I must hang up . . .'

4

Although slightly lame from a childhood's illness—his characteristic movement in walking closely resembling descriptions of the manner in which Lord Byron appeared never to set the heel of one foot to the ground —Lambert was a great walker. One Sunday afternoon in the summer we had tea together, probably in his flat over The Varda Bookshop, after-wards, I can't imagine why, strolling east to have a drink at The Tiger on Tower Hill, a pub of attractive interior standing opposite the main gate of the Tower itself.

Licensed premises opening only at seven in the evening on a Sunday, it must have been towards eight, perhaps later, when we left The Tiger, and continued to press eastward. The immediate object was to inspect the bas-reliefs of the Seasons, supposedly executed by Caius Cibber (Danish-born father of the 18th century dramatist, Colley Cibber, much derided by his own contemporaries), to be seen on the exterior walls of a house (formerly the Danish Embassy, I think) in Wellclose Square, some way beyond the Mint. The sculptor himself is buried nearby in the former Danish–Norwegian Church.

Having inspected these elegant plaques (now divided between the Danish Seamen's Church, Commercial Road, the Danish Church, Regent's Park, and the Norwegian Embassy, Belgrave Square), we moved on through the twilight into Wapping and Shadwell. Dinner was eaten rather late at a Chinese restaurant in Limehouse. In general I found Chinese food tolerable only in Lambert's company, because (his cult for the Orient particularly biased towards China) he justly regarded himself as an authority on Chinese food procurable in London. He had formerly claimed a taste for Chinese wine, but, becoming disillusioned with celestial vintages (examples of which had been given him), made over his Chinese cellar to Tommy Earp. After the first draught, Earp enquired in his piping voice: 'Rather an aphrodisiac effect?' Lambert replied he had never noticed that. Earp thought the matter over. 'Perhaps it coincides with my annual erection,' he said.

Continuing our journey, there was almost certainly a visit to The Prospect of Whitby; the pub of which the French writer, Paul Morand, wrote that, whenever English friends said they were taking him somewhere he had never been before, he knew he was on his way to The Prospect of Whitby. Several other riverside pubs, less widely known than The Prospect, were included in our survey. Skirting the Isle of Dogs, we crossed the River by the Blackwall Tunnel in order to make a return journey along the South Bank. By this time it was past midnight, the domes and towers of Wren's Greenwich illuminated by the moon. This is a sight worth seeing, but it would be hypocritical to pretend that the walk back did not become a little exhausting.

Between Rotherhithe and Bermondsey a miracle took place. There was a rattle of wheels along metal lines, and, altogether unaccountably, a tram drew up beside us. Perhaps it was a ghost tram. No one else seemed to be using it as means of transport, and, even at that date, its outlines and method of locomotion appeared noticeably antique in the gloom. Nevertheless we were grateful, entering the tram, and riding as far as possible. It turned south just before one of the bridges. We alighted. The spectral tram disappeared southwards into the night. I do not recall where the River was recrossed. The hour was past four when, rather footsore, I descended the steps of the area in Tavistock Square.

There were also long walks, taking in such outlying areas as the Buttes Chaumont, during a Christmas Lambert and I spent together in Paris. A visit to Père Lachaise was marred by the keeper at the gate of the cemetery immediately asking if we wanted to know the way to the tomb of Oscar Wilde, naturally our goal, but a question unacceptable in its implications. On the same Paris visit, one café provided not only an orchestra, but catalogue of the various musical pieces offered 'on request'. Lambert—who used to describe orchestral players as 'arming' (in contrast with 'disarming')—took a sadistic pleasure in demanding performances of those scores most complicated to render. Speaking of sadism is a reminder of the little opening-and-closing wire brush for tapping drums possessed by Lambert, which he called 'the sadist's vade-mecum.'

5

Lambert took me once or twice to see his friend, Philip Heseltine (Peter Warlock, the composer), who lived with a mistress in what was then a very rundown area of Pimlico. Heseltine, in his early thirties, had by taking thought turned himself into a consciously mephistophelian figure, an appearance assisted by a pointed fair beard and light-coloured eyes that were peculiarly compelling. His reputation, one not altogether undeserved, was that of *mauvais sujet*, but I always found him agreeable and highly entertaining; though never without a sense, as with many persons of at times malignant temper, that things might suddenly go badly wrong.

Heseltine had been model for Halliday in D. H. Lawrence's novel, *Women in Love*; for Coleman in Aldous Huxley's *Antic Hay*. Coleman (a name perhaps chosen from the Victorian pornographer) is given Heseltine's beard, taste for composing limericks, intellectual anarchism. If exact portraiture of an existant individual is what the reader requires from a character in a novel (and many novel-readers seem interested in little else), Coleman conveys quite a good idea of what Heseltine was like to meet.

Halliday, on the other hand (much reduced in scope after a libel action brought by Heseltine himself), is chiefly to be identified (before legal pruning of the novel) by Heseltine's habit of speaking of his girls as if they were cats; animals for which—like Lambert—he had a passionate affection. As a character in a novel, Halliday embodies that overheated unrealized air that envelopes so many of Lawrence's projections of his own acquaintances, especially if he had fallen out with them. In that connexion the generalization might be risked that envy, hatred, and malice (of which Lawrence must have had at least his fair share) can build up a reputation for journalism, but in less ephemeral writing, especially the novel, are almost always disadvantageous.

Elizabethan pastiche was Heseltine's musical speciality, which included an exceptional knowledge of musical history's obscure bypaths; for example, the compositions of Gesualdo Prince of Venosa, that sinister Italian contemporary of Shakespeare. In such esoteric musical regions Lambert certainly learnt a lot from Heseltine, who has also been represented as a deleterious influence on him. One of Heseltine's pen-names was Rab Noolas (Saloon Bar in reverse, a precinct often his background), and he was certainly not a friend to preach moderation in drinking or other dissipations. At the same time, Lambert's career, not easy to envisage taking a different course, was essentially one guided by his own temperament, rather than anything imposed from the outside. I doubt of Heseltine's ferociously destructive critical faculty having much effect, Lambert, even at his most satirical, possessing a creative rather than eroding intelligence, which almost always offered critical alternative to whatever he opposed in the arts.

Heseltine was an outstanding instance of that particular kind of alcoholic (comparatively uncommon), who has drunk so much in the past that the smallest amount of drink puts him under. At this period he was not drinking at all heavily, when he wanted to work having no great difficulty in knocking off, at least considerably modifying, what had been at moments a terrific consumption. After one of these Pimlico visits, Heseltine, saying he had not touched drink for days, accompanied us, with his girl, to a pub in the neighbourhood. Arrived there, he had scarcely got through a quarter of his half-pint of bitter (possibly mild-and-bitter) before he became so drunk he almost fell off his chair. Heseltine always felt very strongly about the quality of the beer offered, forever inveighing against publicans who did not 'keep their beer-engines clean'.

In December, 1930, choosing a moment when his mistress was away from the flat (they had possibly had a slight quarrel, but not a serious one), Heseltine put the cat outside the door one night, so that it should not be a fellow victim, and turned on the gas. He was hard up at the time, though not desperately so; simply tired of the business of living. This climax, which came about just before our planned Christmas jaunt to Paris, greatly upset Lambert. Heseltine was the first person known to me, as an acquaintance of that sort, to do away with himself.

6

Heseltine's short unhappy but not unproductive life was recorded by another of Lambert's friends, the music-critic, Cecil Gray. Gray had also belonged to the D. H. Lawrence circle (during the interlude in Cornwall), and was Lambert's chief link with Wyndham Lewis.

A plump bespectacled rather unforthcoming Scot, Gray possessed considerable acuteness over and above musical matters. He was comfortably off, married (in the event, several times), with a small neat house in Bayswater facing the Park. His wife, at this moment, was Russian, daughter of a musician, her mother having later run away with a cavalry officer, then a Grand Duke (marrying him *en troisièmes noces*), who was at one brief moment during the Revolution declared Tsar. That was a side of life in which Gray himself was totally uninterested, as he detested anything that threatened the imposition of conventional social life, even in so exotic a form. He had a capacity for putting away a great deal of whisky without visible effect.

Gray (unfit for military service) had inhabited a Cornish cottage near the Lawrences during the first war. He was (as indicated by his marital career) a thorough-going heterosexual, indeed somewhat intolerant of inversion, but he was fond of telling the story of how, one afternoon in Cornwall, a knock had come on his cottage door. He opened it to find Lawrence standing there. 'Gray,' asked Lawrence. 'How long have you been in love with me?'

Gray shared Lambert's intermittent contacts with Wyndham Lewis, but I am not sure if he had actually introduced Lambert to Lewis. At this period much preoccupied with personal projection as The Enemy, Lewis was naturally doing little to increase his own popularity. He inhabited a house in Ossington Street, Notting Hill, the very locality kept as a supposed secret from all but certain carefully selected associates, who themselves never knew when they might not fall out of favour. Lambert seems to have been one of the few from his age group whom Lewis was from time to time prepared to meet. Although within reason an admirer of Lewis's work (the writing more than the pictures) Lambert always treated the relationship as rather a joke, often telling stories to illustrate Lewis's perpetual nervous tensions.

On occasion Lewis would give a drinking party at Ossington Street— so Lambert reported—amongst whom might be numbered Lambert, Gray, Earp, perhaps one or two more. Heseltine would have been too much of an unknown quantity for Lewis, lacking the capacity of the others to accept even for a short time somebody else's idiosyncrasies. The guests would sit round a table on which were placed a bottle of gin, a bottle of whisky, and (I think) a bottle of brandy. Then there would be high-powered conversation. Lambert noticed that, whenever in the nature of things he and Gray sometimes exchanged musical technicalities, Lewis's hands, lying before him on the table, would clench with nervous irritation at the invoking of an art in which he was himself unversed.

Another story of Gray's that turned on the opening of his own front-door, very different from the Lawrence one, took place at the Bayswater house. Sitting in the window one evening reading, he saw Wyndham Lewis turn in from the street, mount the steps as if to pay a call. Gray waited for the bell to ring. He continued to read for some moments, no sound coming from bell or knocker. After allowing several minutes to elapse Gray went to the front door and opened it. Lewis, apparently unable to nerve himself to knock or ring, was standing on the doorstep. Lewis said nothing. He did not look at all at ease. Gray said: 'Won't you come in?' Lewis still did not speak, but slowly entered the house. In the hall he broke his silence. 'Lambert has got something against me,' he said. The matter of whatever Lambert supposedly had against Lewis was, so far as I know, never further ventilated.

Tendencies in Lewis not far from paranoiac (doing him grave damage as a writer) were well on the way by the time of the publication of *The Apes of God* (1930). The huge cast making up this satirical novel must represent a considerable proportion of all the people Lewis had ever met in the intellectual world, most of whom had for one reason or another caused him irritation. There are no obvious versions of, say, Lambert, Gray, Earp, but no one who knew Lewis—as Lambert was fond of pointing out— could ever be certain that he (or she) had provided no searing detail of behaviour or appearance.

Notwithstanding the brilliance of much of the language, the unrelieved subjectivity of *The Apes of God* defeats its own specifically satirical ends. If the prototype of the 'ape' in question is known personally to the reader, the description, however unjust in omitting all redeeming features, is at the same time so vivid that the victim might almost be in the room. On the other hand, if Lewis is dealing with a personality the reader has never encountered in the flesh, there is a total breakdown in communication. The obsessive venomous prose crackles away, but carries little or no meaning. Through a fog of imagery and vituperation the ape's outlines cannot be clearly described. Clouded in the author's verbosity, the object of Lewis's attack is not merely obscured as an individual in a particular social world that is being satirized, but even as a generalized entity inhabiting that world.

7

I did not come across Wyndham Lewis himself until about twenty years after this period. I had written a piece about satire in the 1920s for the *Times Literary Supplement*, then edited by Alan Pryce-Jones. This article had spoken in praise of *Tarr*, but some sort of a correspondence followed, Lewis denying that he had used the phrase (which occurs in the preface to the novel's 1928 edition) 'the first book of an epoch'. As nothing had been printed that was not entirely favourable to Lewis (except his own forget-fulness of what he had written), Pryce-Jones, thinking this might be an opportunity to persuade him to become a *TLS* contributor, invited Lewis and myself to luncheon *à trois* at the Travellers' Club.

Big, toothy, awkward in manner, Lewis behaved with an uneasy mixture of nervousness and hauteur. In his white shirt and dark suit he looked like a caricature of an American senator or businessman, causing one to remember that his father had been born a citizen of the US, and that, during the war, Lewis had described himself in books of reference as 'of American parentage.'

There was also a touch, if only a faint one, of Crowley's moments of thaumaturgical majesty of demeanour, though Lewis was, of course, a considerable artist, not a sinister if gifted buffoon. The comparison seems worth making simply because some aspect of a shared megalomaniac egotism may have accounted for a sort of resemblance. From time to time in the course of the meal Lewis swallowed what were presumably digestive tablets. I had come prepared to admire, but found some difficulty in doing so.

In consequence of the civilities offered by Pryce-Jones, Lewis was induced without too much difficulty to write a 'front' for the *TLS*, the subject of which I do not remember. In those days *Times Literary Supplement* articles were unsigned, as indeed they remained long after that date. Lewis had apparently never noticed this essential rule of the paper, in his own piece using the first-person throughout, a method obviously inappropriate, if the reader has no idea who 'I' may be.

Pryce-Jones, as editor, naturally had to return what Lewis had written for alteration; at the same time, wishing to save Lewis as much trouble as possible, pencilling in a few suggestions as to where, without change of sense, the first-person could easily be altered to a general statement.

The effect of Pryce-Jones's letter on Lewis was utterly unforeseen. A reply came back expressed in scarcely sane terms. Legal action was threatened from Lewis's solicitor, interspersed with personal abuse, and bitter complaint of the way he had been treated. This explosion was brought about simply by a request to make at most half-a-dozen minor variations of phraseology in an article of four or five thousand words. The impression of some years past that all was not well with the balance of Lewis's mind could not be avoided.

Lewis died in 1957. Towards the end of his life he began again to write the art criticism in which he had been engaged when much younger. He did that exceedingly well. In 1969 I had for review a collected volume of Lewis's writing on painters and painting. Re-examining this book, I am struck by the manner in which passages that seemed worth marking with pencil in the margin end about 1929; then begin again some twenty years later. In the interim period Lewis is usually giving way to a sense of rage and persecution; a few years before the end of his life the early critical energy, acute whether or not hostile, returned with a new burst.

During the middle period of Lewis's writing he is forever concerning himself with trivialities, which, even if granted as deserving momentary attention (often doubtful), were no excuse over a long period for not getting on with his own creative production. One suspects the trouble was to some extent a certain weakening in that very area; something that can similarly be observed in the painting. With all his gifts there was an insufficiency of some sort in Lewis as an artist; a lack of warmth; of intellectual magnanimity; a flaw hard to define yet disturbing. Nevertheless, Wyndham Lewis is one of the figures of the Twenties who left a very distinct impression on my own approach to writing.

8

John Heygate married Evelyn Gardner in August, 1930. They continued to live for a time at the Canonbury Square flat, the lease of which belonged to her. The first act of the Heygate parents on hearing that their son was involved in a divorce had been to cut off his allowance; while the baronet uncle (somewhat impotently, since the Ulster property was entailed on the heir to the title) declared that he would disinherit his nephew out of hand; proceeding to do so in whatever manner lay within his power.

Sir John Reith, on his pontiff's throne in Langham Place, did not recognize divorce (nor was there any form of BBC annulment to be sought), so Heygate resigned from the Corporation before pressure was applied to enforce that. Shortage of money brought about by these two eventualities, loss of his job, cutting off of parental supplies, caused Heygate to set about writing a novel, with the object of earning at least a little, while he looked about for something to do. In due course, indeed fairly soon, Heygate's relations with his parents were restored to a fairly normal footing, and, when the lease of the flat fell in, he and Evelyn Gardner would take cottages in the country, where I often came to stay for weekends.

Heygate's novel, *Decent Fellows* (1932), had an Eton background, and was first published as an experimental paperback. The book made a certain stir on account of its supposed impropriety, though why, even in those days, anyone should have been at all shocked, is hard to understand. The plot, a plausible one, if schoolboys are to be written of in novels at all, outlines how a quiet hardworking boy gets into a badly behaved set, becomes idle, is concerned in various mishaps, jeopardizes a scholarship at the university.

References to public school homosexuality—a subject by then treated comparatively openly for at least fifteen or twenty years—were of the mildest. Nevertheless, *Decent Fellows* outraged certain people, and very silly things were written and said of it. Lambert read Heygate's novel simultaneously with *The Enormous Room*, alleging that he got the two books hopelessly confused in his mind, causing perpetual surprise at how uncomfortable were circumstances at Eton.

Disapproval of *Decent Fellows* did no harm to Heygate professionally, indeed probably helped in finding employment later as writer of film scripts, a vocation he undertook for a time with a certain amount of success. He worked with the German film company, UFA, at Neubabelsberg, outside Berlin, where he was engaged on trilingual pictures (with the English actress, Lilian Harvey, as star); continuing to write books, when these employments came to an end. I visited Germany in 1932, and some relics of this glimpse of the film industry, experienced through Heygate, found a place in *Agents and Patients*.

X

That Just Divides the Desert from the Sown

In contrast with earlier attempts at writing a novel, *Afternoon Men*, once begun, moved fairly steadily forward, though probably with more recurrent cutting than subsequent books. One weekend, leaving the flat only for meals, I worked throughout Saturday and Sunday well into the night; a concentration of energy exceptional then, altogether unattainable in two or three years' time. My first novel was set down with a pen, some of the proceeds of its sales devoted to buying a typewriter. In due course I began to find writing achievable only in an accustomed room (usually the bedroom, as less distracting), a typewriter also becoming a necessity, the operation of the machine somehow diminishing too strong a consciousness of inscribing words on paper; giving the process a touch of automatic composition, almost of drawing or sculpture. Subject always to severe revision of what has been first put down, that is the ideal course for writing to take. At the outset, less capricious, I could work in places far away from my permanent base.

Without being at all a precise record of what actually happened, *Afternoon Men* gives a picture reasonably in focus of the kind of life I was living at this time. When the novel appeared I was a little surprised by the manner in which reviewers treated, as a savage attack on contemporary habits, what had seemed to me something of an urban pastoral (if that is a permissible concept), depicting the theme of unavailing love.

2

Some of this first novel was written in Toulon, a delightful place in those days, impressions of which occur in *What's Become of Waring*. The naval port, with its small inner harbour, row of cafés along the *rade*, was quite separate from the business quarter of the town. A paddle-steamer plied several times a day between this roadstead and the agreeably unsophisticated *plage* of Les Sablettes.

Lambert had recommended the Hôtel du Port et des Négociants, where he had himself stayed several times, though we were never in Toulon together. The hotel, far from luxurious, very reasonable in price, was placed conveniently for cafés and paddle-boat. No doubt the local *négociants*, to whom the Hotel du Port was partly dedicated, made use of its facilities; French intellectuals also stayed there for summer holidays that included opium smoking and chasing sailors.

I set out alone for Toulon, intending to work hard on my novel, but in the event undertook little more than a few pages of revision. That was because of the company found at the hotel. At the Tavistock Square party the year before, guests had included several of the Ballet, among them the two dancers, Frederick Ashton (now famous choreographer, knighted, OM), William Chappell (later stage-designer and theatrical director), both friends of Lambert's. Chappell turned out to be spending a holiday at the Hôtel du Port with two cronies from art-school days: the painter, Edward Burra, and Irene Hodgkins ('Hodge'), an extremely pretty girl, who was also a painter and model.

After meeting in the hotel, we all used to have meals together, bathe together at Les Sablettes. Hodge, whom I may have come across rather vaguely at parties, was to be collected in about ten days' time by the middle-aged publisher, C., to whom she was engaged; for whose sake she had joined the Jewish faith. I knew Ed Burra hitherto only by name, and a few stories about his eccentricities. Billy Chappell did most of the organizing of the Toulon day, and did it very well.

Burra never sunbathed (then the rage), his skin retaining its constitutional tint of parchment, appropriate to an air of having just stepped out of a Cruikshank engraving. Like the rest of the party, Burra was in his middle twenties, but seemed prematurely old; truer perhaps to say that he resembled a prisoner just brought out into the sunlight after years of confinement in a pitch-dark subterranean dungeon. He spoke rarely, but always with devastating aptness.

Burra, something of a reproach to myself, spent a great deal of time at Toulon working. His method—anyway in those days—was one of the most unusual I have ever observed in a painter. He would sit in an hotel bedroom on a rickety hotel chair at an equally rickety hotel table— possibly even a dressing table—dozens of extraneous objects round about him (including the remains of petit déjeuner), while he executed his pictures. What was always an immensely complicated design would be begun in the bottom right-hand corner of a large square of paper; from that angle moving in a diagonal sweep upward and leftward across the surface of the sheet, until the whole was covered with an intricate pattern of background and figures. If not large enough, the first piece of paper would be tacked on to a second one—in fact would almost certainly be joined to several more—the final work made up of perhaps three or four of these attached sections.

At this period Burra's pictures were likely to be brightly coloured grotesque images of Firbankian fantasy, often Negroid, the forerunners of those 'bulging husky leathery shapes' described by Wyndham Lewis in a much later critique. In middle age Burra was also to explore in his own disturbing fashion a very unnaturalistic English countryside; a sphere where he was perhaps finally at his best.

Burra was reputed to engage in no sexual activities at all, nor to feel emotional attachments of any kind; a view of himself to some extent confirmed from his own lips, when (I think) Hermione Baddeley, a great comic star of those days and frequenter of parties, cross-questioned him on the subject.

'Have you ever loved a man?'

'No.'

'Have you ever loved a woman?'

'No.'

'Not even your mother?'

There was a short pause while Burra considered the matter. A conclusion was reached.

'No.'

This singularity in his own affections did not prevent Burra from making apt comment on the sexual behaviour of others. His remarks, in any case, had a quality all their own. Once, at a party, the sound of such frightful retchings and vomitings came from the lavatory that the host, disturbed that one of his guests should be in such an unhappy condition, tapped on the door to ask if first-aid was needed. From the far side Burra's voice faintly answered: 'It's *only* Madame.'

3

About a week had passed at the Hôtel du Port in this tranquil manner, when half-a-dozen persons, some known, some unknown, appeared by boat from Cassis—then a centre for artists—for a night out in Toulon.

One of the girls who turned up was the heroine (or anti-heroine) of *Afternoon Men*. She was known to Hodge—who supported life in much the same manner—but I don't think Hodge had previously met any of the men, two of whom were painters. We all (probably excluding Burra, who liked to retire to bed early) joined up for an evening at the *bal-musette*. No doubt several of these dancing places were visited, during which it became clear that Hodge was having a success with one of the painters. In due course, the night having clearly nothing to offer from my own point of view, I returned to the hotel, leaving some of the others to seek yet further haunts to dance.

The following day, by the time I was up and about, the Cassis group had shipped themselves back to base. That afternoon, or the next, Hodge's middle-aged publisher, C., appeared by train in Toulon. He was a very nice man, whom I was to meet on and off for many years; indeed he was to publish *Brief Lives; and Other Selected Writings of John Aubrey* (1949), which I edited.

The morning after C.'s arrival I found him at a café table on the *rade*, where it was customary to have breakfast, rather than in the hotel. We talked of this and that. I asked when he and Hodge were to return to England.

'I'm leaving tomorrow,' he said. 'Hodge isn't coming with me. She's going off to live with this fellow who came over from Cassis the other night.'

It was not easy to know how to reply. This was not (as I knew) the first rough ride C. had experienced in matters of love; nor, as it turned out, was it to be the last. There is no particular point in the anecdote, except, like others recorded here, to convey the atmosphere of the period. It also adds force to C.'s recipe for writing a good Jewish novel: write a good novel; then change all the names to Jewish ones.

The story illustrates the manner in which persons like the *Afternoon Men* heroine (and, of course, all sorts of other people too) will recur inconsequently in the lives of those whose hearts they have disturbed. I shall give a further instance in this particular case.

4

The following year, again with the object of working on a novel (*Venusberg*), I set off once more alone, this time going to Sainte-Maxime, a resort then consisting, so far as I can remember, of little more than a largish hotel, and a couple of café-bars, one at each end of the *plage*. I found an obscure dump called something like Robinson's Universal Hotel et Pension Osaki, where for a day or two I worked at my book; between times lying on the beach, sitting in alternate bars, since there was nothing else to do. Seeing me writing in the bedroom, learning I was engaged on a novel, the *femme de chambre* told me that her brother-in-law also wrote novels, but, in contrast with my own (which I admitted to be about *l'amour*), in the style of Pierre Loti.

Becoming bored by myself, I moved up the coast again to Toulon, where I knew various friends were to take a holiday. This time there was quite a crowd at the Hôtel du Port; with several more from both sexes, Billy Chappell, Freddy Ashton, their great crony, Barbara Ker-Seymer, then an avant-garde photographer. I don't remember whether Ed Burra had reappeared, but there was said to have been one Toulon holiday from which Burra, Ashton, Chappell, all returned on the same train, travelling respectively First, Second, and Third. Other friends of mine present were Wyndham Lloyd; Beatrice 'Bumble' Dawson, another photographer in those days, later a successful stage-designer; several more acquaintances too.

Also staying at the hotel on this occasion were Cocteau and his entourage. I never met him personally, though they were all to be seen playing about together at Les Sablettes. It was said that the bittersweet fumes of opium were discernible on the staircase of the hotel, but I was myself not able to distinguish the scent among a variety of others hanging about there; nor did I ever find on the base of my bedside table drawer the charred marks of what was said to be the opium pipe's accustomed resting place.

I left Toulon with a week in hand, wanting to travel back slowly through Provence, stopping at Arles and Avignon. The Arlésiennes are spoken of as particularly attractive. Sitting alone in an Arles café one evening, my attention was riveted by the appearance of a girl strolling through the crowd. I thought how true was what had been written about this tradition of local beauty at Arles. Then, as she looked straight at me and waved, I became aware that here again, passing through the town by car—ratifying once more the inexorable law of coincidence—was the girl of *Afternoon Men*.

5

During these years I stayed twice with the Sitwells in Derbyshire. The exterior of Renishaw Hall, a long low sombre crenellated house, lying in country where park land, mining village, pit-head, the dales, all march together, at first sight suggested something not much short of decay, an atmosphere melancholy, even sinister. This impression was much modified on the far side of the mansion, where elaborately laid out Italian gardens swept down in tiers, their lawns traversed in the centre by a flight of steps, towering baroque statues flanking this descent.

Initially, Renishaw's interior offered a similar contrast between comparative neglect—at least no more outward show than to be expected of any run-of-the-mill country house of that size—then, a moment later, splendid tapestry, unexpected pictures, much else unusual. One wing, for example, was left permanently out of commission on account of the aggressive nature of its ghosts. That was not to imply that the rest of the house, especially the bedrooms, was outstandingly free from all menace of spectral appearance.

Osbert Sitwell's famous account of his father given in *Left Hand, Right Hand!* does not at all overstate the case. Indeed, in depicting the figure of Sir George Sitwell, 4th baronet—always known among his children and their friends as Ginger—less pleasant sides are toned down, rather than exaggerated. No one who reads the letters reproduced in his son's Memoirs could disagree that Sir George sailed at times uncomfortably close to the condition of madness. That did not prevent him from mustering an exceptional array of abilities in many different fields—a fact he himself was never tired of affirming, modesty not being one of his handicaps—gifts manifested through a nature equally likely to express itself in the wildest prodigality, with shrewd business sense, or a grinding stinginess that would have shamed Scrooge.

By this period Sir George had been built up by his children—anyway among their friends—as a supremely comic creation. In a sense he certainly was a comic personality, one of the most notable of the day, but that was by no means the whole picture. This version of their father as a kind of Pantaloon, Justice Shallow, prototype of unrivalled pomposity and grotesqueness, fitted well into the Sitwell scene as consistently projected; an ornate and satirical extravaganza, half-poem, half-burlesque.

Nevertheless, notwithstanding a tone that seemed on the whole to avoid the deeper notes of tragedy, not much more than a dozen years before a disaster of Dostoevskian dimensions had occupied this same stage; a calamity that goes far to interpret need to escape from too grim a realism, into the stylized glitter of the harlequinade. It might be insisted that plenty of Sitwell satire was bitter enough, but only Osbert Sitwell—then in direct narrative, rather than sublimated in novel or poem—treats in his work of the dark cloud in the background that overshadowed the house, accounting not only for its melancholy, but much else in Sitwell essences.

Lady Ida Sitwell (daughter of the 1st Earl of Londesborough) had been married off to Sir George at the age of seventeen. Her own daughter has left some account of her. A beauty, frivolous, not at all intellectual, rather absurdly conscious of her lineage (perhaps because it also had its less grand aspects), she was linked to a husband the most understanding of wives might have found a trying companion for life. Once, when Osbert Sitwell was speaking of his parents, I asked if there had ever been a moment when they had got on well together. 'Oh no.' he said. 'Not for a moment. I don't think so.'

Although Lady Ida may not have been cast for the rôle of Sir George's wife, discord had been of a financial sort, rather than involving a third party on either side. Utterly imprudent about money, a compulsive gambler, deep in debt, she found herself caught in the snare of a professional swindler. This man—himself convicted more than once—trapped her into signing papers that led to a prison sentence. The circumstances are set out in Osbert Sitwell's memoirs, but no judgment is passed on his father, whose behaviour was perhaps equivocal. Certainly some people thought so at the time; others asserting that, the papers having been signed, the Law could take no other course. Those who supposed Sir George might have averted the débâcle disapproved of him accordingly.

Edith Sitwell used to say that, whatever her father's faults, the outward appearance he displayed of a Renaissance tyrant was splendid. He was certainly not a man to be overlooked. Unusually tall, good features, the pointed red beard that gave him his nickname, Sir George's manner was abstracted, distant, not much short of hostile. He might have been an accomplished actor playing for a laugh among the more subtle of his audience.

It was an exterior that made one think of Osmund in *Portrait of a Lady*. There was something 'wrong' about Sir George Sitwell, badly wrong, and for me he always lacked the air of distinction possessed by his children; indeed also by his unhappy wife. The eccentricities were certainly genuine enough, not in the least assumed to make an impression; yet he was in some manner an actor dressed up to play a part; that part perhaps a not very pleasant one.

6

Among the guests at Renishaw on my first visit was Arthur Waley, invited with his maîtresse en titre, Beryl de Zoete. Waley, now famous for having translated and promoted the literature of Japan and China, to the extent of almost introducing the classical literature of those countries to the English-speaking world, worked in the Print Room of the British Museum. Though not one of Bloomsbury's highest inner praesidium, he ranked as an authentic Bloomsbury of the next grade; in Waley's case perhaps appropriately to be described as a Mandarin of the Second Button.

Slight, sallow, among other accomplishments an expert skier, Waley spoke always in a high clipped severe tone, as if slightly offended, quiet, but essentially smacking-down. He habitually refused to make the smallest compromise in the way of momentarily lowering intellectual standards in the interests of trivial conventional courtesies; demeanour that could produce in a room an extraordinary sense of social discomfort.

It has been suggested that Waley himself was unaware of his disconcerting manner. I do not believe that to be true. I think he was perfectly conscious of its impact. Waley possessed his fair share of aggression, even if that was also to some extent a barrier of rather agonized self-defence against people who might underrate his own abilities. A story he once told me seems to confirm this appreciation of the effect he made.

The occasion was Waley's introduction to F. F. Urquhart (Sligger, often described Dean of Balliol), a meeting that must have been enjoyable for anyone else who might have been present. Waley, accordingly to his own account, 'not wishing to appear Cambridge', made some trite remark. Urquhart, in general noted for the mildness and banality of his conversation, replied: 'Need we talk about the weather?' Here, on both sides, one perhaps glimpses the collision of bitterly opposed forces, a well-sensed mutual antagonism jockeying for position.

Tête-à-tête, Waley was an amusing talker, who loved gossip. At the same time one never knew when a friendly tone would be withdrawn, and he would re-enter his carapace of disassociation. After our meeting at the Sitwells' he rang me up once or twice, asking me to dine with him, though himself never apparently available for playing a return. On one of these occasions he took me to see Patrick Hamilton's play, *Rope* (a dramatization of the Leopold and Loeb case, two undergraduates who murder a third), insisting on paying for both tickets. When we left the theatre I expressed a word of thanks for this gesture. Waley listened for a second, as if to find out what I was talking about, then, without replying, quickly turned away and withdrew into the night.

Beryl de Zoete, somewhat older than Waley (then about forty), was rumoured, perhaps an exaggeration, to have been divorced from her first husband before 1887. At this period she and Waley looked much of an age. Beryl de Zoete, also a fairly formidable figure, was an accomplished translator. She had rendered Sacheverell Sitwell's *The Rio Grande* into German, when the poem was set to Lambert's music. Her version is said to to have improved Svevo's *Confessions of Xeno*, by freeing the novel, in English, from the too Triestine Italian of the original.

The last time I saw Arthur Waley and Beryl de Zoete was in the late 1950s; at an art gallery showing paintings executed by two chimpanzees. Waley, hardly at all altered from earlier days, must have been about seventy by then. Beryl de Zoete, still brisk enough in her movements, had shrivelled in the manner almost of Tithonus, making her seem older than the hills. We all three agreed that the female ape was the more sophisticated painter; the male, an artist of deeper feeling.

One of the Sitwells' favourite stories was of their friend Ada Leverson (The Sphinx) saying: 'I expect, Mr Waley, you often go to *The Mikado*.'

7

I have heard people remark, in a jocular manner, that the 'Sitwells' best book' was, in fact, a work by their father (author of several botanical, historical, genealogical, and other studies), entitled *An Essay of the Making of Gardens*. This assertion is not to be taken seriously, Waley, while at Renishaw, clinching the matter by observing: 'Ginger writes like an eighteen-eighty don.'

How far, if at all, Sir George apprehended the extent to which, behind what was undoubtedly a barrier of fear, his children made fun of him, is impossible to guess. Certainly he found their literary activities in many respects a mystery, but, adapting his own behaviour accordingly, he was possibly aware of more than they supposed. He would from time to time utter a protest. On reading a poem written by his daughter which included the line 'the poxy doxy dear' (*Rustic Elegies*), he remonstrated: 'To anyone conversant with Elizabethan idiom, or the low speech of our own day, etc. etc.' Not long before the publication of *Before the Bombardment*, he observed to Lambert, when staying at Renishaw: 'It would be a strange novel that Osbert would write—there will be no love and no buried treasure. I fear it may not find great favour with the public.'

On one Renishaw visit I was strolling with Walton on the lawn before luncheon. Sir George approached. 'I have just been reading about medi-aeval painted chambers . . . strange . . . very strange . . . rather horrible at times . . .' He paused, contemplating the horror of mediaeval painted chambers. Taken off our guard, Walton and I gave way to involuntary nervous laughter. Sir George showed no sign of noticing this response, inadequate, not very well-mannered. Nevertheless he said no more on the subject, striding moodily away.

Sir George Sitwell felt a strong prejudice against drink, so that at

Renishaw was none of the vinous plenty to be found at Carlyle Square. A house party of perhaps twenty persons sitting down to dinner would be individually lucky to get more than a glass of white Bordeaux that certainly did not startle the connoisseur by its pretensions. When the ladies withdrew, the men would sit gloomily round the white tablecloth, draining the dregs of their coffee, while Sir George, who did not consider want of port or brandy a reason for cutting short the traditional male interlude spent in the dining room, held forth on one of his favourite topics, such as Nottingham in the Middle Ages.

Such austerity was not at all to the taste of the rest of the family, and picked guests would be secretly bidden to assemble before dinner in Lady Ida's upstairs sitting room, where, unknown to Sir George, a clandestine apéritif was provided for those deemed worthy. Traces of Lady Ida's former beauty remained, but, never wholly recovered from her ordeal, she would disconcertingly address one as 'Osbert' or 'Sachie', during a dinner-table conversation. She said to me: 'I love Paris so much, but I daren't ever go there, because I spend so much money.' She always pronounced *Façade* with a hard 'c'.

Osbert Sitwell liked to describe how on some occasion, no guests at Renishaw, he and his mother decided one afternoon to sample a bottle of Maraschino together in her sitting room. Suddenly, altogether unexpectedly because in general he never showed himself there, Sir George stood in the doorway. Seeing the bottle he started dramatically back.

'*Not* Maraschino!'

His voice was agonized. Lady Ida answered her husband in a fashionable Edwardian drawl.

'What djer mean—Maraschino?'

If *Left Hand, Right Hand!* does not exaggerate the peculiarities of the author's father, neither does it overestimate the remarkable qualities of the Renishaw butler, Henry Moat, of whom many stories are told there. Moat, who looked like pictures of the traditional John Bull, and seemed rarely in less than the highest spirits, once observed to Lambert: 'Sir George is the strangest old bugger you ever met, and as for poor old Ida, she doesn't know whether she's coming or going.'

Nevertheless, the final word on the subject is perhaps owed to Cecil Gray. Travelling by himself in Italy, staying for a night in a small provincial hotel, Gray had been kept awake all night by maniacal laughter from the bedroom next door to his own. When he paid the bill the following morning, he enquired at the hotel desk who his neighbour might have been. '*Inglese*.' The clerk pointed to the register. The name inscribed there was that of Sir George Sitwell.

8

Matlock, in Derbyshire, is only about twenty miles away from Renishaw, and, when I was sent there to attend an army course, I managed, on Osbert Sitwell's invitation, to get over to the house one weekend for luncheon, a rare treat in the circumstances. By that time Sir George had already made over the estate to his elder son, he himself, more eccentric than ever, living in retirement at his Castle of Montegufoni in Tuscany; an alien in an enemy country, but still sustained by the indomitable Moat. It was said that the two of them never bothered to wind up the castle's innumerable clocks, so that their estimate of the time of day was sometimes as much as five or six hours out.

Later in the war, Violet and I stayed at Renishaw for my week's leave, a happy civilized interlude during those grim years. Only Osbert and Edith Sitwell were there. It was winter, snow on the ground, the statues of the Italian garden clad, appropriately for wartime, in their seasonal garments of sackcloth. On the lawn we constructed a giant snow-woman representing Mary Queen of Scots.

Contrary perhaps to the popular picture of her, Edith Sitwell loved feminine chat, clothes, shopping, where to get your hair done, if that chat was carried on with a sympathetic woman friend. Discussion of the last of these matters led to the arrangement of an expedition to Sheffield. The Sitwells recommended that I should accompany the party in order to see a town with its own particular fascination, especially the steeply pavemented streets high above the roadway. As the Sheffield group was leaving the house, Osbert Sitwell drew Violet aside. 'We're a little short of food,' he said. 'Don't bother Edith about it, but should opportunity arise, visit Mr So-and-so, the fishmonger, who sometimes gets hold of a salmon. He might have one today.'

When we were in the car Violet put forward this possibility. Wartime shortages, as I have already remarked, making food an ever absorbing topic, Edith Sitwell—who left all the housekeeping in the competent hands of her brother—asked how best to cook the salmon, if the fish proved available, so that it went as far as possible. Violet offered some sort of an exposé on this subject, ending with the words: 'Then you make the tail into kedgeree.'

In one of the high-banked streets that give Sheffield its unique character we stopped at the fishmonger's. A queue, not one of great length but perceptible, waited on the pavement outside. For this foray into town Edith Sitwell had gone to some trouble in her outfit, which included a high cylindrical hat, something between an archimandrite's and that of a Tartar horseman in *Sohrab and Rustum*. She was a person who would never have deliberately jumped a queue, but, her head full of her brother's instructions, Violet's words on the culinary uses of salmon, she swept forward, disregarding the people waiting patiently outside, and seized the fishmonger—who was wearing the traditional straw boater of his trade— by the hand.

'Mr So-and-so, what a long time since I have been in to see you. How are you? How are your family? You are looking well yourself. Mr So-and-so, I have come to ask something, whether by any chance you have a salmon? *We want a salmon for making kedgeree.*'

The fishmonger went pale. Had the days of the Bourbons returned? Lucullus himself might have thought twice before devoting a whole newly caught salmon to kedgeree; anyway while Rome was at war. Notwithstanding, a salmon was produced. By some extraordinary mischance it was also left behind in another shop, while further purchases were packed up; but all was well in the end, the salmon being put on a train just in time to reach Renishaw for dinner.

9

One of the essential drop-scenes of my early London life was Castano's, an Italian restaurant in Greek Street, Soho, where in principle I used to lunch every day. I was introduced there, when still an undergraduate, by John 'The Widow' Lloyd. It was then called Previtali's (presumably after the Bergamesque painter), a name that occurs quite often in the Waugh Diaries during the period 1924/25, though I don't think I ever heard Waugh mention eating there.

Some have attempted to identify Previtali's with the Restaurant du Vingtième Siècle, where Max Beerbohm (*Seven Men*) consorted with Enoch Soames and the Devil, but such cannot be. The Vingtième Siècle is specifically described as French, the tables (in the Beerbohm illustration) arranged in an altogether different manner. Nevertheless, Previtali's seems always to have had some sort of a literary clientèle, George Gissing's Letters showing him as inviting H. G. Wells to dine there in the Nineties.

The restaurant (now no more) stood three or four doors south of the archway leading from Manette Street (called after Dr Manette in *A Tale of Two Cities*, or vice versa?) into Greek Street. The ground-floor room was entered through a curtain of coloured beads strung together; eight or ten tables, perhaps the same number upstairs, though relegation to the first floor was regarded as exile by habitués. The walls of both rooms were without decoration, painted white in the Italian manner. There was one waiter, Pino, a man of lively personality, who looked a little like the elder Grimaldi.

Castano (Pietro, sometimes Peter), the proprietor, always dressed in great style, had renamed Previtali's after himself. Small, round, with a little moustache, he had served during the first war as cook to one of the battalions of The Sixtieth or The Rifle Brigade, I forget which. Castano had never taken out papers of naturalization—'After all, look at me, I am not an Englishman'—but his wife was English, and they had a beautiful daughter, who would lend a hand in the restaurant; later also in the club established on the first floor, which was to prove Castano's ultimate downfall.

A genre picture of Castano, his restaurant, the club, appears in *A Dance to the Music of Time*, as Foppa's. Castano was far the nicest restaurateur I have ever come across. He was a compulsive gambler, and used to play cards with his friends in the club on the first floor, when it was established, where headwaiters and the like would gather. There was a Russian-billiards table, as in the novel, and it was true, as represented there, that Castano occupied his spare time with trotting races, in which he himself took part. Unfortunately these expensive pursuits constrained him at last to give up the Greek Street restaurant. I last heard of him, just before the outbreak of war, running a coffee-stall in Battersea. I have often thought of him, and hope things looked up again; though that would not have been easy for an Italian in wartime.

Castano's was frequented by a miscellaneous collection of friends and acquaintances, including The Widow Lloyd, his brother Wyndham Lloyd (Cambridge and Medicine, an accomplished photographer, who took some of the pictures that illustrate these memoirs), Lambert, Daintrey, the Heygates, a certain influx from the Ballet, many more. A plateful of Castano's minestrone was likely to knock the customer out for the next course, and, when minestrone sometimes seemed desirable on a cold day, Lambert would say: 'No, no, you mustn't live for the moment. You'll regret it later.' Lambert would sometimes sign his bills at Castano's, and once when he asked for the account of whatever he owed, the sheaf of bills pinned together was marked in pencil at the top with the reference 'Maestro'.

Castano's served only *espresso* coffee, the deposit of which some find distasteful, so that a tradition grew up of drinking *café filtre* at Legrain's in Gerrard Street. At Legrain's, a shop to the right sold coffee and all that pertained to coffee; to the left, existed a room where coffee could be drunk at tables. The café, dark, crowded, claustrophobic, yet somehow sympathetic, was presided over by a magnificent white-haired French woman, who seemed to have come straight out of a painting by Manet. Legrain's provides the opening scene of *Agents and Patients*. When I married in 1934, Castano, in ironic reference to my rarely if ever drinking coffee in his restaurant (though I have, in fact, no particular objection to *espresso*), presented us with a self-straining coffee-pot as a wedding present.

10

Gerrard Street, in those days not wholly Chinatown, included Maxim's Chinese Restaurant, to some small extent model for Casanova's Chinese Restaurant, in the volume of that title. The street, something of a centre for itinerant musicians, at times echoed with the marvellous voice of the very pretty blonde crippled girl, with whose singing *Casanova's Chinese Restaurant* (1960) opens, though she is there represented as passing through another area of London, since she might suddenly appear in almost any neighbourhood. The blonde singer would certainly have been heard in opera had she not been lame.

Other occasional performers outside Legrain's were three or four ageing male transvest dancers, wearing sequined ball dresses, in which they would do high kicks to a barrel organ. They were said to be relics of Splinters, a theatrical group entertaining overseas troops during the first war.

Another peculiar Gerrard Street figure was a man with a broad-brimmed black hat, long black coat, got up to look perhaps like The Sheriff in a Western. This effect, if aimed at, was diminished by one of his legs being shorter than the other, the short leg terminating in an appliance that looked rather like an iron door-scraper. The pockets of the black coat were always stuffed to overflowing with newspapers and periodicals, and one day Lambert pointed out to him—smoke pouring upwards like mediaeval representations of the Foul Fiend—that some of these papers were on fire. This odd personage was not in the least grateful for the warning. Easily recognisable from a photograph reproduced beside the paragraph reporting the case, he was later in some trouble about pornography; also appearing in a view of Gerrard Street (captioned 'Piccadilly'), published in a Soviet illustrated paper to demonstrate the rundown state of London.

At the east end of Gerrard Street, in the open space behind the Shaftesbury Theatre (then dedicated to farces about the Royal Navy) was a street market: a cat's meat stall with a placard *Pussy's Butcher*; a huge Negro vending patent medicines at the top of his voice ('You drink quinine, you go blind! You drink quinine, you go deaf!'); the two performers in chains and padlocks, who also figure in *Agents and Patients*. One of this couple— chosen as example of the agent-and-patient relationship—with much cursing, would fetter his partner, who would then, after superhuman effort, free himself from his shackles, while the hat was taken round by his oppressor.

II

As a London Italian, Castano certainly did no more than flick the minimum pinch of required annual incense at the shrine of Mussolini (a fact made clear by his demeanour when drawing my attention to an unusually absurd photograph of the Duce), but that minimum included his daughter's ownership of a black tasselled Fascist cap, on her head cute in effect, which she would sometimes assume for fun in the restaurant. Some member of the Sadler's Wells Ballet—Freddy Ashton, Billy Chappell—borrowed this paramilitary headguar for Ashton to wear as The Officer in Rieti's *Barabau*, revived at The Wells in 1936.

At this performance of *Barabau* (a choral ballet originally composed for Diaghilev), costumes and décor were by Ed Burra, but some sort of dress had to be laid down for the female choir, which appears on the stage for occasional bursts of singing. Someone suggested they should wear hats. The redoubtable Miss Baylis (mentioned earlier in connexion with Bobby Roberts) showed her accustomed flair for combining improvisation with economy by saying she herself could produce the hats. Years before, so it appeared, Miss Baylis had been presented with a collection of old hats—some possibly going back to Edwardian days—for use in the Theatre's wardrobe. In these hats the *Barabau* choir was fitted out. This antique headgear was meant to be a joke, but one music-critic wrote in his notice: 'The choir was in good voice, but wore rather depressing mufti.'

12

In the first volume of these memoirs, I spoke of Gerald Reitlinger—then painter, writer, editor, collector; later historian of Hitler's extermination of the Jews, and oracle of the economics of aesthetic taste—in connexion with Robert Byron's journey to Mount Athos, when Reitlinger had been one of the party. He belonged to a slightly earlier Oxford generation than my own, contemporary of The Widow Lloyd, like him very briefly enrolled in the army during the first war. Even without active service this could impose a sense in some of remaining in the pre-war period, but both of these two belonged essentially to the post-war vintage.

Reitlinger appears in *The Station* as Reinecker, a profile not wholly complimentary (there had been differences with Robert Byron on the Holy Mountain), which defines Reinecker as 'financially independent; and emanating from a large house of his own in Kensington filled with rare and austerely disposed Oriental potteries.'

This pen-picture, so far as it provided a rough outline for Reitlinger too, was no less than the truth. We did not know each other at the moment when Duckworth's published *The Station*, but (probably brought together by the Lloyds or Daintrey) must have met soon after that, because I visited the large Kensington house, with its austerely disposed pots, an inherited residence, shared with an elder brother, and sold by its owners soon after the appearance of Robert Byron's book. Reitlinger himself was in due course to become a Duckworth's author, with *The Town of Skulls*, a work describing a journey in Turkey and Persia.

The brother with whom the Kensington house had been shared, appreciably older than Reitlinger himself, was also a collector, something of an eccentric. I probably met him at least once, but he remains a memorable figure not on account of that so much as for the stories his younger brother would tell. The best of these gave rise to the nickname 'Captain Teach', by which the initiated always referred to him.

According to Reitlinger, he was sorting family papers on some occasion —possibly on leaving the Kensington house—when he came across a letter from a Swiss publisher, rendering a royalty statement for a book written by Reitlinger's brother, and complaining that sales had been disappointingly small. The book itself seems to have been a work of dubious tone, entitled *Slavey*, the author appearing pseudonymously as *Captain Teach*.

This might have been thought a piece of pure (or impure) fantasy, a story invented or exaggerated by a younger brother to entertain the company at dinner. The tale was, however, borne out in a curious manner. Lambert—describing the act as a moment of weakness—disclosed that, when in Paris on some occasion, he had himself bought a copy of *Slavey* from one of the bookstalls along the quays of the Seine, which—with other more humdrum works—used to display a good many publications of that genre.

This authenticated purchase of his brother's book by a friend might have been thought sufficient embellishment to Reitlinger's story, but additional flavouring was added by Lambert.

A few minutes after buying *Slavey*, Lambert ran into Lytton Strachey, also on a visit to Paris, and taking a stroll along the quays. Lambert, understandably, did not wish this recent acquisition to his library to fall under Strachey's satirical eye, and make a good story for spreading about Bloomsbury. Concealment was fairly easy in the street, where he tucked the book well under his arm.

Strachey now complicated matters by inviting Lambert back to whereever he was staying in Paris. Even then *Slavey* might have been kept hidden without too much difficulty, had not something not at all bargained for by Lambert taken place; the making by Strachey of a determined physical pass. Nevertheless, all was well. Lambert managed to repulse Strachey—too concerned with his objective to think of other things—and escape without the detection of what appears to have been Captain Teach's sole publication under that pen-name.

13

I think of Gerald Reitlinger chiefly as giving weekend parties in the country, but in those days, after abandoning the South Kensington house, he also retained a studio in London; a large one at the bottom of Glebe Place—in which he and various other owners gave parties—then, nearby in Chelsea, a much smaller establishment in Bramerton Street, where for a time Adrian Daintrey also came to live and paint. This coalition was comparatively soon dissolved, to some extent on account of the architectural unserviceableness of this last house's interior.

At Bramerton Street, Daintrey's studio was entered from the hall; then came the bathroom; beyond the bathroom, Reitlinger's studio. Reitlinger would be the first to start work in the morning; Daintrey as a rule rising later. Accordingly, Daintrey, on using the bathroom, would lock not only the door leading out of his own studio, but that leading into Reitlinger's. On leaving the bathroom to begin his morning's work, Daintrey did not always remember to unlock the far door.

That omission might not particularly matter, if Reitlinger stopped work first, because he could bang on the door to obtain release; but, if Daintrey went out to lunch early, there was always a risk that Reitlinger might be imprisoned in his own studio until Daintrey's return; not unlikely to be in the small hours of the morning. So far as I know nothing like such a long confinement was ever imposed, though Reitlinger was on more than one occasion under restraint for shorter periods.

As owner of the house, Reitlinger demurred at being locked in, even for an afternoon, and for this and other reasons it was mutually agreed, on a perfectly friendly basis, that Daintrey should find somewhere else to live. I saw Daintrey soon after this decision had been reached.

'Have you heard Gerald and I are getting a divorce?' he said.

'On what grounds?'

'Extreme cruelty.'

When I first knew Reitlinger he had a country cottage—in fact, two cottages knocked together—at Iden, not far from Rye and the coast. It was called Thornsdale, and stood well away from the road, beyond several fields, on the edge of where the country sloped down to the Romney Marsh; a romantic spot, not another building in sight.

Later he moved a short way into Sussex; Woodgate House, Beckley, a red-brick farmhouse in the local tradition, to which a stucco Regency façade had been added. Soon after this rather more impressive change of address, Reitlinger became widely known among his friends as The Squire.

The entertaining at these country seats was very much *sui generis*, free and easy, without being outstandingly luxurious. Lambert used to complain that, no looking-glass in the bedroom, he had to shave round his face in the glass reflections of a framed watercolour by Meninsky; The Widow Lloyd, that one of the beds caught the innmate's shoulder, when turning over, in an iron grip between its springs, from which it was impossible to obtain release.

The oriental pots were transferred to Woodgate, and, among the many pictures in the house, was an unusual 18th century representation of three couples, the children in middle life, the parents both as young and old, with the caption:

> 'My Father and my Mother that go stooping to your grave,
> Pray tell me what good in this world I may expect to have?'
> 'My son, the good you may expect is all forlorn.
> Men do not gather grapes from off a thorn.'

Daintrey used to say that, when driving a car, Augustus John always kept to the right, except in France. Reitlinger's driving could also discompose nervous guests, and he himself recalls some altercation on this subject with Lambert, who suddenly snapped out: 'Well, I've dismantled a chain transmission drive, and that's a damn sight more than you've ever done'; thereby revealing an altogether unexpected knowledge of mechanics, particularly surprising in one who did not drive a car himself, and always denied, in his own case, the supposed connexion between musical and mathematical abilities.

14

After dinner at Woodgate the game of *bouts-rimés* was often played. It will be remembered that each player writes down a line of heroic verse, which (after a single line by everyone has been passed to the next player in the first instance) rhymes with the verse above; then turns down the paper, so that the verse cannot be seen, only a second new line visible, which has to be rhymed; and so on. To get the best results in building up these extempore epics, at least one player is required who is no more than barely competent. Too much dexterity shown by everyone participating seems to defeat the ends of the game.

This *bouts-rimés* playing was the basis of a squib of mine, which occasionally comes on the market nowadays, and requires a word of explanation. It may even have begun with lines composed during these after-dinner games.

At about this period several books written in a somewhat self-applauding tone by Scotchmen on the subject of Scotland (or condescendingly humorous about the rest of Great Britain) had been published. A counter-satire in the 18th century manner seemed required. I used to compose verses in this vein during hours of insomnia, from which I suffered in those days. They would be repeated, sometimes improved, at the Castano luncheon table; Lambert writing the section on Scotland's music.

Caledonia, as this pastiche came to be called, knocked about as a rough typescript for a time; being read aloud—in the Elizabethan manner of publication—to anyone who might want to hear it. When I married (at the end of 1934), Desmond Ryan, a friend who possessed control over a small printing press, said he would pull off some hundred copies as a wedding present. He arranged for the production, which was bound in tartan boards, to have a black-and-white frontispiece by Ed Burra, another friend of his.

Like Ryan himself, the printer was somewhat given to the bottle, and *Caledonia*, a treasure-house of long forgotten topical references, is also notable for its misprints. Ryan, a delightful fellow, whom I saw only intermittently throughout his life, as he lived largely abroad, was (at the time of which I write) later to give a party greatly to influence my own life; but that was some years on, and subject for a subsequent volume of these Memoirs.

15

In 1931, probably after a celebration of the appearance of *Afternoon Men*, Lambert had gone down on one knee in my Tavistock Square flat, and proposed marriage to the beauty he had found on that Sunday in St John's Wood. In August of the same year (when I was in Toulon) they were married; in due course going to live in the top flat of 15 Percy Street, where I often used to visit them.

During the two years or more that Lambert had kept his future wife fairly well concealed from his friends, he had talked to her of what concerned his own work, the books he was reading or admired, the pictures he liked. In fact it might almost be said that, at an age when most girls were still at school—she was very young indeed at the time of their first meeting —Flo Lambert was reading only 'good' books, seeing only 'good' art, listening to only 'good' music. This should not, of course, be over-exaggerated, but to her beauty she certainly added a quite remarkable appreciation of such things.

The Lamberts were staying at Woodgate on one of the occasions when planchette was played; the little board shaped rather like a painter's easel, equipped with two rollers and a pencil, that writes automatic 'messages'. Reitlinger's other guests that weekend were Wyndham Lloyd and myself. Lambert was always interested in the Occult in any form, but Wyndham Lloyd, as a man of science, disapproved of planchette or any other frivolous contacts with the extra-sensory; an attitude that roused Lambert to protest: 'You're talking like the editor of a radical rationalist paper in 1880.'

Whether or not Wyndham Lloyd's disapproval—said to be an inhibiting factor—helped to bring about planchette's refusal to function, the pencil at best merely made scribbles on the paper, usually refusing to move at all. Lambert, becoming bored, sat down to write letters at a desk in the corner of the room. The others picked up books or papers. Reitlinger and I, almost without thinking what we were doing, had continued to rest our fingers on the board.

Suddenly planchette began to move, then to write. The 'influence', transcribed in a long sloping 18th century hand, announced itself as Mozart. Neither Reitlinger nor I being much up in musical matters, we asked Lambert to suggest an appropriate question for the great composer.

'Enquire who was his favourite mistress.'

We did so. Planchette wrote a reply.

'*La petite Carlotta.*'

'When did this love affair take place?'

'*À Napoli en* 1789.'

I think that was the date given, but could not swear to the exact year, which was certainly in the 1780s, so far as I remember.

'What was she like?'

'*Comme une guenon.*'

This last word had to be looked up, no one present sure of its meaning. The French dictionary gave: 'she-monkey, ugly woman, strumpet'.

Some of the subsequent replies were in English, some in French, some in German; the last language known to Reitlinger, but not at all to myself, nor to Lambert, who, as the only musician present, seemed in some manner telepathically concerned. His attention caught by these Mozartian manifestations, he had ceased to write letters, but was still playing no tactile part in relation to the board.

The statements about *La petite Carlotta* were noted down, and in due course Lambert looked up the story of Mozart's life to see if the name occurred there. These efforts were unproductive, except in establishing that Mozart could not possibly have been in Naples on whatever date was specified.

16

A fairly frequent guest at Woodgate (he did not date back so far as Thornsdale) was Basil Hambrough. Outwardly a typical Guardsman, brushed-up moustache, Brigade tie, indefectible turnout on all occasions, Hambrough concealed under this stylized exterior not only a genius for mimicry and improvisation, but an essentially individual manner of attacking life. His stories—especially those about himself—were likely to merge into fantasy, but, so odd had been his genuine experiences, the point at which fantasy took over was always hard to establish.

Hambrough claimed to be half—in some moods, three-quarter—Russian. His father, undoubtedly an eccentric too, had owned a large house in the Isle of Wight, long thought to be an invention of his son's, but now certified as the truth. One of Hambrough's stories described his expulsion from Sandhurst after some escapade, but my own father could remember him in 1913 as a subaltern in The Welch Regiment, who had entered the army through the Militia. This was perhaps not wholly incompatible, as, after being sacked from the RMC, he might have approached a regular commission through the Militia. In any case Hambrough transferred from The Welch Regiment to The Welsh Guards on their formation in 1915.

During the first war, no doubt because his origins gave him some knowledge of the language, Hambrough (before the Revolutionary Government made peace with Germany) had been attached to a Cossack unit or formation in Russia. How much Russian he knew was never clear, but his rendering of an Orthodox priest intoning the liturgy could be altogether convincing. Hambrough was far from impressed by the manner in which the Cossacks had looked after their horses, negligence that would never for a moment have been tolerated in the British Army.

Hambrough also served with the Guards in France, and, after the war, as assistant military-attaché in Greece. He hoped to follow up this Greek appointment with a similar one in Rumania (where the Queen was known to have a penchant for British officers), but did not bring that off. Not long after returning to England and his regiment, financial embarrassments (he was something of a gambler, with atrocious luck, I have seen him hold four kings under four aces) led to his resignation from the army.

Basil Hambrough had met Gerald Reitlinger through Dorothy Warren (married to Philip Trotter, another former Welsh Guardsman), lively founder of the Warren Gallery in Maddox Street, scene of many avant-garde shows, not a few controversies, though by then Dorothy Warren had, I think, herself given up the Gallery. Hambrough was parted from three wives (of whom he would sometimes tell stories in a detached manner), and lived modestly in Sussex, at Bosham, where he did a certain amount of sailing.

During the period when I first knew him, a characteristic Hambrough incident took place in the Bosham neighbourhood, when he was returning from a pub-crawl. Prudently deciding that he had consumed more drink than made it fitting to drive a car, he drew up by a church (as it happened, an undistinguished late 19th century edifice), and, with the object of resting for a time, sobering up, entered the building. Sitting in one of its pitch-pine pews, he went to sleep.

When Hambrough woke, night had fallen. Surrounded by darkness he could not at first remember where he was, and, possessing no watch, or unable to see its face in the dark, did not know the time. He had the impression of having slept for several hours. He groped his way to the door. It was locked. He found another door. That was fastened too.

By now quite sober, Hambrough saw he must devise some means of avoiding a night spent in the church. There seemed only one possibility. He looked about for the belfry.

> And lo! the great bell farre and wide
> Was heard in all the country side
> That Saturday at eventide.

The trouble was the hour being not so much eventide, as well into the night, and, while Hambrough tolled away, for a long time nothing happened. Then a key turned in the lock. Hambrough went to the door. It was the vicar. He was white with fear. When he saw Hambrough, fright turned to anger.

'What are you doing here?'

Hambrough thought from the tone that he was going to summon the police.

'I saw your beautiful church, and stopped to look round it. Then I sat down to meditate for a moment or two. In the atmosphere of peace I must have dropped off to sleep. I can only offer my deepest apologies for having had to summon you from your bed in this manner.'

The vicar did not look at all convinced. Hambrough quickly said good-night, and made off towards his car.

Being locked in, like his bad luck at cards, seems to have been Hambrough's fate, though the second occasion I know of was in very different circumstances. He was spending a weekend at Woodgate, Reitlinger's other guests being two good-looking young women, neither known well by their host, and I think not at all to Hambrough. In the course of the evening Hambrough showed signs of making an excellent impression on one of the girls. When the company retired, at a fairly late hour, the key of Hambrough's door must have been on the outside (or Reitlinger, with memories of his own incarcerations by Daintrey, quickly transposed it), because, at some stage after entering the room, Hambrough heard the lock quietly turn.

Hambrough said nothing. He dressed, packed his bag, broke down the door, had a final drink below, got out his car, drove to London. The following day, on the appearance of his elderly housekeeper, Reitlinger began to adumbrate the nature of the damage upstairs. She cut him short at once.

'You don't have to explain, Mr Reitlinger, I was married to a drunkard.'

Friendship survived this incident; others scarcely less tricky. It may have been at Woodgate that Hambrough met his fourth wife, Monica Nickalls, whom he married—this time with resounding success—at about the time of the outbreak of war in 1939.

Monica Nickalls, a charming young woman then making a career for herself in advertising, had been staying with Reitlinger on one occasion, when a mother and daughter were 'doing' for him; the mother as cook, the daughter, Cath, undertaking the housework. Cath, of fairly mature age, somewhat woebegone appearance, suffered from 'nerves', the reason why mother and daughter sought employment together. One day, Monica Nickalls alone in the sitting room, the mother approached her in a somewhat conspiratorial manner.

'Miss Nickalls, may I ask you something?'

'Of course, Mrs So-and-so.'

'Miss Nickalls, I hope you won't mind my speaking about this, I wouldn't do it only it's such a worry to Cath. She wants Mr Reitlinger to do something for her, and she doesn't like to ask him herself. You don't mind my mentioning this, Miss Nickalls?'

'No, no, please go on.'

Cath's mother braced herself to speak of her daughter's need.

'Miss Nickalls—Cath wants Mr Reitlinger to give her a little goblin.'

Monica Nickalls was too startled by this announcement to make any answer. Cath's mother mistook astonishment for disapproval.

'Oh, Miss Nickalls, do tell him. It isn't all that of a thing to ask of Mr Reitlinger, and Cath does want it so. It would make all the difference to Cath's nerves, it really would. If *you* speak to Mr Reitlinger, I'm sure he'll listen—he'll give her a little goblin, he really will.'

Only later in the conversation did it turn out that financial action, rather than physical or magical, was required; a Little Goblin being a make of vacuum-cleaner, well-known, but, as it happened, unfamiliar to Monica Nickalls.

Hambrough (a captain at the outbreak of war), when he returned to the army as a Reserve officer, exchanged from the Foot Guards to the Pioneer Corps, where prospects of promotion were better for one of his age. His subsequent adventures included being torpedoed, and spending several days in an open boat. He said the most painful part was later, on the ship that rescued him and his companions, the whistle always going, with a shout of 'Survivors'. In due course he rose to the rank of lieutenant-colonel, commanding a large formation of Basutos in Africa.

'Do they talk English?' somebody asked.

'Talk English? They've been so worked over by missionaries, they say "Thanks awfully" whenever they answer you.'

After the war Basil and Monica Hambrough settled in Kenya, where Hambrough lived into his eighties.

Some of Hambrough's extraordinary imaginary projections—which he would produce without warning and continue for several minutes—remain for ever in my mind: for example, the old man who looked after a lighthouse. The old fellow (who had a ne'er-do-well son) lived quite alone. He said he didn't want a radio. He listened to the sound of the wind and the sea; 'God's music, he called it.' The seagulls would fly about him, when he looked out from the top of the lighthouse, getting caught up in his long white beard and hair . . .

XI

Twilight in Henrietta Street

In its opening stages, the scheme agreed between my father and Balston had been that, if the three years apprenticeship at Duckworth's proved fruitful, my father would invest a modest sum (not precisely specified) to constitute some sort of partnership for myself in the firm. It was never stated that the shares were to be made over to me, my father, in fact, probably envisaging them as remaining in his own hands; from his point of view an ideal focus for making trouble; from Duckworth's, a risky disposition in the light of his unforeseeable permutations of mood.

The question did not arise, because, when the time came, my father refused to produce any money at all. He gave no reason for this change of tactics, beyond objection that the security offered was insufficient; although, as a publishing house, the status of the business, as such, was certainly better than when things had been first talked over. By this time, of course, my father had left the army, and was becoming at a rapid rate increasingly cantankerous. He and Balston (according to Balston) had a colossal row about this disclaimer, which involved shouting abuse at each other while crossing Trafalgar Square.

I am inclined to think my father never intended to go through with the deal. The plan had at first seemed a good one for settling my future, and goodness knows what otherwise would have happened to me, had not its initial framework been, so to speak, delivered on the doorstep by the existence of the Balston link. Now the original project had at least to some extent taken shape, my father wished to carry matters no further; certainly not in the form of parting with money. He was by no means incapable of generosity, especially if in a manner flattering to his self-esteem; my own independence, something he had never encouraged, was another matter. By the end of his life he became exceedingly close about money, complaining so much about his financial condition that, accepting assertions of dire poverty, I would refuse the offer of a glass of sherry before lunching with him.

Negotiations with Duckworth's—that is to say with Balston—therefore began again, this time solely on my own part. Balston offered £250 a year; raising the bidding to £300, when I too made a fuss; feeling—as Lambert put it—'Either say: "Push off, you get the place a bad name", or pay a respectable wage.' Accordingly I found myself in a job not remarkable for the munificence of the pay (though jobs at the moment were not at all easy to get), and virtually without prospect of rising within the firm. The situation seemed unsatisfactory at the time. In the long run, from the point of view of becoming a writer, to have no financial involvement whatever with Duckworth's was certainly for the best.

It was convenient for Balston to have on the premises a young man more or less capable of reporting the literary activities of his contemporaries; one of the things unforeseen in early life being the near impossibility in middle-years of keeping in touch with the writing of a younger generation. Over and above that aspect, Balston, I suspect, even if momentarily put out by failure to increase the firm's capital, wished as little as my father for any such alteration in my own status quo. A useful subordinate was one thing; an additional director to meet on more or less equal terms, quite another. The two partners with whom Balston was already saddled irked him enough in their different ways; a third—unless he combined adequate capital, hard work, complete passivity—would be nothing but an additional burden.

After the three years of my novitiate, Balston may well have conceived a particular wish that I, personally, should not move into the position of being one of his fellow directors. Such sentiments on his side are by no means out of the question. There are indications (which need not be gone into here) that he played with the possibility of substituting another youngish man (Alan Harris) for myself in such a capacity; abandoning him from desire to have no other competitor as an active force. This is no mere conjecture, but rests on certain remarks made to me by Balston himself after he had left the firm.

Like Lewis in a purely managerial capacity, Balston, although not outstandingly good at taking decisions, wanted to decide everything himself. Perhaps all publishers are like that. Certainly all publishing houses are scenes of violent internal struggles for power; in that respect probably not very different from other commercial enterprises or official employment. The contrast with other businesses is that publishers traffic in goods of a very special sort. Selling books is not like selling insurance or varnish. In their own day, the qualities of contemporary writers are only very approximately assessable, and always subjectively. This invests publishing with a peculiarly enigmatic character.

2

To my own relationship with the firm was now added the fact of becoming one of its authors. *Afternoon Men* (advance £25) was published in the spring of 1931; the production of the book itself—with the natural admonition that everything about it must be cheap—left in my own hands. I think the final result not discreditable, showing the extent to which a volume of decent appearance could be achieved at that date without undue expense; something Duckworth's did not always bring about in their list.

In the course of several years spent interviewing a steady stream of diversified callers at Henrietta Street, I had been impressed by the portfolio of a rather tousled young man, looking like an art student and even younger than myself, whose designs for book jackets included several schematized through the medium of photography; then rarely used except in a straightforwardly representational way. He was called Misha Black (in due course knighted, architect and industrial designer of some fame), to whom I unfolded the theme I had in mind for the jacket of my novel. This was an artist's wooden-jointed lay-figure (which I still possess), posed drinking a cocktail against a plain background. Black executed this subject to perfection. He was to carry out similar designs for my next three novels.

Afternoon Men was, on the whole, not at all badly received (Edith Sitwell wrote kindly of it in a general article not long after publication), though praise, from some quarters for being up-to-date, was mixed with complaint about too much drinking and sex ('thinly veiled pornography') from others. I had been infected by Cummings—to some extent also by

Wyndham Lewis and Hemingway—with the then fashionable antagonism towards capital letters, so that proper names used adjectivally were (as in France) printed in 'lower case' lettering. This innovation, which proclaimed at the time an aggressive modernity, agitated a few reviewers, a race with strong resistance to the most trivial mutations of habit.

Since my first three novels appeared within the space of three years, they may be briefly dealt with together here and now. All belong to the same genre of writing, one I have earlier called 'lyrical', because, although much hard work is always required to get any book into proper order, the strain in these was not primarily on the faculties of the imagination. The dammed up reserves of twenty-five years were there to be drawn on; the problem, how to use these with best advantage.

When this store—a kind of Original Sin—is used up, the writer must consciously look about for new material. This means an essential change in the sort of book written; the setting in motion of what one hopes to be a self-renewing system of continuous imaginative development. The novelist, too, is of course changing, losing the flush of youth, not only in the literary field, but in daily life as well; while also inevitably affected as a person by the fact of having published a book or two. In my own case, the second war set its own particular barrier between pre-war and post-war writing, but, even without World War II, change would certainly have had to take place.

3

In the first volume of these memoirs I touched on the extent to which *Venusberg* (1932) owes—and does not owe—material to Oxford vacations spent in Finland, together with other experiences of undergraduate travel. New themes approached in this second novel were adultery and political violence.

Quite recently (1977) I read Maurice Baring's novel, *Friday's Business* (an Eton phrase), which appeared in the same year as *Venusberg*, and also deals with a small diplomatic society. (Baring's novel is founded on the story of J. D. Bourchier, an Eton master, who gave up teaching because he could not keep order among the boys, became *Times* correspondent in the Balkans, where, especially in Bulgaria, his influence was so much revered that to this day a boulevard in Sofia is named after him.) It was interesting to note how many period similarities existed in a novel written about a small imaginary country (Balkan rather than Baltic), by a man thirty years older than myself, who had himself been a professional diplomat.

Venusberg also received for the most part well disposed notices (with the habitual undercurrent of disapproval from those who disliked books being 'modern'), several critics commenting that the stiff hurdle of a second novel had been satisfactorily cleared. The book sold about the same as *Afternoon Men*, which was perhaps something approaching 3000, by the time the cheap edition was expended.

An American publisher, Holt (represented by an agreeable Southerner, Herschell Brickell, also a literary critic), had taken the first novel (sales and reception about the same as in Great Britain), but the slump much altered the picture when it came to British writers placing their books in the US. *Venusberg* did not cross the Atlantic for twenty years.

4

From a View to a Death (1933), the scene laid in the English countryside, fuses a mixture of experiences, varying from the 'Orphans of this Town', street-musicians drawn from life in the streets of Salisbury (when I was living there with my parents), to a day's hunting in Northern Ireland (a field where I had not distinguished myself) that must have taken place while the book was actually being written.

For those interested in how novelists find their characters, the two Passenger sisters in *From a View to a Death* (the elder, in her thirties, separated from an unsatisfactory foreign husband; the younger, a deb with slight intellectual leanings) were modelled on a couple met for an hour at tea, on being taken by friends to a neighbouring country house; never otherwise known. I mention this only to emphasize the haphazard nature of a novelist's ragbag.

The reviews of *From a View to a Death* continued in a reasonably favourable trend, some liking it better, some worse, than its predecessors. Sales remained about the same, perhaps a shade improved. At first there seemed no hope of placing the novel in the US. Then a rather eccentric American publisher, James Henle, of the Vanguard Press (somewhat Left Wing books, and 'juveniles'), taking a fancy to a minor character in the novel called Fischbein, bought a thousand sheets. *From a View to a Death* appeared in America under the slightly bizarre title, *Mr Zouch : Superman*, and was a disaster, so far as sales were in question. Henle, quite unconcerned by that, would afterwards send me an occasional playful telegram on such occasions as the Fourth of July.

The title and epigraph of *From a View to a Death* required, on publication, establishment of the authentic words of *John Peel*, a song of several versions. The most correct rendering of the relevant lines, historically speaking, seemed to run:

> From a drag to a chase, from a chase to a view,
> From a view to a death in the morning.

When the book appeared, the kibitzers—to use that expressive Yiddish phrase for those (particularly familiar to writers) who offer gratuitous advice—questioned the pedantry of this choice, persuading me to alter the first line to the more accustomed wording:

> From a find to a check, from a check to a view,
> From a view to a death in the morning.

Nowadays, the term 'drag'—meaning a man wearing woman's clothing —is to be seen in newspaper headlines, but forty years ago it was used only in the theatrical world, or the sort of intellectual society that included a high proportion of homosexuals. 'Drag', in that sense, would have been incomprehensible out of those milieux; liable, at best, to be taken as deliberate indication that the speaker himself was homosexual.

In short, by substituting 'find' for 'drag' (the latter restored to recent reprints of *From a View to a Death*), I had also eliminated an undesigned, but now generally intelligible, reference to Major Fosdick's taste for transvestism. This point seems worth noting, if only as an example of the manner in which what is initially written in a novel can develop, with the passing of time, changing of language, other things, in an altogether unexpected manner.

5

Since there was not much pattern to these early years in London, I can introduce some of those who played a part only in a rather disjointed manner; though perhaps the chain of acquaintance that led to certain byroads in itself illustrates the sort of life I was leading.

A rather rackety young White Russian woman (whose father had been in Kerensky's brief Cabinet), met with Reitlinger at Thornsdale, introduced me to Carl Bechhofer Roberts, an amusing adventurer, who should not go unrecorded. I continued to see him on and off, until his death in a car accident at the end of 1949. One of Bechhofer Roberts's several backgrounds was in White Russian circles, in consequence of having served towards the end of the first war in South Russia on a Military Mission; later returning to the country as newspaper correspondent.

When a young man, Bechhofer Roberts—who looked a little like the film actor and director, Erich von Stroheim—had devilled for F. E. Smith, 1st Earl of Birkenhead (of whom he wrote a study); later turning out a continuous stream of miscellaneous writings, mainly political; a comparatively remunerative Grub Street existence, which he conducted with a good deal of zest.

(At a much later period, during the second war, Bechhofer Roberts brought me into touch with a writer who deserves not to be forgotten, Hugh McGraw, by profession an engineer, who wrote several novels [*The Lads of the Village, Rough Island Story,* etc] of a sort then rather rare, which give a lively picture of, usually provincial, office life. Within his own terms of reference, McGraw had the makings of a goodish writer. Unfortunately he had trouble with love affairs, and committed suicide.)

Birkenhead had caused all his 'young men' to take the required preliminaries for being called to the Bar. Among them, Bechhofer Roberts had 'eaten his dinners'. He had never proceeded further with the Law, though in a position to qualify at any moment he passed the examination.

At the beginning of the second war, outlets for books and journalism limited, not likely to improve, Bechhofer Roberts got together a few legal treatises, studied them for a month or two, sat for the examination, managing to scrape through at the lowest possible level. He then set up as a hedge-barrister, attending the court daily, prepared to take on anything that was going. In his first year he made a few pounds; by the end of the second, that amount had increased to what were encouraging returns; at the third, a respectable sum was coming in.

Bechhofer Roberts's methods in court were buccaneering. A case between two refugees—both wanting a divorce, in those days not allowed if collusive—had dragged on till a late hour one afternoon, everyone, including the judge, longing to finish off and go home. The husband could not be persuaded to say under cross-examination that he had 'come to England to get justice'; instead, prosing on about the possibility of emigrating to South Africa, Brazil, a dozen other countries. Bechhofer Roberts jumped up.

'M'lud, do you think it possible his wife desired a divorce from my client because he was such an unconscionable bore?'

'Maybe,' said the judge. 'Petition granted.'

6

When he heard I lived in Tavistock Square, Bechhofer Roberts said I must meet Theodore Besterman, then secretary of the Society for Psychical Research, the premises of which were also in the Square, only a few doors from my flat. Besterman and Bechhofer Roberts were first in touch, it appeared, because Bechhofer Roberts had written at least one book attacking psychical research as nonsense, but they were nevertheless friends.

Besterman himself wrote several works on psychical research (other subjects too); in consequence of our meeting, doing a book for Duckworth's about the Druce/Portland case; the long drawn out Victorian lawsuit regarding the absurd allegation that the 5th Duke of Portland had staged a sham burial of himself in the character of a Baker Street upholsterer. Later Besterman became an authority on Voltaire, writing Voltaire's biography, and being appointed Director of the Voltaire Institute and Museum at Geneva.

The Society of Psychical Research, an organization of the highest respectability, undertook its experiments in a manner to give every facility for those present at a 'sitting' to detect anything that might even hint at the possibility of a medium contriving faked effects. To get the best results, reasonably large sittings—at least seven or eight persons—were considered preferable, and, after meeting Besterman, I would sometimes be invited to attend the Society's rooms simply in order to make up numbers.

At the premises of the SPR the mediums were always regarded as, in principle, reliable, the merest apparent twitch of a curtain treated as a significant incident. On one occasion, however, the sitting took place in a private house—quite why, I can't remember—and on the way there Besterman issued a warning that the medium of the evening was looked on as not above all suspicion in producing artificial effects.

The routine of these sittings was to sit in the dark holding hands, sometimes singing, until the medium 'went under', usually with a great heaving and snoring. On this occasion the medium went under quite quietly, and once or twice, while he was in this state, unaccountable patches of light flickered in different parts of the room. After a time the medium came to, commenting that he was not in at all good form that night. To prevent the sitting being a dead loss, he offered to go round the room individually, trying to be clairvoyant about everyone present.

When he came to me, the medium said: 'You are going away to stay with friends. An older man, whom you do not find very easy to get on with, will put you in touch with a business opportunity. So far as I can see, that might be worth proceeding with.'

I spent that Christmas staying with the Yorkes at Forthampton, their house in Gloucestershire. Henry Yorke's father (whom it was true I never found very easy) had business interests in Mexico, a country from which he had recently returned. Quite unexpectedly, he gave me a novel (translated into French) by a Mexican writer, a former politician, which he suggested might be worth publishing in England. The book was based on an abortive revolution observed from ministerial level. There was an account of a Cabinet meeting, at the end of which several of the ministers slipped away to a low brothel; the chapter ending with the words (which I have often recalled when reading of politicians): 'These were the men who ruled Mexico.' The novel had points, but on balance the decision at Duckworth's was negative. Some of these psychical odds and ends found their way into *What's Become of Waring*.

In a similar vein at about this moment I read J. W. Dunne's *An Experiment with Time*, which suggests future events may be prefigured in dreams. The only way to establish this possibility was to keep a note-book by the bed, and record a dream at the moment of waking. I did this for about three months, the chief difficulty being to describe a given dream satisfactorily even for my own use. I noted only two faint plausibilities: one (probably too complicated to explain) I have forgotten; the other, I dreamt that I was in a Paris theatre watching a play. I was, in fact, taken some days later to see a French company of actors performing in London, of whose presence in England I had certainly been unaware. Perhaps the chief use of this exercise was to summarize dreams in an intelligible manner.

7

Not long after the publication of *Venusberg*, that is to say later in the summer of 1932, I received from Balston, at my private address, a letter, written in his own hand, that was unambiguously menacing. It was to the effect that recent sales at Duckworth's had been very disappointing; the directors had agreed to halve their own fees; severe retrenchment was to take place all round at Henrietta Street.

Publishing is always apt to be a precarious business, but, in spite of the depression, the firm had until then not being doing too badly, at one moment my wage having been even slightly raised. Now, where money was concerned, two alternatives were presented: that I should return to £300 a year, for the continuance of which no guarantee could be offered; be reduced to an annual £200, attendance at the office required only in the morning.

The veiled threat, implied by the statement that full-time employment might not be possible to maintain, underlined the prudence of accepting the halftime proposition. Less money would at least mean less office hours. I had by now written two books. The new arrangement would give additional time to write more; strike out into journalism. A reorganization of life therefore took place. In point of fact I found in due course that I hardly ever worked in the afternoon, not as a rule a fruitful time of day to write a novel; while literary journalism was at that period far from easy to come by.

In the same year, having overstayed by a few months the original three-year lease of Tavistock Square, I decided to move. The flat was sympathetic, but existence had gone on long enough in a basement. In the course of looking about for other accommodation, an opportunity was offered which I have always a little regretted not to have tried out, anyway for a time.

8

In the first volume of these memoirs, I spoke of Michel Salaman, one of the most good-natured of men, whom I did not see very often, though he was known to a great many people I knew. He had a Lutyens house—the first, I believe, built by that architect—in Surrey; Ruckman's, a secluded place not far from Leith Hill. Salaman's circumstances were comfortable, and he was fond of describing how, when he first sought her daughter's hand in marriage, his future mother-in-law's opening words had been: 'Of course, Mr Salaman, we can never forgive you for crucifying Our Dear Lord.' Later, hearing how agreeably he was situated, she agreed to overlook this culpability.

At the Slade, Salaman had been friends with Augustus John (who later painted a portrait of him as Master of Foxhounds, grasping a hunting horn), but, if country pursuits occupied one side of Salaman's tastes, John had also bequeathed a touch of his own bohemianism and disorder, and Ruckman's combined homelife of a most domestic sort with an atmosphere not unlike that of the house party represented in Noël Coward's *Hay Fever*, with its recklessly assorted guests invited by various members of the family. In spite of his domesticity, Salaman liked plenty of girls about the place whom he found attractive: Varda; Juliet and Helen Wigan; many of the corps de ballet; an occasional star like Gertrude Lawrence.

Salaman owned a flat (possibly the whole building) on the top floor of the north-east corner of Haymarket, which brought in £100 a year from an advertisement hoarding set in front of its windows. He said, if I wanted to occupy the premises at the same rate, he would be glad to remove the hoarding.

To have lived in that flat would have meant looking steeply down on to Piccadilly Circus; a kind of watch-tower, from which one could find endless entertainment. Indeed, a good deal too much time might have been spent gazing out of the window on to the scene below. There were objections too. Thought of an almost perpetual clatter of traffic, the inconvenience of parking (by this time I owned my small car), the miles of stairs to be climbed, in combination caused me to reject Salaman's offer, and instead to remain in Bloomsbury.

I found a slightly more expensive two-room flat at the top of 26

Brunswick Square, the sitting room looking out on to the Square's garden. Here things were slightly less ascetic than at Tavistock Square. Certainly the view was pleasanter.

In the flat below mine lived E. M. Forster (a writer whose books have never greatly appealed to me), but we never met. He once sent me a note to apologize for repairs being made to his ceiling, which, Forster said, might involve workmen coming up through my sitting-room floor. This did not happen, and there were no further contacts. Another resident in the Square reported that Forster was to be seen at his window each morning first thing, waving to the policeman setting out on his beat.

9

In August, 1933, after the publication of *From a View to a Death* earlier in the year, I had the offer of a holiday in a car driving through Spain. August, owing to the heat, is not an ideal month for Spanish travel, but the season of the trip was decided by some concatenation of circumstances now forgotten. Among these was certainly a crisis in the recent marriage of the car's owner, an old friend, with whom relations on the trip were merely those of friendship, though the other couple making up the party formed a ménage.

The weather was very wet driving down to the coast. The car skidded, turning a semicircle, so that we faced the opposite direction, but without worse effect. This was bad for everyone's nerves, and there were re-criminations; by no means the last on that expedition.

Spain was to be entered by Catalonia; vacated through the Basque lands; taking a sweep through the centre, which would include Madrid. There were pleasant drives through an unexplored French countryside, during which took place the only occasion when, speaking for myself, I have experienced that much adumbrated, seldom in practice achieved good fortune, of stopping at what was literally a pull-in café for lorries, and being provided there with a literally splendid meal.

At Perpignan, already in the shadow of the Pyrenees, I went for a stroll by myself after dinner. It was a dark night. I wandered through an old part of the town that seemed in ruins. Possibly archaeological excavations were taking place there. There was not enough moon to light up what was happening. All round about was completely deserted and silent.

I was thinking that we were now in the country of the Troubadors, when these reflexions were all at once echoed in a manner not wholly comfortable. Moving pensively through the night, leading on a leash two tall greyhounds, glided a mediaeval lady. She was not actually wearing a pointed cap and wimple (costume certainly too late for the Troubador era), but her dress was no less essentially of the Middle Ages, set off by the brace of hounds. For a second I wondered whether I was to have something like the experience of the two ladies at Versailles in *An Adventure*, flattering myself that perhaps I was observing an apparition. Only after the lady and her greyhounds had passed quite close did I take in the fact that she was a tart; France perhaps the only country where so delicate a contemporary tribute would be paid to a regional past.

10

'Spain,' says Wyndham Lewis, in *The Wild Body*, 'is an overflow of sombreness . . . a strong and threatening tide of history meets you at the frontier.' Nothing could better describe the country's impact, particularly at this juncture, administration breaking down everywhere, people already hinting that violence could not be long delayed. No doubt such is the impression Spain has given to the newcomer for centuries, but certainly the air at that moment seemed loaded with menace of the conflict that was to come in less than two years' time.

In Barcelona (where we unwisely crossed the bay in the rusty cable car spanning it, which broke down in transit), the German lift-boy at the hotel obligingly took us round the city's *quarter reserve*, the celebrated Barrio Chino. The tour began with The Sacristan's Bar, a homosexual *bal-musette*, frequented, so it seemed, exclusively by Spaniards (perhaps one should say Catalans), though no difficulties were made about the female members of our party, the only women present.

Nor was objection taken (as sometimes in France) to women visitors in a large brothel, the interior of which had the air of dating back to the 18th century, the main reception salon of almost ballroom proportions and considerable height. The lofty ceiling was no doubt designed to accommodate the boxes, like those of a theatre, constructed round the upper half of the room. In front of these boxes, for the benefit of occupants who wanted to see without being seen, grilles could be drawn.

Some little way below, girls in long white flounced dresses moved among the clients; at the moment of our arrival only two in number, a couple of small somewhat embarrassed Indo-Chinese (they looked) in very neat white naval uniforms. From time to time a girl would lift the front of her frilled skirt, while she rested her hand on her hips; perfectly embodying the delicately suggested brothel scenes in drawings by Constantin Guys.

At Saragossa (again the fact noted only for its coincidence, because we did no more than have a drink together, go our separate ways), we ran into Constant and Flo Lambert in the street; neither of us knowing the others were visiting Spain.

Stendhal loved *espagnolisme* in all its forms. An initial coldness (as in England) can often mask behaviour that shows understanding. There is, of course, a violent side too. In Toledo, a child of about four, selling lottery tickets, declined by one of our party in a café, hit her as hard as he could on the back before running away.

In Madrid was a demonstration of *espagnolisme*. We had gone into a bodega for a drink, the toughness of its clientèle—who looked like the smugglers' band in *Carmen*—not manifest from the outside. While in there, the other male of our party asked at the counter if they sold cigarettes. The answer was negative. A character standing nearby, with all the appearance of a professional bandit in reduced circumstances, indicated that if given the requisite sum, he would get the cigarettes from round the corner. There seemed no alternative but to say good-bye to a note covering the price of a packet of cigarettes.

On the contrary, the bandit reappeared within about five minutes with the cigarettes. He brushed aside a tip. Cheap Spanish cigarettes were (perhaps still are) simply the grains of tobacco necessary to make a cigarette, enclosed in a screw of paper; the smoker rolling his own in cigarette-papers kept on him for the purpose—perhaps Orwell developed that habit in Spain. Not knowing this Spanish custom—though surprised at the supposed cigarette being sealed at each end—our companion made several efforts to light up. Finally, seeing this foreigner was a hopeless case, the bandit—a charming gesture—presented one of his own cigarettes.

It was hot enough in Madrid already, but that day or the next a heat descended, said to be the most grilling since 1918; too hot to cross the street, too hot even to make plans for getting away. Water ceased to flow from the taps. Like Mrs Porter and her Daughter in the poem, we literally washed our feet in soda water, somehow at last managing to leave Madrid's baked streets and squares for the north.

At the Escorial nothing so worthy of note happened as when I visited that palace twenty or more years later. On that occasion, after the guide had expatiated for several minutes on the smallness and austerity of Philip II's own bedroom, an American lady ventured the question: 'You mean he was a democrat?'

Arriving at Aranda, the car drew up on one side of a wide empty square. The engine had scarcely been turned off before five of the most disturbing crippled beggars I have ever seen came racing through the dust towards us. The first to arrive was a truly Goyaesque figure, a youngish girl, quite mad, wearing only a shift; a horror from the *Caprichos* or *Desastres de la Guerra*.

For the last night in Spain we had planned to stay at Zarauz, a small seaside place, much recommended, a few miles from San Sebastian, described as large and not very attractive. The day had been fine, but at about half-past six in the evening, as Zarauz drew near, 'the sky became overcast, and a few drops of rain began to fall.

The first hotel we tried at Zarauz was full; so too was the second; and the third. In short, Zarauz was packed out. The sole accommodation on offer was a room that contained a *cama matrimonial* and a child's cot. In those days—anyway in the south of Spain—Spanish girls in shops would drop their eyes when dealing with a man (then glance up at him under the lids), but the plump handsome young manageress, who made this offer, could not repress a smile.

There was nothing for it but to press on to San Sebastian in what was now heavy rain. San Sebastian, as we had been warned, was a large town. Notwithstanding that, its hotels were even fuller than those of Zarauz. We toiled round the streets, getting more and more drenched in what were now torrents of rain. Many other travellers found themselves in just the same situation. Drawing up at some not yet sampled hotel, we were met by now only too familiar faces coming down the steps in despair, with the news that no rooms were available. A receptionist at one of these hotels suggested the name of an hotel on the far side of the river. We found it with some difficulty. The place was full to overflowing.

At this last hotel someone appealed to the porter for advice. It turned out the porter had a suggestion. He said: 'My sister-in-law keeps a *maison de passe*. She might be able to fit you in there—but mind you, don't grumble. It's not an hotel, it's a *maison de passe*.'

By that time we would all of us have willingly settled for the matrimonial bed and the child's cot offered at Zarauz; a brothel sounded comfort itself, anyway somewhere out of the wet. Unfortunately the *maison de passe* of the hotel-porter's sister-in-law (a sentence all phrase books should include) proved absolutely impossible to locate. In the end, towards midnight—though that means nothing in Spain—we returned to the most expensive hotel in San Sebastian, and took the still vacant honeymoon suite at an altogether ruinous price.

These tribulations improved no one's temper, and, after the French frontier had been crossed, it was at Bayonne, I think, that the row between the car's owner and the other couple—chiefly its male half—broke out in a manner to make further travel together impossible. Instead of returning to England, the ménage left, making for Paris, while the car's owner and I proceeded to the car ferry, and returned across the Channel. The trip had been a fairly gruelling one, but I am always glad to have seen Spain before the Civil War. The next time I looked at the Prado pictures was in Geneva, where they had been taken for safety.

II

A year later, in August, 1934 (after a summer holiday of which I hope to say more in a subsequent volume), an altogether unanticipated upheaval took place at Duckworth's. Balston's hints as to the uncertainty of my own position there had made me feel its balance more than a little precarious, but, in the event, things turned out otherwise. If not precisely a situation in which the dog it was that died, the dog was voted off the board, a circumstance for him almost as disastrous.

At a meeting of the firm's directors to reconsider the still rickety condition of the business, there was a sudden explosion. I think the question at issue was a further cut in directors' fees. Whatever the cause, all Gerald

Duckworth's barely pent up rage over the years on the subject of the Sitwells, Waugh, Beaton, other modern abominations forced on him by Balston, broke out; while at the same instant Balston gave voice to his equally powerful resentment of what he had long regarded as Gerald Duckworth's obstruction and inertia. Both directors seem to have expressed their feelings in the plainest possible terms.

The dramatic climax of this set-to was, so to speak, that General Milsted turned traitor. A decade before Milsted had disconcerted Balston by remaining alive; now, no less unexpectedly, he cast his vote with Gerald Duckworth. There was no alternative but for Balston to resign his directorship. That he did. He left Henrietta Street almost from one day to the next.

This rupture, as might be supposed, was a terrible blow to Balston. The whole of his life had been geared to the ambition of becoming a publisher. He had brought that off, not without a degree of distinction and individuality, for a dozen years. Now, in his fifties, in a kind of reverse process of fairy gold, *Spring Buds* and *Autumn Leaves*, so many of their pages representing Balston's own labours, had turned to dross.

Thereafter, Balston took no further hand in publishing, a trade on which in a small way he had left his mark, even if for himself all ended in dust and ashes. He suffered some sort of a nervous breakdown in consequence of the shock he had received, one not to be underestimated; then, when sufficiently recovered, paid a long visit to Spain with his old chum, protégé, much admired painter, Mark Gertler.

When the second war came, Balston returned briefly to the army as a staff-officer (nearly suffering another nervous breakdown in consequence), and, on relapsing to civilian life, occupied himself henceforth with his hobbies: Staffordshire pottery; amateur painting (his pictures included a symbolic female figure running headlong with a flaming torch); writing an occasional book about his great-uncle, the Headmaster of Eton, or the firm of paper-makers from which the Balstons were sprung; haunting the Garrick Club, where his unquenchable garrulity—especially on the subject of why *Decline and Fall* had slipped through his fingers—achieved a certain fame. He died in his mid-eighties.

12

Balston's passing from Henrietta Street could hardly be said to have improved my own chances there, in one sense leaving me more insecure than ever, since at least in theory he was a personal friend. In another aspect, King Log, a very genuine one, was taking over again from what was, in contrast, broadly speaking King Stork; Gerald Duckworth's preference for making no change whatever in any circumstances including by this time lack of any active inclination to get rid of me. In any case editorial and other odd jobs had to be done by someone. Alan Harris, with whom I was always on the best of terms, also retained his connexion with the firm as 'literary adviser'; and in due course, after Gerald Duckworth's death, was to become an influence in the newly constituted firm.

13

By this time I had been in London some seven years or more, and—to glance again for a moment at the Balzacian or Stendhalian viewpoint for a young man setting out on life—could not be said to have made a dazzling success of things. I was not likely to get any advancement in my present job, although, if a living had to be earned by some means other than writing books, its duties suited me well enough. On the other hand, if publishing were to be regarded as a life work, I should never be much of a hand at 'costing stock', or any of the other business necessities of the trade.

A Stendhalian (rather less Balzacian) necessity had been accomplished in having been romantically in love; also in having experienced some less unsubstantial relationships. I had never proposed marriage. I don't know whether that does a man credit or not. Henry Yorke once said (before he himself was married): 'The fact is everyone gets married who can afford to.' Looking round at friends and acquaintances (even the homosexual ones not to be wholly excluded), one saw a certain truth in this generalization; to which the rider might certainly be added that many married who could not afford to. I had nothing against marriage in principle, rather the contrary, but never felt the moment had come.

On the credit side, I had written three novels, all reasonably well received. They had sold what was respectable for a new writer of serious intent, no more; a number far short of enough to live on. I did not feel any lack of 'creative fantasy'—a useful phrase to cover productive capacity in any of the arts, which I first heard used in connexion with an individual actor at a rehearsal—but an eye must always be kept on this fundamental necessity of a novelist's equipment, the maintenance of which seems to rest chiefly on instinct.

Inability to produce is, of course, the haunting fear of the writer, especially the novelist; a spectre exorcized at the risk of raising the almost equally gruesome one of over-production. Scrutinizing the work of novelists past and present, one ponders this matter. Have novelists simply got a certain amount in them, which (if not cut off by early death) is in due course exhausted, or does some manner of existence stimulate or dry up these powers? Do certain ways of life build up reserves? If so, what are these ways of life; how should they be practised? Is there no rule?

INDEX

Index

203

Index

Index